MATHEMATICS
FOR RETAIL BUYING

seventh edition

BETTE K. TEPPER

Fashion Institute of Technology

FAIRCHILD BOOKS / NEW YORK

Fairchild Books
An imprint of Bloomsbury Publishing Inc

1385 Broadway	50 Bedford Square
New York	London
NY10018	WC1B 3DP
USA	UK

www.fairchildbooks.com

Fourth edition published 1996
Fifth edition published 2002
Sixth edition published 2008
This edition first published 2014

Library of Congress Cataloging-in-Publication Data

Tepper, Bette K.

Mathematics for Retail Buying, 7th Edition

2013935945

ISBN: PB: 978-1-60901-524-4

Typeset by Tom Helleberg
Cover Design by Carly Grafstein
Cover image © Veer Images/Pichet Panyaud

Printed and bound in the United States of America

CONTENTS

LIST OF FIGURES

PREFACE

"When you can measure what you are speaking about and express it in numbers, you know something about it; but when you cannot measure it, when you cannot express it in numbers, your knowledge is of a meager and unsatisfactory kind."

LORD KELVIN 1824–1901

In the first edition of *Mathematics for Retail Buying*, we stated that operating figures are the language of the retail merchandiser, regardless of the size of the store. This has not changed, and in today's highly competitive business environment, it is even more important than ever before to have comprehension of the mathematical factors involved in profitable merchandising. Because profit is the way you keep score. This fundamental mathematical background gives insight into how merchandising problems are solved mathematically and perception as to why merchandising decisions are based on figures. The most experienced and skilled merchandiser knows that the mastery of mathematical techniques and figure analysis is an essential tool. Additionally, persons in related careers who comprehend the mathematics of profit will also benefit by their broader understanding of merchandising situations.

Mathematics for Retail Buying depicts the essential concepts, practices, and procedures as well as the calculations and interpretations of figures related to the many factors that produce profit. The choice of material and the depth of each subject are deliberately confined to that which has practical value for the performance of occupations in or associated with retail merchandising. It concentrates on the mathematical concepts and their relationships to the many activities involved in achieving a profitable retail buying/selling process without the detailed explanation of each process. The book was developed primarily as a learning device to meet the needs of career-oriented students who will be directly, or indirectly, involved in the activities of merchandising and buying at the retail level. In addition to the obvious educational benefits to the students of retailing, *Mathematics for Retail Buying* can serve as a guide in training junior executives and can be a constant source of reference for an assistant buyer or the merchant who operates a small independent store.

When contemplating the writing or revision of any retailing textbook, the question of practical value will inevitably arise. We feel the contents of *Mathematics for Retail Buying* are not only sensible but realistic because it has been based on:

- The personal experience of the author, who was a buyer in a major retail organization.

- The knowledgeable opinions of current retail executives as to the information necessary to prepare prospective retail merchandisers.

- The insights manufacturers have gained that help to provide better service and to communicate more effectively with retailers and merchandisers.

- The tested use of the material by the author and other teachers at the Fashion Institute of Technology, by faculties at other schools, and by retail executives and training departments.

- The favorable comments about the value of the material in relation to career performance by the alumni of the Fashion Merchandising Management curriculum at the Fashion Institute of Technology.

The study and comprehension of the principles and techniques contained in *Mathematics for Retail Buying* will enable the student to:

- Recognize the basic and elementary factors of the buying and selling process that affect profit.

- Understand the relationship of the profit factors and improve profit performance by the manipulation of these factors.

- Become aware of practices and procedures in stores.

- Become familiar with the applications of computers and computerized forms in retailing.

- Understand and apply the basic mathematical concepts used to solve real-life merchandising problems.

- Comprehend the standard industry terminology employed in retailing and merchandising.

Every effort is still being made to build the contents of the book into a solid foundation for ease of understanding, and not merely to display formulas. Without sacrificing completeness, the material has been structured and restructured into a simplified outline form. This step-by-step presentation uses brief explanations stated in basic terms and precise definitions, demonstrated clearly in examples that express the mathematical principles discussed in that section. Within each unit, after a major topic, a series of problems is presented that tests the understanding of the fundamental principles discussed in that section. Contained at the end of each unit, there is a large collection of problems and case studies that utilize practical retailing situations and common obstacles and difficulties encountered in real-life merchandising.

The majority of these problems focus on ready-to-wear as the kingdom of fashion goods is explored. Among these are problems designed and designated as spreadsheet problems and cases, which can be calculated manually, with a calculator, or on a computerized spreadsheet. Included is a CD-ROM with all the problems and cases that pertain to the fundamental concepts of profitable retailing. These features further reinforce comprehension of the specific section

For the revised Seventh Edition, particular attention has been paid to the comments of the various users, including their own teaching experience, as well as the author's, and also the comments of the people in industry interviewed for the book.

The significant changes in this edition are:

- The Introduction continues to connect the text contents with an overview of the growth of retailing and the mega trends of the times, accelerated by the use of computers and the cardinal principles of successful merchandising.

- "Using Computerized Spreadsheets" has been added. It explains the advantages and usage of spreadsheets in retail mathematics. All the concept problems are now expressed in spreadsheet as well as traditional arithmetic format.

- The sequence of units has been revised. The content of some units has also been altered to better present the relationship of the profit indicators.

- Sales became Unit I to show the relationship and impact of this element on the function of a retailer offering merchandise profitably for sale.

- At the beginning of each unit, a list of Key Concept Formulas has been added for immediate reference and information. In addition, there is now a complete Glossary of Concept Formulas at the end of the book that should be an easy reference.

- At the end of each unit, the review and practice problems, which help student comprehension of presented material, continue to apply industry terminology and retain the feature of illustrating realistic current merchandising situations.

- The included CD-ROM now contains the Practice Problems and Case Studies of each unit, and its organization mirrors that of the textbook. The purpose is that all practice problems can now conveniently be worked on the computer.

- The adaptation of spreadsheets to the mathematical concepts gives maximum comprehension while solving more sophisticated problems without complicated, tedious calculations.

- "Quick Tips for Setting up Your Computer Spreadsheets" is now included as an appendix.

- Selected answers continue to be given at the end of the book.

- The Answer Manual corresponds to the revision of all Practice Problems and Practice Problems for Review.

- The comprehensive Answer Manual for the entire text also includes the computations and answers to the Practice Problems and Case Studies for each unit.

- At the end of Units I–VI, Case Study problems demonstrate the use of material in realistic, practical merchandising situations.

- Problem-solving situations throughout the text illustrate the basis for decision-making.

- The most common Key Performance Indicators, KPIs, have been included in Unit I.

- The Profit Components section in Unit VI has been restructured with detailed definitions, including an abbreviated example problem and solution using this concept, reinforcing an additional explanation of net operating profit.

- A section explains the criteria used to evaluate a buyer's performance.

- Data on gross margin, operating profit margins, and annual turnover illustrates the accepted basis for comparison.

- Explanations are included on the relationship of basic pricing factors to profit, and the effect of merchandising policies to the pricing of goods.

- Important key words continue to be highlighted throughout the book to facilitate the student's understanding of important key concepts.

- A Glossary of Terms, defining the highlighted terms throughout the book, facilitates student understanding of important key words.

- Industry terminology and data are updated and reflected in the text and problems presented.

- The sequence within some units has been altered to accommodate additional and/or more detailed explanations.

In developing and changing the book for this revised Seventh Edition, I have tried to be sensitive to and concerned about comments from colleagues and students at the Fashion Institute of Technology, and from many other colleges relating to the sequence of study units in our book. The old puzzle about "the chicken or the egg" has surfaced time and time again. Why the Sales unit first? Why not the Retail Method unit? Or Dollar Planning? Or Pricing?

There is a rather basic principle about the buying/merchandising process: There is no one beginning and no one end. It is a circular process: an unending, interrelated continuum within which all factors influence all other factors. Even though the units are interrelated, each chapter can be used as a separate topic of study, and each can be shifted without losing the continuity of the process. The various facets of the merchandising cycle are an ongoing procedure of monitoring, analysis, and evaluation, directed to the purpose of meeting the merchandiser's objective of achieving a predetermined gross margin, which should, in turn, generate an appropriate net profit. This is mentioned to point out to instructors and students alike (and to merchants who use our book for in-service training purposes) that the study of retail mathematics may begin at any point on the "circle."

In this revised Seventh Edition, the material is divided into six units. Each unit covers a particular, basic mathematical factor that affects the profits of a retail store. The relationships among these profit factors are stressed throughout the book. The units of study and their subject matter are:

- Unit I, Analysis of Basic Sales Elements—Defines, analyzes, and shows the calculations pertaining to basic sales elements vital to the function of a retailer.

- Unit II, Retail Pricing and Repricing of Merchandise—Discusses and illustrates the basic pricing factors used in buying decisions and presents the calculations used when pricing and/or repricing retail merchandise.

- Unit III, Basic Markup Equations Used in Merchandising Decisions—Explains the importance of markup to profitable merchandising and illustrates the calculations of the various types of markup (i.e., cumulative, initial, and maintained) that, when understood and implemented, achieve the desired results.

- Unit IV, The Retail Method of Inventory—Presents and explains this proven, reliable procedure as a mechanism and system for determining the total value of the stock-on-hand and shortages.

- Unit V, Dollar Planning and Control—Includes the analysis of possible sales, the planning and control of stocks and purchases, and the techniques used to accomplish these objectives.

- Unit VI, Merchandising for a Profit—Examines the basic profit elements, and defines, calculates, and shows their relationship to one another in profit and loss statements.

The idea for this book originated with the many faculty members who helped develop some of this material to meet the needs for teaching merchandising mathematics at the Fashion Institute of Technology. The author is indebted to those faculty members for their contributions, and to the many students and alumni for their constructive criticism and suggestions that were used in preparing this book. For this revision, my special thanks to Paula Thompson, who inspired me to revise the sequence of the units of study. The enthusiastic response provided the incentive to complete this revision. Special thanks go to my coauthor of earlier editions, Professor Newton E. Godnick. He was actively involved in sharing and participating in all phases of the original and subsequent editions. Many of his contributions are still evident in this book.

In the revision of this book, it was mandatory to include information, conforming with current general practice, regarding the adaptation, preparation, and use of computerized spreadsheets as they pertain to the text's fundamental mathematical concepts of each unit of study, and the effect on profit and/or any other important decision-making process required in a variety of retail merchandising situations. In order to present this material, I had to enlist the aid, guidance, and knowledge of an expert. So I am deeply grateful and indebted to my daughter, Rebecca Citron, consultant and principal of Sunnybrook Consulting, who was able to fulfill these requirements. She is solely responsible for expressing all concepts in computer notation, problems in spreadsheet format, and preparing the section "Quick Tips for Setting up Your Computer Spreadsheet." In addition, she saw the value of summarizing Key Concept Formulas at the beginning of each unit and including a complete Glossary of Concept Formulas at the back of the book for easy reference. She also assisted in editing to make the Seventh Edition more readable and user-friendly, adding delightful quotes to make mathematics more gratifying.

I want to acknowledge and give special thanks to the following people for their valuable input into the revision of this edition: Sibyl Webb, Store Manager, Peebles Department Store, Barkhamsted, Connecticut, for conveying current duties and activities of a store manager; Dr. Georg Mehl, for researching the sales volume by various store types available from the U.S. Department of Commerce; Michael Stone, Director of Retail Services Group and a member of Cushman Wakefield, real estate firm, for emphasizing the importance and effect of store size and location on sales volume achieved; Peter Herink, General Merchandise Manager of Global Retail at Tory Burch, who stressed the importance of dollar stock investment for the classifications that are major contributors of sales volume; Larry Bienenfeld, President of Jildor Shoes, Cedarhurst, New York, for conveying the effect of prompt invoice payment while achieving the appropriate markup and markdown percentages. Additional thanks go to the acquisitions reviewers selected by the publisher for their thorough and insightful recommendations: Marla Green, LIM College; Donna Duffey, Johnson County Community College; Eun Jin Hwang, Indiana University of Pennsylvania; Shubha Bennur, Ph.D., University of Nebraska, Lincoln; Janis Shaffer, Indiana University; Evonne Bowling, Mesa Community College; Deborah D. Young, Ph.D., Texas Woman's University; Lorynn Divita, Baylor University; Theresa Mastrianni, Kingsborough Community College; Soyoung Kim, Ph.D., University of Georgia; and Janice E. King, Ph.D., Western Illinois University. And last, but hardly least, my thanks go to Fairchild editors Olga Kontzias, Amy Butler, and Linda Feldman, whose helpful recommendations and attitudes were most appreciated.

BETTE K. TEPPER

INTRODUCTION

It is not possible to predict or visualize the various organizational and/or ownership alternatives retailers will pursue or changes that will result from future hi-tech innovations as each retailer struggles for uniqueness in the marketplace. However, we can foresee in the future, as in the past and the present, significant and rewarding career opportunities in the retail industry—in traditional institutions, other diverse developed retail formats, as well as e-commerce. Today, the challenges to be successful are ever increasing due to the rapid increase in the type, size, and number of retailers in plentiful domestic and foreign locations.

In preparation for the revised Seventh Edition of *Mathematics for Retail Buying*, much thought was given to what and how the text's basic mathematical concepts involved in profitable retailing—which have been and will continue to be constant, once learned and calculated to achieve a profit—could be more meaningful today. At best, retailing is volatile, and the environment continues to be exciting, stimulating, and continually changing; successful retailers constantly reinvent themselves to achieve differentiation from competition as they entice customers to their doors. It is recognizable that having learned these mathematical concepts, it is how they are applied that makes for profitable merchandising. The aim of this text is to explore in depth the mathematical concepts and procedures that achieve profitable merchandising in the retail arena. The topics integrated with the buying/selling function—such as store organization; what, when, and where to buy; assortment planning; and vendor relations—are covered fully in other texts that focus only on these subjects. Although the Practice Problems and Case Studies treat a variety of merchandise, fashion apparel and accessories are given the greatest attention, as these are the areas a new trainee or assistant buyer would most likely begin when taking on the responsibility of merchandise selection. The focus still remains on the mathematical concepts and their relevancy to profitable merchandising.

Merchandising strategies are conceived by the retailer and executed by the buyer. The buyer knows that the basic mathematical elements involved in profitable buying must be coordinated with the concepts that are applied to the function of buying at cost, selling at retail, and producing a profit from these activities. The most cardinal principle is that it does not matter what product you buy, or which diverse retailer offers the product, or what the industry is—be it fashion, hardware, or supermarkets—the same set of concepts and mathematical calculations are connected to the three elementary factors of retail, cost, and profit. Their application to any product in any particular store and/or industry is identical. However, the emphasis on these elements may differ because the retailers' policies may not be alike. It is understandable, for example, that the calculation of a markup percentage for a specialty store like Bergdorf Goodman and a discounter like Target Stores is computed identically, yet the markup percentage considered acceptable by each is different. We can better appreciate the interlinking of the retailer, or any other alternate merchandise distribution choice, with the buyer as we consider their common goals and their effect on each other's function.

By definition, retailing is the term used to describe the many activities involved in selling small quantities of goods and/or services, at a profit, to the ultimate consumer. Merchandising combines having the right merchandise, in the right place, in the right quantities, at the right price, at the right time. Performed by the buyer, this task—to go into a market buying what a customer wants and having it ready when it is wanted—seems simple. In practice, retail management today has become quite complex and difficult because the growth of retailers fosters keen competition and has seriously reduced the possible profit margin. Therefore, it is more important than ever that the buyer who fulfills the merchandising function has a basic knowledge of the mathematical factors involved in profitable merchandising. Without this background it is difficult to comprehend the operation of either a small store, a department in a large store, or a non–store-based retailer, such as mail catalog or an Internet operation. This fundamental mathematical background gives insight into how merchandising problems are solved mathematically and why merchandising decisions are based on figures. The financial personnel in many major organizations, such as Sears and Home Depot, use preset programs and spreadsheets for analysis and profit planning. Nevertheless, the buyer's ability to understand and manipulate the profit factors is essential, because everyday problems and situations that arise from figuring profits can be a basis for earning future maximum profits. In a computerized organization, the buyer can instantly retrieve a particular desired merchandising figure. However, if the data necessary to take immediate action is not available, the buyer who can compute and supply the necessary information has a decided advantage.

THE GROWTH OF RETAILING

In America, retailing first began with the Native American trading posts of the frontier days. After 1850, such pioneers as R. H. Macy and Marshall Field established the department stores. By 1900, there were department stores in all major cities, and this was the retail format recognized as the mass distributor of goods. The mail-order houses were given a substantial boost by the adoption of rural free delivery by the post office, while the chain store, established in the middle of the nineteenth century, rose to maturity in the twentieth century.

The consolidation and growth in American retailing occurred during the period between the two World Wars. After 1945, there were revolutionary changes with the appearance of planned shopping centers, which often led to direct competition among retailers. The latter part of the twentieth century saw variation in retailing format, with the inception of discounters, closeout stores, manufacturer's outlets, and warehouse clubs, to name just a few. In addition, direct selling and television shopping channels became the convenient techniques by which to buy merchandise in a non-store environment. There was another unprecedented phenomenon in 1994 when the competitive strategy changed with the acquisition of R. H. Macy's by Federated Department Stores. We currently see that many older, well-known local stores (e.g., Filene's in Boston, Marshall Field's in Chicago, and Famous-Bar in St. Louis, to name a few) have undergone name changes and are now identified as Macy's. Presently, you can find Macy's coast to coast with hundreds of locations, from the city to the suburbs, to Macys.com. Today, independent ownership of department and specialty stores has become a rare phenomenon, as ownership groups consolidate and operate their acquisitions. As many local and regional stores have disappeared, others have appeared on the scene. Competition is keen and takes many forms. While Kohl's, a Midwest specialty department store, successfully invaded the East Coast, UNIQLO, Japan's largest casual-apparel retailer, opened stores in Manhattan with ambitions to become the top clothing retailer in the world, and Walmart looks for future growth from international operations in such markets as China and India. Today, retailing is not only fast paced, but it requires the ability to adapt and be flexible as the basic concepts and principles are applied.

MEGA TRENDS IN RETAILING

Retailing becomes more challenging and fast paced daily. Knowing how the fundamental mathematical elements that produce a profitable operation are affected by the variety of innovative strategies pursued by all retailers is a necessity. A survey conducted by the NRFF (National Retail Federation Foundation) and Bearing Point revealed that the two important messages from the retailers for their future were growth and differentiation. This section will allow the student to better appreciate the realistic retail environment as it currently exists. The graph on pages xx and xxi shows the movement, by volume, by store types according to the grouping by the Bureau of the Census. The trends enumerated will affect all retailers, but how and when will be determined by each organization as it charts its own course of action.

Currently, with the prevalence of multi-units, there is a major trend toward varying degrees of centralizing and organizing buying activities. The choice of how to profitably accomplish the buying/selling functions depends on such factors as fashion vs staple goods, number and size of store units, etc. Regardless of the method chosen, the control of the constant flow of suitable merchandise from the markets to the stores can only be accomplished by extensive records. These records provide accurate requirements of assortment factors that pertain to classification (grouping merchandise by common distinctive features, such as men's, women's, children's, etc.), price lines, and other assortment factors in order to achieve portions consistent with customer demands. It should be noted, however, that there are differences between individual units.

The buyer continues to perform the specialized work of selection and negotiation. The buyer in all organizations makes the buying arrangements that pertain to selection of resources (specific items to be carried), including specifications for private branding, quantities, negotiations of cost prices, terms of sale, method of shipment, and the setting of retail prices or repricing. Deviations from these general principles are decisions of top management.

Introduction. Sales by Store Type, 2003–2009 (Billion $)

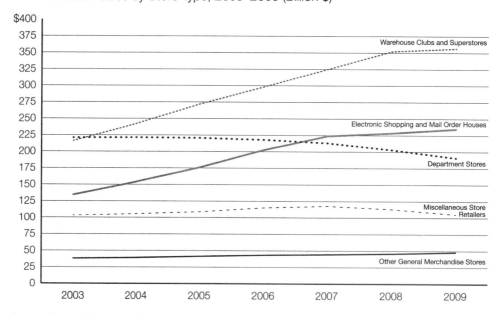

Source: *Census Bureau and Bureau of Economic Analysis, U.S. Dept. of Commerce.*

	Department Store Sales	% of U.S. GDP	U.S. GDP
2003	$221.0 bil	1.98%	$11,142.2 bil
2004	$221.4 bil	1.87%	$11,853.3 bil
2005	$220.7 bil	1.75%	$12,623.0 bil
2006	$218.1 bil	1.63%	$13,377.2 bil
2007	$213.3 bil	1.52%	$14,028.7 bil
2008	$202.9 bil	1.42%	$14,291.5 bil
2009	$190.8 bil	1.37%	$13,939.0 bil

Source: *Census Bureau and Bureau of Economic Analysis, U.S. Dept. of Commerce.*

Warehouse Clubs and Superstores Sales	
2003	$216.3 bil
2004	$242.3 bil
2005	$271.9 bil
2006	$298.0 bil
2007	$325.0 bil
2008	$352.1 bil
2009	$356.5 bil

Other General Merchandise Stores Sales (excluding Warehouse Clubs and Superstores)	
2003	$38.0 bil
2004	$39.2 bil
2005	$41.3 bil
2006	$43.3 bil
2007	$44.4 bil
2008	$45.7 bil
2009	$48.0 bil

Electronic Shopping and Mail Order Houses Sales	
2003	$134.4 bil
2004	$154.1 bil
2005	$175.9 bil
2006	$202.4 bil
2007	$223.9 bil
2008	$228.5 bil
2009	$234.7 bil

Miscellaneous Store Retailers Sales	
2003	$103.1 bil
2004	$105.7 bil
2005	$108.8 bil
2006	$115.1 bil
2007	$117.8 bil
2008	$113.2 bil
2009	$105.4 bil

Source: *Census Bureau and Bureau of Economic Analysis, U.S. Dept. of Commerce.*

A significant happening took place when budget chains from the Midwest and the South opened offices in New York, where bestselling clothing brands are designed. Although the costs of leasing space and luring designers were contrary to the operating budgets of low-cost retailers, they felt a need to focus on fashion trends and increase their fashion relevance. They wanted to discover new looks quickly and incorporate them into their clothing lines. A vast majority of their design staff remains in their corporate headquarters. Well-known designers have shown a growing willingness to sell their clothing and household products at lower prices to a broader audience. This allows the budget-minded consumer to find clothing by Isaac Mizrahi at Target and limited-edition merchandise at H&M by designers such as Karl Lagerfeld, Stella McCartney, and Viktor & Rolf. Macy's is providing affordable luxury as it contracts fashion designers such as Oscar de la Renta, Elie Tahari, and Martha Stewart for signature lines; and J. C. Penney introduced an exclusive lifestyle brand created by Polo Ralph Lauren Corporation's Global Brand Concepts division.

Merchandising policies are constantly shifting as retailers attempt to set themselves apart. The competitive advantage gained by optimizing assortments, products, and prices while minimizing markdowns is appreciated by retailers who recognize the necessity for differentiation. The emphasis on private-label products resulted in international sourcing. Through customer satisfaction, it is possible to achieve comparable store growth. To quote Charles Darwin, "It is not the strongest of the species that survives, nor the most intelligent, but the one most responsive to change."

In the late twentieth century, high-tech made its mark everywhere, including retailing. Success in the contemporary retail environment relies heavily on records that are the basis for analysis, planning, decision-making, and quick action. The first generation of electronic computers started in 1951, when the growth of multistore operations mandated a need for prompt, accurate, and complete data to make merchandising decisions.

Since the 1960s, data processing systems have provided retailers with an uninterrupted flow of information. In more recent years, the increased use of Electronic Data Processing (EDP) systems by department stores and retail businesses, as well as by mass merchandising chains, has had a major impact on the management of merchandise inventories and on other areas of recordkeeping. Today, because retailers locate their stores in distant geographic markets, the computer not only furnishes data that identifies problems but also facilitates and accelerates the decision-making process. Computers assist retailers not only with merchandising functions, but also by providing information that enables them to integrate and improve merchandising, buying, customer service, store operations, and the financial management of the business.

All retailers agree about the value of computer usage in their individual stores. This powerful force that processes information accurately and promptly is particularly appreciated in the volatile retailing industry because it has resulted in much improved control and management of merchandise and finances. The network of computers that allows a continual flow of information to be electronically exchanged between retailers and manufacturers results in this control at a lower cost. Ideally, a computerized merchandising system should provide data about the physical stock that is in tandem with dollar control. Management has an almost unlimited choice concerning which programs should be instituted, maintained, or eliminated. The benefits of the computer to a particular organization can easily be determined through analysis of sales, productivity, and profit.

The quick evolution of technology has become critical to a retailer's success. The major mass retailers of the '90s, Walmart and Home Depot, as well as sophisticated specialty stores such as Saks Fifth Avenue, have a major competitive advantage as they reap the benefits from their capital investments in technology. Their programs touch every aspect of their operations. They include executive information systems that analyze and report the detailed performance of what merchandise is selling, they use historical performance to plan data to determine quantities, and they improve the efficiency of the buying process by providing better distribution of merchandise by the store based on customer profiles. Internal and external communications were changed dramatically by the use of e-mail. Vendor partnerships through development of replenishment systems ensure that the merchandise wanted by the customer is in the store when they want it. Leading companies see results from innovative technologies that help identify regional customer preferences by demographic analysis. The many uncontrollable, external variable factors encouraged retailers to invest in planning and forecasting technologies. In the 1970s, when the standardized bar code printed on tickets and labels was introduced in products of grocery supermarkets, it enabled merchandisers to move quickly from distribution centers to selling floors at lower costs. These bar codes opened up a vast amount of inventory and sales data that reduced labor costs and provided a more efficient checkout process as it changed the relationship between retailers and manufacturers. This standardized, universal product code became a global bar code standard.

Surveillance technology is being utilized for security and loss prevention. New software allows the creation, management, and deployment of in-store digital videos throughout the store or chain as it gives the retailer an opportunity to learn what takes place at all points of the customer's in-store experience. It is a universal fact: consumers are turning to technology to help them shop. E-commerce sales have grown exponentially. By 2006, Internet spending, or electronic shopping, passed the $200 billion mark and has demonstrated continued growth ever since. Marketers and retailers used new technologies to draw customers to the Internet, trying to boost the growth rate of online shopping. Retailers constantly upgrade their e-commerce systems to integrate the customer data across Web, store, and catalog sales. The objective continues to be to have what the customers want, where they want it, and in precisely the right quantity, especially when the competition is just a click away.

History records past events. We know the merits and influences of the computer on the development of retailing today. The future will reveal how this or other major innovations will facilitate the degree or the speed of electronic progress.

Mathematics for Retail Buying delineates the essential concepts, practices, and procedures as well as the calculations and interpretations of figures related to the many factors that produce profit. The choice of material and the depth of each subject are deliberately confined to that which has practical value for the performance of occupations in or associated with retail merchandising. The study of retail mathematics may begin at any point in the buying/selling "circle." The six units in this text are interrelated with the various phases of merchandising; therefore, each unit can be used as a separate topic of study, and each can be shifted without losing the continuity of the process. Here is an overview of the units and their respective roles in the buying/selling process, followed by an explanation of the introductory sections Using Computerized Spreadsheets and Using the Enclosed CD-ROM.

UNIT I: ANALYSIS OF BASIC SALES ELEMENTS

The function of the retail store is to sell merchandise to consumers. The amount of merchandise sold is the store's source of operating income, commonly known as sales or sales volume. However, before merchandise can be sold, it must be bought. The basic elements of sales volume are defined, analyzed, and calculated because their effective understanding is critical to a retailer's success.

UNIT II: RETAIL PRICING AND REPRICING OF MERCHANDISE

This unit presents the relationship and calculations of the basic pricing factors, the various pricing situations used in making buying decisions, the techniques involved in repricing goods, and the effect of each on gross margin (the difference between the sales and the cost of those sales) and profit. The approach to pricing is presented from the standpoint of who sets the selling price on goods purchased for resale.

The buyer, guided by a prescribed price line structure, plans purchases and merchandise offerings that fit into this framework. The buyer sets the retail price on each item purchased.

UNIT III: BASIC MARKUP EQUATIONS USED IN MERCHANDISING DECISIONS

The overall effectiveness of buying and pricing is measured by the buyer's ability to achieve a markup established by management, designed to produce the desired profit. As merchandise is purchased, it is neither common nor desirable to require that each item be retailed with the same markup percentage. The results would be disastrous! Yet it is the buyer's responsibility to meet the overall target figure for profit. Never can the buyer forget that goods must be priced to sell. Therefore, during a season there are many considerations that affect the pricing of merchandise at the time of purchase, and many of these actually cause goods to sell at a lower price. The ability to recognize that this results in different markups allows the buyer to make the necessary adjustments. The buyer constantly has the opportunity to average high and low markups to reach the required predetermined average.

UNIT IV: THE RETAIL METHOD OF INVENTORY

An essential feature of retail merchandising is to determine the total value of stock-on-hand. The value of inventory is significant for planning specifically how much to buy and for the determination of the proper valuation of inventory for profit figuring purposes. Unit IV discusses the retail method of inventory because it is the accepted, proven system that provides this information. We familiarize ourselves with the general procedures used in implementing this system, and the calculation and records required to maintain it. A probable amount of stock-on-hand can be known at any time without counting the merchandise, and a shortage figure can easily be derived through a comparison between the actual physical inventory and the computed records. The mathematical calculations involved in this method are not performed by the buyer, but the accuracy depends on the buyer's prompt and accurate classifying of records that pertain to price changes. This system helps the buyer to constantly track the amount of stock-on-hand while protecting the gross margin (the difference between sales and the cost of those sales to be attained).

UNIT V: DOLLAR PLANNING AND CONTROL

The most talked-about topic in retailing is the budget of stocks and sales, more commonly known as a six-month dollar plan. This is the subject of Unit V. The six-month plan is an attempt to set in advance realistic projected goals for stocks in ratio to sales, the amount and timing of markdowns, an average markup for the season, and the correct amount and proper timing of purchases. This "calendar" plans, forecasts, and controls the purchase and sale of merchandise. It is designed to protect the store's inventory investment and produce a profit as it controls the above factors. The projection of planned sales is the hub of the buying/selling wheel, and all of the other elements are predicated on this figure. Although the estimation is based on actual past performance plus external and internal sales-related conditions, it is not an exact process. It is a judgmental decision, and therefore it is not always possible to predict all contingencies.

The buyer, who is responsible for interpreting and achieving the goals set, constantly monitors the sales in order to adjust the elements of the plan that rely on the amount of sales generated. The six-month dollar plan, in action, helps the buyer to keep score of whether the correct balance between sales and stocks is maintained. The procedure of planning the various elements and the calculations that produce the desired outcome give insight into why and how this technique produces a profitable operation.

UNIT VI: MERCHANDISING FOR A PROFIT

Logically, the study of mathematics involved in retail buying should begin with the analysis of a profit and loss statement. This statement reports a summary of the achievements of a particular department, store, or company, revealing whether or not the activities involved in operating this unit for a specific time period have been profitable. Profits are mainly the result of how much merchandise is sold (known as sales volume), the cost of the merchandise sold, and the expenses incurred in buying and selling this merchandise. The buyer is the force that buys, prices, reprices, and negotiates the merchandise found in a retail store and/or featured on the Internet. These functions are the responsibilities of the buyer, who must understand the linkages of the profit elements. The fundamental relationships among the profit factors are repeated throughout the book.

The Practice Problems, Case Studies, and Spreadsheet Solutions to be solved in *Mathematics for Retail Buying* focus mainly on situations prevalent in the women's, children's, and men's apparel and home furnishing industries, because fashion is such an important factor in our economic system. It affects the major industries of retailing, manufacturing, and marketing. Practical and realistic examples follow the theories, principles, concepts, and calculations that through application test the reader's understanding of the fundamentals of each major topic discussed in that section.

USING COMPUTERIZED SPREADSHEETS

Just as we have become more and more accustomed to using computers and smart devices in our everyday activities, so too it becomes apparent that the use of computerized spreadsheets in doing retail mathematics offers many advantages. Computerized spreadsheets can make repetitive, lengthy mathematical calculations quick, easy, and accurate. Organizing data in spreadsheet format provides a visual summary of important information that is easily read and understood. They are particularly valuable when there is a large amount of data to organize and assimilate. Once spreadsheets are set up, key assumptions and/or variables can be changed in order to do quick "what if" analyses, testing various scenarios, thereby resulting in better decision-making. Using these spreadsheets will enable the user to test sensitivities such as:

- "If we make a small change in the price, how much will it impact our profitability?"

- "If we take a larger markdown, what will be the impact?"

- "What effect will it have if we reduce the markdown percentage slightly?"

Using computerized spreadsheets will test your ability to understand mathematical concepts, while reducing your need to do basic arithmetic. Concept formulas must be entered absolutely correctly, and once they are properly entered your answers will always be correct. If your answers are not right, you did not enter the concept formula correctly.

In this edition of *Mathematics for Retail Buying*, solutions to the concept problems are also given, where appropriate, in both spreadsheet and the more traditional arithmetic format. Not every concept problem lends itself to preparing a spreadsheet, and those problems are given only as an arithmetic solution.

When solving the concept problems, we cannot easily show the spreadsheet formulas in the written text. When a spreadsheet is open on the computer, however, and a specific cell is highlighted, the formula that was used to compute the number appearing in that cell will appear at the top of the page in the formula bar. So that you will be able to check the concept problem spreadsheet formulas, these concept problems appear on the enclosed CD-ROM, in the appropriate unit. These problems are solved using Microsoft Excel 2010. With Excel, as well as other spreadsheet software, please remember that there may be multiple ways in which a particular spreadsheet can be set up and a problem solved.

USING THE ENCLOSED CD-ROM

The enclosed CD-ROM is a learning tool to be used to practice the concepts presented. Its organization mirrors that of this textbook, with each unit having a matching folder on the CD-ROM. Thus, as one moves through the textbook, the corresponding concept problems and Practice Problems can be easily found. All of the Practice Problems found in the text appear on the CD-ROM so that you can work the problems directly.

The CD-ROM is protected and therefore cannot be permanently changed. You have the freedom to play with the concept problems' numbers to see how the concepts work, as well as to work the Practice Problems, but you cannot save your work on the disc. If you need additional space to work the problems, go to Home – Insert and insert additional rows, columns, or even pages. Some problems do not warrant the development of a spreadsheet. Even so, the computer can be useful to do basic arithmetic calculations to solve the problem.

Remember: Be sure to save your review problems to your hard drive.
You cannot save your work on this disc!

In the future, the function in retailing of maintaining assortments appropriate for selected customers, in quantities that provide efficient use of investment, at prices that create a constant flow of merchandise, while ensuring a profit focused on the buying/selling process, will continue. The principles by which this will be achieved will remain constant as they adjust to the mode and tempo of life in the twenty-first century. As additional traditional retailers join Macy's, Walmart, and Internet-only retailers with the development of websites, online selling will grow. New rules and standards that pertain to return policies and company-wide coordination will have to evolve. However, the basic profit elements as we know them will continue to guide and measure success.

BETTE K. TEPPER

*Because of her encouragement,
contribution, assistance, and support,
I would like to dedicate this edition to
my daughter, Rebecca Tepper Citron.*

ANALYSIS OF BASIC SALES ELEMENTS

"The entrepreneur always searches for change, responds to it, and sees it as an opportunity."

PETER DRUCKER, ONE OF THE 20TH CENTURY'S MOST INFLUENTIAL AND RESPECTED THINKERS ON MANAGEMENT THEORY AND PRACTICE

OBJECTIVES

- Definition and dissection of the basic sales elements in the buying/selling process.

- Calculation, analysis, and measurement of the performance of operating income, known as net sales.

- Identification of the most common retail key performance indicators (KPIs) that measure sales performance.

- Determination and calculation of the costs of goods sold when purchasing merchandise.

- Recognition and calculation of the net cost (terms on the conditions of sale) agreed upon when making purchases, i.e., types of discounts, dating, and shipping terms.

KEY TERMS

advanced dating (postdating)	dating	inward freight
alteration and workroom costs	direct expenses	list price
	discount date	loading
anticipation	EOM dating	net cost
billed cost	extra dating	net loss
cash discount	FOB retailer, factory, city or port of destination, prepaid	net payment date
COD dating		net profit
cost	gross margin	net sales
cost of goods sold	gross sales	net terms
customer returns and allowances	indirect expenses	operating expenses

operating income

quantity discount

regular (ordinary) dating

retail

ROG dating

sales volume

terms of sale

total cost of goods purchased

total cost of goods sold

trade discount

KEY CONCEPT FORMULAS

Cost of goods sold

$$\text{Total cost of goods sold} = \text{Billed cost} + \text{Inward transportation charges} + \text{Workroom costs} - \text{Cash discount}$$

$$\text{Cost of goods sold \%} = \frac{\text{\$ Cost of goods sold}}{\text{Net sales}} \times 100$$

$$\text{\$ Cost of goods sold} = \text{Cost of goods \%} \times \text{Net sales}$$

Billed cost = List price − Trade discount(s)

Customer returns and allowances

$$\text{Customer returns and allowances \$} = \text{Total of all refunds or credits to the customer on individual items of merchandise} \times \text{Number of units actually returned}$$

$$\text{Customer returns and allowances \%} = \frac{\text{\$ Customer returns and allowances}}{\text{Gross sales}} \times 100$$

$$\text{\$ Customer returns and allowances} = \text{Gross sales} \times \text{Customer returns and allowances \%}$$

$$\textbf{Department's net sales \% of total store sales} = \frac{\text{Department's net dollar sales}}{\text{Store's total net dollar sales}} \times 100$$

Gross sales

$$\text{Gross sales} = \text{Total of all the prices charged to consumers on individual items} \times \text{Number of units actually sold}$$

$$\text{Gross sales} = \frac{\text{Net sales}}{(100\% - \text{Customer returns and allowance \%})}$$

Gross margin

Gross margin = Net sales − Total cost of goods sold

$ Gross margin = Gross margin % × Net sales

Net cost

Net cost = Billed cost − Cash discount

Net cost = List price − Trade discount(s) − Cash discount

Net sales = Gross sales − Customer returns and allowances

The function of the retail store is to sell merchandise to consumers. The amount of merchandise sold is the store's source of operating income, commonly known as sales or sales volume. However, before merchandise can be sold, it must be bought. In this opening unit, the basic elements of sales volume are defined, analyzed, and calculated, because their effective understanding is critical to a retailer's success.

UNIT 1.1
DEFINING THE BASIC SALES ELEMENTS

The function of the retail store is to sell merchandise to consumers at a profit. These sales are the store's source of operating income. Before merchandise can be sold, however, it must be bought. Even in a computerized organization in which financial personnel may preset programs and spreadsheets, the buyer is ultimately responsible for creating a merchandise assortment. This selection occurs after planning and predicting what, when, where, and how much to buy, and what to pay for these purchases. **Cost** is the amount the retailer pays for these purchases. **Retail** is the price at which stores offer merchandise for sale to the consumer.

Because the buyer buys and prices the merchandise offered for sale in a retail store, the buyer must have the ability to understand and manipulate the five basic profit factors: **operating income**, also known as sales or **sales volume**, indicates in dollars how much merchandise has been sold. **Cost of goods sold** shows the amount paid for the goods sold. This results in **gross margin**, in which the total cost of goods is subtracted from the net sales. **Operating expenses** refer to those expenses, other than the cost of the goods, incurred in the buying/selling process. When all of the operating expenses are deducted from the gross margin figure, the result is called **net operating profit** or **net profit**.

To properly compare profits among retailers, it is necessary to know how the expenses are treated. In accounting, there are acceptable variations in how expenses are recorded. In this text, expenses will continue to be listed individually or referred to merely as operating expenses. In performing the calculations necessary to answer the practice problems that apply to the profit concepts and principles, the focus is on adjusting the proper element to the appropriate basic profit factor. For example, cash discount is an adjustment to the cost-of-goods factor. When there is other net income that does not result directly from the everyday operation of the retail business, it is added to or subtracted from net operating profit to get "net profit before taxes." This income does not result from the everyday operation but rather reflects financial or nontrading earnings and deductions.

Gross sales are the entire dollar amount received for goods sold during a given period. This total sales figure is calculated by multiplying the retail price of the individual items of merchandise by the number of pieces actually sold to consumers. The accurate calculation of gross sales, however, must also take into account adjustments due to returns and price reductions. Stores typically give customers the privilege of returning merchandise. When merchandise is returned to stock and the customer receives a cash refund or a charge credit, these returns of sales are called **customer returns**. In addition, if a customer receives a price reduction after the sale is completed, it is known as a **customer allowance**. These two adjustments are referred to collectively as **customer returns and allowances**. When a customer return or allowance takes place, the previously recorded sale must be canceled and subtracted from the gross sales amount. When customer returns and allowances are subtracted from gross sales, the resulting total is the net sales figure. Thus, **net sales** are the sales total after customer returns and allowances have been deducted from gross sales. Net sales represent the amount of goods that actually stay sold. When retailers calculate profit, the net sales figure is the more significant because a firm can only realize a profit on goods that remain sold at the retail price. For this reason, the term "sales volume" is always a **net sales figure**.

Merchandisers must determine and balance the retail price for the items they purchase for sale to customers with, among other factors, how much they can afford to pay a vendor for merchandise. Cost of goods sold is simply the cost of the merchandise that has been sold during a given time period. This concept is simple, but the actual calculation is complex because other necessary adjustments must be made to the cost or purchase price that appears on the bill or invoice (vendor's bill). These adjustments are: transportation costs, also known as **inward freight**, which is the amount a vendor may charge for transporting merchandise to the designated premises of the retailer; **alteration and workroom costs**, which is a charge made to a selling department when it is necessary to treat merchandise so that it will be in condition for sale (i.e., assembling, polishing, making cuffs, etc.); and **cash discounts**, which is a percentage deducted from the invoice cost that vendors may grant for the payment of an invoice within a specified period of time.

Gross margin is the difference between net sales and the total cost of merchandise sold. It is a figure that indicates the buyer's ability to purchase the "right" merchandise, negotiate the "right" cost and credit terms, and put the "right" retail price on these purchases.

In addition, the retailer must maintain a place of business from which the goods are sold, and to maintain this place, it must incur operating expenses. Operating expenses usually fall into two major categories and are charged to a merchandise department to determine the net profit for that department. Expenses that are specific to a given department, and which would cease if that department were discontinued, are called **direct expenses**. These include salaries of the buyer, assistant buyer, and salespeople; departmental advertising; selling supplies; and customer delivery expenses. Store expenses that exist whether a department is added or discontinued are **indirect expenses**. These include store expenses that are prorated to all selling departments on the basis of their sales volume, such as store maintenance, insurance, and salaries of top management.

The operating expenses, which refer to those expenses, other than the cost of the goods, incurred in the buying/selling process, are deducted from the gross margin, resulting in net operating profit or net profit.

ELEMENTS OF BASIC SALES VOLUME

Each of the basic sales elements needs to be dissected, because each consists of factors that contribute to profit. The calculations involved highlight the meaning and importance of each element.

Sales (Operating Income)

Gross Sales

Gross sales are the total initial dollars received for merchandise sold during a given period.

CONCEPT

$$\text{Gross sales} = \begin{array}{c}\text{Total of all the prices charged to}\\\text{consumers on individual items}\end{array} \times \begin{array}{c}\text{Number of units}\\\text{actually sold}\end{array}$$

PROBLEM

On Monday, a toy department sold 30 dolls (Group A) priced at $15 each, 25 dolls (Group B) priced at $25 each, and 5 dolls (Group C) priced at $30 each. What were the gross sales for that day?

SOLUTION:
Spreadsheet format

Item	Quantity	Unit retail price	Income
Dolls (A)	30	$15	$450
Dolls (B)	25	$25	$625
Dolls (C)	5	$30	$150
Gross Sales			$1,225

SOLUTION:
Arithmetically

30 dolls @ $15 each	=	$450
25 dolls @ $25 each	=	625
5 dolls @ $30 each	=	150
Total gross sales	=	$1,225

Customer Returns and Allowances

Customer returns and allowances are profit factors because the customer receives either a complete refund of the purchase price or a partial rebate. Thus, the retailer must make a corresponding deduction from the gross sales figure because these transactions result in some cancellation of sales. This dollar figure is usually expressed as a percentage of gross sales.

Although these transactions many seem insignificant and are considered a daily happening in the buying/selling process, they should be scrutinized and evaluated. If they are excessively numerous, they can ultimately affect profit because it is "costly" to sell, return, and, hopefully, resell merchandise. The causes of returns should be examined, and an attempt should be made to reduce them to a reasonable percentage, which is the yardstick used for comparison.

CONCEPT

$$\text{Customer returns and allowances \$} = \text{Total of all refunds or credits to the customer on individual items of merchandise} \times \text{Number of units actually returned}$$

PROBLEM

On Saturday, the junior petite department refunded $98 for one leather jacket, $75 each for two wool skirts, and $55 each for two knit tops. Other returns for the week amounted to $400, and the weekly total of allowances given was $57. What was the dollar amount of customer returns and allowances for Saturday? For the week?

SOLUTION:
Spreadsheet format

Item	Quantity	Unit retail	Customer returns and allowances
Leather jackets	1	$98	$98
Wool skirts	2	$75	$150
Knit tops	2	$55	$110
Saturday total			$358
Other weekly returns			$400
Weekly customer allowances			$57
Total customer returns and allowances			$815

SOLUTION:
Arithmetically

$98	×	1 Leather jacket	=	$98
$75	×	2 Wool skirts	=	150
$55	×	2 Knit tops	=	110
		Customer returns for Saturday	=	$358
+		Total weekly customer returns	=	400
+		Total weekly customer allowances	=	57
		Customer returns and allowances (for week)	=	$815

CONCEPT

$$\text{Customer returns and allowances percentage} = \text{Dollar sum of customer returns and allowances expressed as a percentage of gross sales}$$

$$\text{Customer returns and allowances \%} = \frac{\text{\$ Customer returns and allowances}}{\text{Gross sales}} \times 100$$

Last week, the junior petite department had gross sales of $20,375. Customer returns and allowances for the week totaled $815. What was the combined percentage of allowances and merchandise returns for the week?

PROBLEM

$$\text{Customer returns and allowances \%} = \frac{\$815 \text{ Customer returns and allowances}}{\$20,375 \text{ Gross sales}} \times 100$$

Customer returns and allowances % = 4%

SOLUTION

Conversely, the dollar sum of customer returns and allowances can be computed when the gross sales and customer returns and allowances percentage are known.

$$\text{Dollar sum of customer returns and allowances} = \text{Gross sales} \times \text{Customer returns and allowances percentage}$$

CONCEPT

Last week, the junior petite department reported gross sales of $20,375, with customer returns and allowances of 4%. What was the dollar amount of customer returns and allowances?

PROBLEM

$$\text{Dollar sum of customer returns and allowances} = \$20,375 \text{ Gross sales} \times 4\% \text{ Customer returns and allowances}$$

Dollar sum of customer returns and allowances   = $815

SOLUTION

Net Sales

Net sales are the sales total for a given period after customer returns and allowances have been deducted from gross sales.

Net sales = Gross sales – Customer returns and allowances

CONCEPT

A shoe department sold $65,000 worth of merchandise. Customer returns were $6,500. What were the net sales of this department?

PROBLEM

Net sales = Gross sales – Customer returns and allowances

Net sales = $65,000 – $6,500

Net sales = $58,500

SOLUTION

In retailing, the operating income is known as net sales. The net sales figure, also called sales volume, is used to designate the size of a particular store or merchandise department. For example, last year Department #37 had a sales volume of $1,000,000. This dollar figure is generally the sales volume for the year.

Retailers use net sales to measure a department's performance or productivity. It is common practice to calculate the percentage of sales that an individual department has contributed to the store's net sales. This type of analysis allows a retailer to compare a particular department of one store with other departments or stores within the company, as well as to compare this selected department's sales with industry figures.

CONCEPT

The individual department's net sales are expressed as a percentage of the store's total net sales.

$$\frac{\text{Department's net sales}}{\text{\% of total store sales}} = \frac{\text{Department's net dollar sales}}{\text{Store's total net dollar sales}} \times 100$$

PROBLEM

The costume jewelry department had net sales of $900,000. For the same period, total store sales were $45,000,000. What is the costume jewelry department's net sales percentage of the total store's net sales?

SOLUTION

Department's net sales = $900,000

Total store net sales = $45,000,000

$$\frac{\text{Department's net sales}}{\text{\% of total store sales}} = \frac{\$900,000}{\$45,000,000} \times 100$$

Department's net sales % of total store sales = 2%

Because net sales are determined by the adjustment of customer returns and allowances to gross sales, it is also possible through this relationship to calculate, when desired, a gross sales amount—provided that an amount of the dollar net sales and the percentage of customer returns and allowances are known.

CONCEPT

$$\text{Gross sales} = \frac{\text{Net sales}}{(100\% - \text{Customer returns and allowance \%})}$$

PROBLEM

The net sales of Department #39 were $460,000. The customer returns and allowances were 8%. What were the gross sales of the department?

Net sales $\quad=\quad$ \$460,000

Gross sales $\quad=\quad \dfrac{\text{Net sales}}{100\% \text{ (Gross sales)} \quad - \quad 8\% \text{ Customer returns and allowances}}$

Gross sales $\quad=\quad \dfrac{\$460,000}{92\%}$

Gross sales $\quad=\quad$ \$500,000

MOST COMMON RETAIL KEY PERFORMANCE INDICATORS (KPIs) PERTAINING TO SALES PERFORMANCE

Sales vs Plan and Last Year Sales

The first performance indicator of sales is the comparison for sales this week vs plan sales for this week, and sales year-to-date (YTD) vs plan sales YTD. Are sales sufficient to cover expenses and leave a profit?

Same Store or Comparable Store Sales

This refers to sales this week or month vs the same period last year, or sales YTD last year only, comparing stores open in that year. Store openings or closings do not impact this comparison. Online channel sales are handled in different ways for each company.

Sales per Square Foot

This figure is calculated by dividing the dollar gross sales figure by the square footage of selling space. A retailer can improve return on the total space their stores or departments occupy by:

    a. Allocating more space to selling.

    b. Increasing sales from existing space.

    c. Selling more profitable items.

Sales per Linear Foot

This figure measures the selling space by linear feet and is used mainly by food and cosmetics retailers.

Inventory Turnover

Inventory turnover refers to the number of times, usually in one year, that the average inventory is sold.

Sell through Percentage

This is calculated by dividing the number of items sold by the number of items bought, and multiplying by 100. The mathematics required to calculate these performance indicators will be examined in appropriate units of study that pertain to each topic.

COST OF MERCHANDISE SOLD

The control of the cost of goods sold is crucial to profitability. The buyer, who decides what merchandise to buy, also makes decisions regarding the cost, transportation, and credit terms as they relate to these purchases. In actual practice, to determine the accurate **total cost of goods sold**, there must be a complete calculation to represent the **total cost of goods purchased**, which begins with an invoice or **billed cost**, to which the following factors are adjusted:

Calculation of Total Cost of Goods Sold

Billed Cost
This is the purchase price that appears on the invoice (i.e., vendor's bill).

PLUS

Inward Freight or Transportation Costs
This is the amount that a vendor may charge for delivery of merchandise. Inward freight or transportation costs plus billed cost is called the billed delivered cost.

PLUS

Alteration and Workroom Costs
It is accepted practice to treat this figure as an additional cost, because it applies only to merchandise that has been sold and not to all purchases.

MINUS

Cash Discounts
These are discounts that vendors may grant for payment of an invoice within a specified time. For example, a vendor may offer a 2% cash discount (deducted from the billed cost) if payment is made within a designated time period. The discounts are offered in the form of a percentage and are deducted from only the billed cost, but the dollar discount earned is used in the calculation of the total cost of sales. For example, a 2% cash discount given on a billed cost of $1,000 translates into a $20 cash discount or deduction:

$1,000 Billed cost $\times$ 2% Cash discount = $20 Cash discount

CONCEPT

$$\text{Total cost of goods sold} = \text{Billed cost} + \text{Inward transportation charges} + \text{Workroom costs} - \text{Cash discount}$$

PROBLEM

An activewear department, for the first month of the period, had billed costs of merchandise amounting to $80,000, inward freight charges of $2,000, earned cash discounts of 7.5%, and workroom costs of $500. Calculate the total cost of merchandise purchased.

Billed costs	=		$80,000
+ Inward freight	=	+	2,000
Billed delivered cost	=		$82,000
+ Workroom costs	=	+	500
Gross merchandise costs	=		$82,500
− Cash discount (7.5% × $80,000)	=	−	6,000
Total cost of goods sold			$76,500

GROSS MARGIN

The difference between the total amount of goods sold (net sales) and the total cost of the goods sold is the gross margin. It is calculated for a given period of time by subtracting the total cost of goods from the net sales for the period under consideration. It is a critical profit factor because it can be an indicator of the final results, and it is frequently known as **gross profit**. This figure must be large enough to cover operating expenses and allow for a reasonable profit. If the difference is not large enough to cover operating expenses, a **net loss** will result. It is a yardstick to measure the performance of a buyer.

Figure 1. Most Recent Fiscal Results of Gross Margin Performance*

Gross Margin	Percent of Companies
Less than 20%	0%
20–30%	13%
31–40%	25%
41–50%	34%
51–60%	19%
Over 60%	9%

Source: Tenth Annual Retail Horizons: Benchmarks for 2011, Forecasts for 2012 (KPMG/NRF Foundation)

Gross margin = Net sales − Total cost of goods sold

A department had net sales of $300,000, with the total cost of goods sold at $180,000. Determine the gross margin.

Net sales	=	$300,000
− Total cost of goods sold	=	− 180,000
Gross margin	=	$120,000

Operating Income Practice Problems

1. Customer returns and allowances for Department #620 came to $4,500. Gross sales in the department were $90,000. What percentage of merchandise sold was returned?

2. The gross sales for Store B were $876,500. The customer returns and allowances were 10%.

   a. What was the dollar amount of returns and allowances?

   b. What were net sales?

3. The net sales of Department X were $46,780. The customer returns were $2,342. What were gross sales?

4. The gross sales of Store C were $2,500,000. The customer returns and allowances were $11,360. What were net sales?

5. The net sales of Department Y were $36,000. The customer returns and allowances were 10%. What were gross sales?

6. After Mother's Day this year, the loungewear department had customer returns of 10.5%. The department's net sales amounted to $635,380. As the buyer reviewed last year's figures for the same period, the customer returns were 12.5%, with gross sales of $726,149.

    a. Compute the department's performance in dollars and percentages for this year and last year, in regards to gross sales, customer returns, and net sales.

    b. Compare this year's results to last year's performance. Discuss the performance from a profit viewpoint.

7. For this year, Store G's sales volume was $550,000,000. The juniors' dress department had net sales of $8,250,000, and the misses' dress department had net sales of $24,750,000. What were the net sales percentages of each department to the total store?

8. Branch Store H had total sales of $30,000,000. The small leather goods department's sales were 1.9% of Store H's total sales. The handbag department's sales were 2.1% of the total branch sales. What were the dollar net sales for each department?

9. Discussion Problem: Explain why a merchant should be alarmed if customer returns are excessive. How does a merchant determine what is an excessive percentage of returns? What can be done by the department itself to correct a problematic rate of returns?

10. The customer returns for the Fall season were 10% on gross sales of $900,000. For the Spring season, gross sales were $850,000, and customer returns were $70,000. What was the percentage of customer returns for the entire year?

Cost of Merchandise Sold
Practice Problems

11. The petite sportswear buyer placed the following order:

    - 36 pants costing $10.75 each.

    - 48 pants costing $15.50 each.

    - 24 pants costing $17.50 each.

    Shipping charges (paid by the store) were 6% of the billed cost. Find:

    a. The dollar amount of shipping charges.

    b. The delivered cost of the total order.

12. A luggage buyer purchased 72 attaché cases that cost $40 each. The cash discount earned was 2%, and the store paid inward freight of $95. Find the total cost of the merchandise on this order.

13. A gift shop has workroom costs of $575. The billed cost of merchandise sold amounted to $59,000, with cash discounts earned of $1,180, and freight charges of $650. Find the total cost of the merchandise.

14. A specialty dress shop made purchases amounting to $3,700 at cost, with 8% cash discounts earned, workroom costs of $100, and no inward freight. Determine the total cost of the merchandise.

15. A sporting goods buyer placed the following order:

    • 18 nylon backpacks costing $22 each.

    • 12 two-person tents costing $54 each.

    • 6 camp stoves costing $55 each.

    Shipping costs paid by the store were $60, and a cash discount of 1% was taken. Find:

    a. Billed cost on the total order.

    b. Total delivered cost of the merchandise.

16. Discussion Problem: Explain why control of inward freight costs and workroom (alterations) costs is vital. Can a merchandiser help to control these factors? If so, how? Why is cash discount calculated on billed cost?

UNIT I.II
INVOICE MATHEMATICS: TERMS OF SALE

The retailer should be able to identify and recognize the different types of discounts offered, as well as understand the different types of dating and shipping terms involved in buying goods, because much of the secondary negotiating between vendors and retail buyers revolves around these three factors.

When retail buyers select merchandise, they not only agree on the cost price, but they also negotiate other factors that influence final cost. These conditions of the sale that are agreed upon when the merchandise is purchased are called **terms of sale**. These terms deal with discounts granted, dating for payments, transportation arrangements, and shipping charges. When the discounts granted are deducted from the billed cost, net cost remitted to the vendor is the resultant figure. When shipping charges are to be paid by the retailers, they are added to the net cost that is due to the vendor, and the final or total amount to be sent to the vendor is determined. Lack of familiarity with terms of sale is a serious handicap, because one of the best ways to improve profits is to lower the cost of goods, assuming other factors remain constant. Consequently, any factor that will increase the ever-significant gross margin figure is essential.

DIFFERENT TYPES OF DISCOUNTS

A discount is a deduction (expressed as a percentage) off the quoted or billed cost of the merchandise. Discounts are granted by a vendor to a purchaser for various negotiated terms. While discount practices and schedules vary from one industry to another, and from firm to firm, and even within different merchandise classifications, there are three basic types of discounts. Generally these discounts are taken in the following order: (1) trade discounts, (2) quantity discounts, and (3) cash discounts. These three types of discounts are examined in the following sections.

Trade Discount
Trade discount is a percentage or a series of percentages deducted from the **list price** (i.e., the theoretical retail price recommended by the manufacturer). The price that a buyer pays for merchandise is determined by deducting this trade discount percentage from the list price. It is a means of establishing the cost price of the goods. The number and/or amount of trade discounts varies according to the classification of the purchasers (i.e., retail stores, jobbers, other middlemen, or industrial buyers) and the amount of marketing services performed by that group. For example, a flashlight manufacturer quotes trade discounts to general retailers at 35%, department stores at 40%, chain stores at 45%, and wholesalers at 50%.

Trade discounts are deducted regardless of when the invoice is paid. In merchandise lines that customarily offer trade discounts, the list price minus the trade discount(s) is a way of quoting the cost. In some cases, this type of discount is quoted as a single percentage (e.g., $100 list price, less 45%), or it is offered as a series of discounts (e.g., $100 list price, less 30%, less 10%, less 5%). Generally the clothing industries do not use the trade discount approach to determine the cost of an item; usually cost prices are quoted directly (e.g., style #332 costs $18.75 each, or scarves cost $120/dozen). Trade discounts deducted from an established list price provide a vendor with a mechanism for changing cost easily. For example, when a supplier shows and describes merchandise through a catalog, the price change is done expeditiously by printing new price lists with a change in the discount. It is a device whereby the various middlemen in the channels of distribution can get larger and/or more discounts than retailers, either because of the functional services they provide for the manufacturer or because of the larger quantities that they purchase. On the same item, a wholesaler might receive discounts of 40% and 10%, while the retailer may receive a discount of 40% only.

CONCEPT	Billed cost = List price – Trade discount(s)

PROBLEM	Trade discounts on a lawn mower that "lists" at $200 are 25%, 10%, and 5%. Find the billed cost.

SOLUTION: Spreadsheet format

	Price	Discount	Discount amount	Resultant figure
Lawn mower list	$200.00	0.25	$50.00	$150.00
1st discount	$150.00	0.10	$15.00	$135.00
2nd discount	$135.00	0.05	$6.75	$128.25

SOLUTION: Arithmetically

List price = $200

Less 25%	$200.00	List price
–	50.00	($200 × 25%) = 1st discount
	$150.00	(resultant figure)
Less 10%	$150.00	
–	15.00	($150 × 10%) = 2nd discount
	$135.00	(resultant figure)
Less 5%	$135.00	
–	6.75	($135 × 5%) = 3rd discount
	$128.25	(resultant figure)

Billed cost = $128.25

Note that even though the list price is $200, it is common practice for the retailer to use the billed cost and the appropriate markup percentage to calculate the retail price of the merchandise.

Quantity Discount

Quantity discount (QD) is a percentage off the billed cost given by a vendor when a stipulated quantity is purchased, and it is deductible regardless of when invoices are paid. Usually the purchase of a large amount of goods is involved. Although quantity discounts are not customary practice in the fashion industries, they are common in home furnishings and hard goods lines. Depending on custom and practice within individual industries, this kind of discount is offered either when the stipulated quantity is purchased or for accumulated purchases over a specified period of time. The amount of discount is based on a sliding scale (i.e., the larger the purchase, the greater the percentage of quantity discount). A quantity discount is offered as an incentive for buyers to commit to purchasing large amounts of goods. This is a legal practice under specific provisions of the Robinson-Patman Act of 1936, federal legislation regulating wholesale pricing. Additionally, it is the buyer's responsibility to judge the merits of savings through this quantity discount against the risks of tying up more than the normal planned amount of open-to-buy money.

$ Quantity discount   = $ Billed cost   ×   Quantity discount %

$ Net billed cost   = $ Billed cost   –   Quantity discount

CONCEPT

A cookware manufacturer's established price schedule is:

- A minimum initial order of $500 receives a 1% QD.
- An initial order of $1,250 receives 1.5%.
- An initial order of $2,500 receives 2%, and so on.

On an order of assorted cookware amounting to $2,000, use this discount schedule to determine:

a. The quantity discount.
b. The net cost of this order.

PROBLEM

Item	Billed cost	Quantity discount	Discount amount	Net cost
Cookware	$2,000	0.015	$30	$1,970

SOLUTION: *Spreadsheet format*

Quantity discount = $2,000 Billed cost × 1.5% Quantity discount

$2,000 × 1.5%

Quantity discount	=	$30
Billed cost	=	$2,000
Quantity discount	–	30
Net cost	=	$1,970

SOLUTION: *Arithmetically*

Cash Discount

Cash discount, the most common kind of discount, is a stated percentage of the billed cost allowed by a vendor if payment of the invoice amount is made within a stipulated time. The full utilization of cash discounts is another approach to decreasing the total cost of merchandise that results in an increased profit potential. Although any invoice or bill must be paid within some specified time, the intent of the cash discount is to offer the purchaser an incentive to make an early payment. The vendor sacrifices a fraction of the cost that is due in order to receive payment more rapidly. Cost prices that are subject to quantity and/or trade discounts may also be subject to cash discounts. Eligibility for a cash discount is contingent on the time element only. The cash discount percentage is not only written on the purchase order, but also on the vendor's invoice (e.g., 8/10 terms refers to an 8% discount if the invoice is paid within 10 days).

CALCULATING NET COST

Billed Cost and Cash Discount Are Known

CONCEPT

Net cost = Billed cost – Cash discount

PROBLEM

The cost of a microwave oven is $60. The cash discount earned is 6%. What is the net cost paid to the manufacturer?

SOLUTION:
Spreadsheet format

Item	Billed cost	Discount	Discount amount	Net cost
Microwave oven	$60	0.06	$3.60	$56.40

SOLUTION:
Arithmetically

Cash discount = $60.00 Billed cost × 6% Cash discount

$$\begin{array}{r} \$60.00 \\ \times \quad 6\% \\ \hline \end{array}$$

Cash discount = $3.60

Billed cost = $60.00

– Cash discount – 3.60

Net cost = $56.40   (Amount to be remitted)

List Price Is Quoted and Cash Discount Is Given

When the cost of goods is stated by quoting a list price with a series of trade discounts, and the buyer is also eligible for a cash discount, the amount to be paid is determined by calculating the billed cost first, and then deducting the cash discount.

Net cost = List price – Trade discount(s) – Cash discount

The list price of a lawn mower is $200 less 25%, less 10%, less 5%. There is a 2% cash discount offered for payment within 10 days. What is the amount to be remitted if the cash discount is earned?

	Price	Discount	Discount amount	Resultant figure	Cash discount	Cash discount amount	Net cost
Lawn mower list	$200	0.25	$50.00	$150.00			
1st discount	$150	0.10	$15.00	$135.00			
2nd discount	$135	0.05	$6.75	$128.25	0.02	$2.57	$125.68

List price	$200.00	$200.00	List price
Less 25%	× 25%	– 50.00	1st dollar discount
	$50.00	$150.00	
Less 10%	$150.00	$150.00	Intermediate price
	× 10%	– 15.00	2nd dollar discount
	$15.00	$135.00	
Less 5%	$135.00	$135.00	2nd intermediate price
	× 5%	– 6.75	3rd dollar discount
	$6.75	$128.25	
Billed cost		$128.25	Billed cost
		× 2%	Cash discount
		$2.57	Cash discount
		$128.25	Billed cost
		– 2.57	Cash discount
Net cost		$125.68	Amount remitted

Quantity and Cash Discounts Must Be Considered

When the purchase is large enough to become eligible for a quantity discount, and a cash discount is offered, the amount to be paid is calculated by first deducting the amount of the quantity discount and then deducting the cash discount.

CONCEPT

Net cost = Billed cost – Quantity discount – Cash discount

PROBLEM

A cookware manufacturer has established price schedules of:

- A minimum initial order of $500 receives 1% QD.

- An initial order of $1,250 receives 1.5%.

- An initial order of $2,500 receives 2%, etc.

In addition, there is a 3% cash discount offered for payment made within 10 days. Based on this discount schedule, what is the net cost for a $2,000 order of assorted cookware if it is paid within 7 days?

SOLUTION:
Spreadsheet format

Item	Order	Quantity discount	Discount amount	Resultant figure	Cash discount	Cash discount amount	Net cost
Cookware	$2,000	0.015	$30	$1,970	0.03	$59.10	$1,910.90

SOLUTION:
Arithmetically

Quantity discount	=	$2,000.00 Billed cost × 1.5% QD	
	=	$2,000.00	
	×	1.5%	
Quantity discount	=	$30.00	
Cost	=	$2,000.00	Billed cost
	–	30.00	QD
Cost	=	$1,970.00	
Cash discount	=	$1,970.00	
	×	3%	Cash discount
Cash discount	=	$59.10	
Net cost	=	$1,970.00	
	–	59.10	Cash discount
Net cost	=	$1,910.90	

List Price Is Quoted and Quantity Discounts and Cash Discounts Are Allowed

When the cost of goods for some types of merchandise is stated by quoting a list price with a series of discounts, and the buyer is granted a quantity discount and is also eligible for a cash discount, the amount to be remitted to the vendor is calculated by:

- First, deducting the series of trade discounts to find the billed cost.

- Second, determining the eligibility for the quantity discounts offered and deducting the percentage of dollar amount from the calculated billed cost.

- Third, subtracting the cash discount from this amount.

The reason for this order is that when merchandise is quoted with trade discounts, the cost price of the goods must be established first. Only then can the buyer determine if the amount purchased satisfies the quantity specified for the quantity discount, regardless of when the invoice is paid. After this cost price is calculated, the cash discount is then subtracted—but only if payment is made within the stipulated time. Savings realized by these discounts alone have an impact on the department's profit margin and should be thoroughly understood for what they are and how they are calculated to determine the remitted cost price.

CONCEPT

$$\text{Net cost} = \text{List price} - \text{Trade discount(s)} - \text{Quantity discount} - \text{Cash discounts}$$

PROBLEM

A silverware buyer purchases 75 pairs of sterling salt and pepper shakers directly from a manufacturer who quotes the list price of this item for $125 less 25%, 10%, and 5%. The vendor's price schedule is as follows:

- A minimum order of $4,000 receives a 3% quantity discount.

- An initial order of $4,500 receives a 4% quantity discount.

- An initial order of $5,000 receives a 7% quantity discount.

In addition, there is a 2% cash discount offered for payment made within 10 days. What is the net cost of this order if it is paid in 8 days?

SOLUTION: Spreadsheet format

Item	List price	Quantity	Billed cost									
Sterling S+Ps	$125	75	$9,375									

			Discount	Discount amount	Net cost	Quantity discount	Quantity discount amount	Discounted cost	Cash discount	Cash discount amount	Net cost remitted
Total list price	$9,375		0.25	$2,343.75	$7,031.25						
1st discount	$7,031.25		0.1	$703.13	$6,328.12						
2nd discount	$6,328.12		0.05	$316.41	$6,011.71	0.07	$420.82	$5,590.89	0.02	$111.82	$5,479.07

List price: $125 × 75 pairs	=	$9,375.00
− 1st trade discount 25%	×	25%
	=	$2,343.75
Total list price	=	$9,375.00
− 1st $ discount	−	2,343.75
1st intermediate price	=	$7,031.25
	=	$7,031.25
− 2nd trade discount 10%	×	10%
	=	$703.125
1st intermediate price	=	$7,031.25
− 2nd $ discount	−	703.13
2nd intermediate price	=	$6,328.12
	=	$6,328.12
− 3rd trade discount 5%	×	5%
	=	$316.406
2nd intermediate price	=	$6,328.12
− 3rd $ discount	−	316.41
Billed cost	=	$6,011.71
	=	$6,011.71
− Quantity discount 7%	×	7%
	=	$420.82
Billed cost	=	$6,011.71
− Quantity discount	−	420.82
	=	$5,590.89
− Cash discount 2%	×	2%
Cash discount	=	$111.8178
Billed cost	=	$5,590.89
− Cash discount	−	111.82
Amount remitted	=	$5,479.07

(Note: Difference in spreadsheet format solution is due to rounding)

NET TERMS

Net terms is the expression used to refer to a condition of sale if a cash discount is neither offered nor permitted. When an item is sold under these conditions, it is expressed as a "net" arrangement.

PROBLEM

A buyer purchases an item costing $500 with net terms. The invoice is dated October 5 and the bill is paid within 30 days. What is the amount of the bill that was paid?

SOLUTION

$500 billed cost with net terms means no cash discount is allowed, so $500 is paid.

DATING

Dating is an agreement between the supplier and retailer whereby a specified time period for payment of an invoice is arranged. Dating arrangements vary within any particular industry and from one industry to another. Dating usually implies a cash discount and is expressed as a single term of sale (e.g., 2/10). This means that the buyer will deduct a 2% cash discount from the billed cost if the payment is remitted to the manufacturer on or before the stipulated 10-day period. For example:

Industry	Common dating practice
Ready-to-wear	8/10 EOM
Jewelry	2/10, net 30
Home furnishings	2/10, net 30

EOM dating will be described later in this section. In the jewelry and home furnishings examples, "2/10, net 30" means that a 2% discount off the billed cost is permitted if the invoice is paid within 10 days following the date of invoice. If payment isn't made in the 10-day discount time period, the payment of the net amount (i.e., total amount of billed cost) is required between the 11th and the 30th day following the date of the invoice.

PROBLEM

An invoice, dated March 1, for 10 folding chairs at a cost of $24 each carries terms of 2/10, net 30. If the bill is paid on any day from March 1 to March 11, 2% may be deducted. How much should be paid if the invoice is paid on March 8?

SOLUTION	Each chair		$24.00	
	× Quantity	×	10	
	Total cost	=	$240.00	
			$240.00	Billed cost
		×	2%	Cash discount
	Cash discount	=	$4.80	
			$240.00	Billed cost
		−	4.80	Cash discount
	Net cost	=	$235.20	

However, if the bill is paid on or after March 12, the full amount of $240 is due, as listed in the following payment schedule:

Cash discount period		Net period		Penalty period
Date of invoice	*Last date for cash discount*	*First date for net payment*	*Last date for net payment*	*Penalty period starts*
March 1	March 11	March 12	March 31	April 1

In dating that allows a 10-day discount period, the last day for the net payment can be determined by adding another 20 days to the last discount day (i.e., date). For example:

Starting with a March 1 Invoice date

+	10	Discount days
March 11		**Last discount date**
+	20	Net payment days
March 31		**Last net payment date** (traditional calendar)

or

Last net payment date = March 1 invoice date + 30 days = March 31

Different Types of Dating

There are many different types of dating used in all industries. As stated before, variations can even occur within a particular industry. Generally, the nature of the goods influences the prevalent dating practices. For example, some segments of the apparel industry offer a relatively high cash discount (e.g., 8%) to induce purchasers to take advantage of the savings for early or prompt payment. This is vital in an industry composed of many small businesses that are frequently undercapitalized. From the standpoint of the purchaser (i.e., retailer) who utilizes the cash discount privileges, the cost of the merchandise is considerably reduced, which has potential implications for increased profits. In the determination of when to pay an invoice, the buyer must be able to distinguish between the discount date and the net payment date. The **discount date** is the date by which the invoice may be paid to take advantage of the discount granted, and the net payment date is the date by which the invoice must be paid to acquire a favorable credit rating and avoid possible late penalties.

The previous explanations and problems pertaining to the time period of payment reflect the customary, accepted U.S. practices that are associated with the various types of invoice-payment dating. However, in buyer vs seller markets, and in certain other economic conditions (e.g., a recession), the adherence to these rules can, and frequently does, change. For example, when economic conditions are not favorable, a retailer may be prone to disregard or possibly extend the traditional negotiated time period. Under these conditions, the vendor usually makes exceptions and concentrates on invoice payment, rather than the strict observance of datings. Nonetheless, the most important negotiation is to set a specific date for payment of an invoice, and then be able to calculate the exact payment date. Even though there are different numbers of days in each month throughout the year, to simplify the payment calculations, many businesses will base their calculations on a 30-day month. Businesses that want to take advantage of all possible days in the payment period often prefer using the traditional calendar. Since individual arrangements can vary, for the purpose of the identification and application of the various types of dating, the problems and illustrations used in this text calculate the discount and net payment dates on a 30-day month.

COD Dating

COD dating (cash-on-delivery) is a type of dating that means payment must be made "on the spot" as delivery takes place. Generally, COD dating is applicable to purchasers with poor or unproven credit ratings.

Goods valued at $500 cost are purchased by a retail store under COD dating terms. What amount must be remitted? When?

PROBLEM

Invoice amount = $500; Amount remitted = $500

When = As delivery takes place

SOLUTION

Regular (or Ordinary) Dating

Regular or **ordinary dating** is one of the most common kinds of dating. The discount period is calculated from the date of the invoice, which is usually the same date that the merchandise is shipped.

PROBLEM

What payment should be made on an invoice for $500 dated November 16, carrying terms of 4/10, net 30?

SOLUTION

If paid on or before November 26 (November 26 is 16 + 10 days):

Billed cost		$500
– Cash discount ($500 × 4%)	–	20
Remitted	=	$480

If paid between November 27 and December 17 (i.e., the 20-day net payment period), no discount is permitted, and the full $500 is remitted. The vendor reserves the right to charge carrying fees after the expiration of the net payment period. The exercising or bypassing of this option is done on a case-by-case basis and depends on individual factors (e.g., credit history, the relationship of the vendor with the retailer, etc.).

Extra Dating

Extra dating (written as an X) is calculated from the date of the invoice, with a specified number of extra days granted during which the discount may be taken. Consequently, 2/10–60X means that the bill may be paid in 10 days, plus 60 extra days (i.e., a total of 70 days), from the date of the invoice in order to earn the 2% discount. The full amount is due after the expiration of the 70 days, and the customary, though often unstated, 20-day additional net payment period follows.

PROBLEM

An invoice dated March 16 has a billed cost of $1,800 and terms of 3/10–60X. Determine:

a. The final date for taking the cash discount.

b. The cash discount earned if the bill is paid by June 14.

c. The amount due if paid in full on April 17.

d. The last date for net payment.

a. Final date for cash discount:

   March 16 through 30 = 14 days

   April (entire month) = 30 days

   May 1 through 26 = 26 days

   End of cash discount period: May 26 = 70 days

   Cash discount allowable through May 26 only.

b. **None**

c. Eligible for cash discount:

$1,800	Billed cost
− 54	($1,800 × 3% Cash discount)
$1,746	Amount due
$1,746	**Amount due if paid in full on April 17**

d. Last date for net payment:

   20 days after May 26 = June 16

   Last date for net payment: June 16

EOM Dating

EOM dating (end of month) means the cash discount period is computed from the end of the month in which the invoice is dated, rather than from the date of the invoice itself. Thus, 8/10 EOM (invoice dated April 1, for example) means that the time for payment is calculated from the end of April. Additionally, an 8% cash discount may be taken if the bill is paid by May 10, that is, 10 days after the end of April. Again, an implied 20-day net period occurs from May 11 through May 31, during which the retailer may pay the bill in full.

(Note: Traditionally, under EOM dating only, invoices dated on or after the 25th of any month are considered to be part of the next month's transactions. For example, a bill with 8/10 EOM dated on August 26 is considered a September 1 bill, and the discount period extends to October 10. Of course, arrangements of this kind vary. It is common to apply this concept for invoice dates after the 25th of a month to other types of dating as well.)

An invoice for $1,000 dated March 17 has terms of 8/10 EOM.

a. What is the last date for deducting the 8% cash discount?

b. What amount will be due if the bill is paid on that date?

a. Discount date = April 10 (10 days after the end of March)

Last date for 8% discount: April 10

b. $1,000   Billed cost

 −   80   ($1,000 × 8% Cash discount)
 _____
   $920   Amount due

   $920   Amount due if paid in full by April 10

If this invoice was dated March 26 through to March 31 (using the traditional calendar), the discount date of payment would be May 10.

ROG Dating

ROG dating (receipt of goods) means that the discount period is calculated from the date the goods are delivered to the retailer's premises, rather than from the date of the invoice. This type of dating is often requested by buyers located a considerable distance from the market (or shipping point). These retailers typically receive bills a few days after shipment but may not get delivery of the merchandise itself for a considerably longer time. Therefore, 5/10 ROG, for example, means that the bill must be paid within 10 days after receipt of goods to earn the cash discount.

PROBLEM

An invoice for $100 is dated April 4 and carries terms of 5/10 ROG. The goods arrive at the store on May 7.

a. What is the last date that the discount may be deducted?

b. How much should be remitted if payment is made on that date?

SOLUTION

a. Date goods were received + 10 days

May 7 + 10 days = May 17

Last day for discount: May 17

b. $100 Billed cost − $5 ($100 × 5% Cash discount) = $95

$95 Amount due on or before May 17

Advanced or Postdating

Advanced or **postdating** (seasonal discount) is a type of dating that indicates the invoice date is advanced, so that additional time is allowed for payment to be made and, ultimately, for the cash discount to be deducted. The discount period is then calculated from this advanced date agreed upon by the buyer and the seller. Generally, this type of dating is used by manufacturers to persuade buyers to buy and/or receive goods earlier than they would normally. It is also requested by purchasers who are momentarily short of cash. Consequently, if a shipment was made on February 10, and the invoice date was May 1, terms of 2/10 would mean that payment was due on or before May 11 to qualify for a 2% cash discount. (Note: On invoices with advanced or postdating, the payment of the invoice at net is delayed until the last day of the month in which the cash discount is earned, after which it is considered overdue.)

An invoice for merchandise shipped on August 18 is postdated October 1 and carries terms of 3/10, net 30. When does the discount period expire?

PROBLEM

3% may be deducted if payment is made on or before October 11. The full amount is due at the end of the customary net period on October 31, using the traditional calendar.

SOLUTION

Net Payment Dates

Net payment dates refer to that date by which an invoice must be paid. This date is expressed as n/30. It is considered overdue—and may be subject to an interest charge—if paid after the net payment period. Of course, there are variations for determining the final net payment date of an invoice (see Figure 2). The net payment date is determined by the agreed-upon type of cash discount dating. The commonly used practices are:

- Regular dating: The full amount of the invoice is due exactly 30 days from the date of invoice.

- EOM, ROG, and extra dating: The net payment date of the invoice is determined by adding 20 days from the expiration of the cash discount period.

- Advanced or postdating: The payment of the net invoice is delayed until the last day of the month in which the cash discount is earned.

Figure 2. Summary of Discount Dates

Type of Dating	Invoice Date	Last Date Eligible for Discount	Net Amount Paid between Dates Below	Bill Past Due if Paid on or Later Than
1. Regular (2/10 or net 30)	11/16	11/26	11/27 through 12/17	12/18
2. Extra Dating (X) (3/10–90X)	6/7	9/17	9/17 through 10/7	10/8
3. End of Month (EOM) (8/10 EOM)	3/17	4/10	4/11 through 4/30	5/1
4. Receipt of Goods (ROG) (5/10 ROG; Rec'd 4/16)	4/4	4/26	4/27 through 5/16	5/17
5. Advanced or Postdating (3/10 net 30 as of 10/1)	8/18	10/11	10/12 through 10/31	11/1

Deadline dates used in this chart are based on a thirty-day month.

ANTICIPATION

Anticipation is an extra type of cash discount that is usually calculated at the prevailing prime rate of business interest and is subject to change based on economic conditions. Although not commonly prevalent, this extra discount is often permitted by vendors when an invoice is paid prior to the end of the cash discount period and, again, is subject to change based on economic conditions. For the purpose of illustration only, this text will use a 6% annual rate, which equates to 0.5% per month, or a decimal equivalent of .005 per month.

The number of days of anticipation is based upon the number of days remaining between the actual date of payment of an invoice and the last date on which the cash discount could be taken. While some vendors do not permit an anticipation discount, some alert retailers deduct it, unless a notation on the invoice expressly forbids it. When sending in a confirmed order, many retailers specify "anticipation allowed." Anticipation is taken by retailers because, in effect, the vendor has the use of the retailer's money ahead of the date arranged by the terms of the sale, and because of this the retailer is charging the vendor "interest" for its use. An anticipation deduction is taken in addition to any other discounts that may apply, and the deduction percentage customarily is combined with the regular cash discount percentage.

Currently, however, some retailers are anticipating invoices based on the number of days from the date of payment to the end of the net period. When using this policy, a bill that is paid after the cash discount period has ended can still be anticipated for the balance of the net period.

(Note: In the following practice problems illustrating anticipation, only the more traditional cash-discount-period method should be used. The following example, however, shows the calculations used for both the cash-discount-period method and the net-payment-period method.)

PROBLEM

An invoice for $100 is dated December 4 and carries terms of 2/10–30X. Anticipation is permitted. If the bill is paid on December 14:

a. Calculate the number of days that were anticipated and the remittance due using the cash-discount-period method.

b. Determine the number of days that were anticipated and the remittance due using the net-payment-period method.

a. Using the traditional cash-discount-period method:

The cash discount period is 40 days.

Because the bill is paid in 10 days, the **anticipation period** is 30 days.

Total $ amount of goods	=	$100
Anticipation	=	0.5% for 30 days
Cash discount	=	2%
Cash discount anticipation	=	2% + 0.5% = 2.5%
Total discount	=	$100 × 2.5% = $2.50
Net cost	=	$100 – $2.50 = $97.50
Amount remitted	=	$97.50

b. Using the net-payment-period method or an alternate approach to anticipation:

The cash discount period is 40 days and the net payment period is 60 days.

Because the bill is paid in 10 days, the **anticipation period** is 50 days.

(Note: Using the net-payment-period method, if this invoice was paid after 40 days—that is, after the cash discount period had elapsed—the buyer would still be allowed an anticipation discount for the 20 days remaining in the net payment period.)

Total $ amount of goods	=	$100
Anticipation	=	0.82% for 50 days
Cash discount	=	2%
Cash discount anticipation	=	2% + 0.82% + 2.82%
Total discount	=	$100 × 2.82% = $2.82
Net cost	=	$100 – $2.82 = $97.18
Amount remitted	=	$97.18

The anticipation calculation for the traditional cash discount period and the net payment period is identical. The difference is merely the determination of the number of days anticipated.

LOADING

Loading is a rare practice of a vendor intentionally increasing the amount of an invoice to a price that would allow a theoretically greater cost discount, but that results in the retailer paying the net amount that the vendor quotes. The standardized cash discount percentage arbitrarily set by top management does not reflect the true cash discount allowed by the vendor. When loading is practiced, the retailer may request that the vendor bill a "loaded" cost that is then adjusted by the required cash discount percentage to achieve the true net cost. In other cases, the store will make the adjustments statistically when the invoices are processed.

PROBLEM

A manufacturer quotes the cost of an item at $30 with terms of 3/10, n/30. The buyer desired an 8% cash discount. What is the "loaded" cost?

SOLUTION

Net cost of invoice $= $ $30 Billed cost $-$ 3% Cash discount

$= $ $30 $-$ $0.90 (3% $\times$ $30)

$= $ $29.10

Loaded cost $= \dfrac{\$29.10\ \text{Net cost}}{92\%\ (100\%\ -\ 8\%\ \text{Loaded discount})}$

$= $ $31.63

SHIPPING TERMS

As with dating, shipping charges vary in different industries and in different situations. They are expressed as free-on-board (FOB) at a designated location. The place that is designated defines the point to which the vendor pays transportation charges and assumes risk of loss or damage and the legal title to the merchandise being shipped to a purchaser. Because the factors that determine the total cost of goods include inward freight charges, it is important that the retailer negotiate advantageous shipping terms as a means of reducing the total cost of goods. The buyer should apply ethical but firm pressure on merchandise resources for appropriate and favorable terms of sale and discounts. The most common arrangements are:

- **FOB retailer.** Vendor pays transportation charges to the retailer's store or warehouse and, unless otherwise agreed upon, bears the risk of loss until goods are received by the retailer.

- **FOB factory.** Purchaser pays transportation charges from factory to purchaser's premises and, unless otherwise agreed upon, bears the risk of loss from the time the goods leave the factory.

- **FOB city or port of destination.** Vendor pays the transportation charges to a specified location in the city of destination, and then the purchaser pays delivery charges from that point to the purchaser's premises. Unless otherwise agreed upon, the risk of loss passes from seller to buyer when goods arrive at the specified location in the city of destination.

- **Prepaid.** Vendor pays transportation (freight) charges to the retailer's store or warehouse when the merchandise is shipped from vendor's premises. The FOB agreement, made at the time of sale, determines whether the vendor or purchaser pays the freight charges.

17. The Robner Electronic Company lists a top-of-the-line answering machine for $175. The trade discount offered is 30%. What is the billing price?

18. A guitar manufacturer sells electric guitars at $450 less 30% and 10%. What is the net cost to the buyer?

19. Dealer A sells stereo sets for $975 with a 30% trade discount. Competitor B offers a similar model at $760 with a 15% discount. Which is the better buy? By how much?

20. The quantity discount schedule of a china importer is 0.5% discount on orders for $1,000, 1% discount on orders for $1,500, 1.5% discount on orders for $2,500, and 2% discount on orders for $3,000. A retailer's order of bone china luncheon sets amounted to $2,800. No other discounts were allowed on this particular group. How much should the retailer pay the importer?

21. As an incentive, a supplier of motorbikes offers an additional 10% quantity discount on orders of more than 5 bikes. The normal trade discount offered by the supplier is 40% and 10% on the suggested list price of $250 each. How much would a retailer remit if 8 bikes are purchased?

22. What is the net cost on an $850 order if the cash discount earned is 4%?

23. Calculate the net cost on an order for 6 dozen boys' swim trunks at $84/dozen. The cash discount earned is 3%.

24. If a buyer purchases 120 coats at $52 each and earns an 8% cash discount, what amount must be paid to the manufacturer?

25. A gift store received an invoice in the amount of $8,200, which represents the manufacturer's suggested retail price. The invoice also shows that a trade discount of 45% is allowed, as well as a 2% cash discount. Determine the amount of payment to the vendor.

26. A sporting goods buyer purchased 50 individual golf clubs of one style that cost $35 each. When the merchandise was received, the invoice indicated that an additional 5% quantity discount was allowed when more than 36 clubs of any one style were purchased. Additionally, a 3% cash discount was allowed when payment was made within 10 days. What amount should have been remitted to the manufacturer if payment was made in 7 days?

27. The housewares department placed an order for 2 dozen food processors that have a list price of $300 each, with trade discounts of 30%, 10%, and 5%. The supplier's price schedule is:

    a. A minimum order of $3,000: 1%.

    b. An initial order of $4,000: 1.5%.

    c. An initial order of $5,000: 2%.

    d. Payments within 10 days: 2% cash discount.

    If this invoice was paid in 9 days, what amount should have been remitted to the seller?

28. A retailer has in stock a microcomputer that lists for $1,950. Trade discounts of 35% and 10% were quoted.

    a. What is the billed cost?

    b. At what price would the microcomputer sell if the retailer decided to apply a 48% markup?

29. If you were a buyer with an invoice that came to a list price of $100, which set of series trade discounts would you favor?

      a. 25%, 20%, and 15%

      or

      b. 50% and 10%

      Explain your choice.

30. Determine the final dates on which a cash discount may be taken on invoices dated May 15 for the different terms listed below. Assume that the merchandise is received in the stores on June 2.

    a. 8/10, net 30.

    b. 2/10 EOM.

    c. 2/10–60X.

    d. Net 30.

    e. 3/10 ROG.

31. An electronics retailer buys 3 color TV sets that list for $725 each and is billed with trade discounts of 20% and 10%. Terms are 4/10, n/30.

    a. What is the actual net cost of each TV?

    b. If the invoice is dated November 16 and paid on November 26, what amount should be remitted?

32. Your department receives an invoice dated October 10 in the amount of $6,750. How much must be paid on November 10 if terms are:

    a. 10/10, net 30.

    b. 10/10 EOM.

    c. Net.

33. Merchandise that amounts to $650 at cost is shipped and invoiced on August 14. Terms are 4/10 EOM. Payment is made on August 26. How much should be remitted?

34. A buyer purchased 75 ginger jar lamps at a list price of $40 each. The trade discounts were 30%, 20%, and 5%, with terms of 2/10, net 30. The lamps were shipped and billed on October 18 and were received October 22. The bill was paid on October 31. What amount was paid?

35. An invoice dated March 2 carries terms of 3/10–60X. When does the discount period expire? Explain.

36. Goods are invoiced and shipped on July 1 and received on July 15. Terms are 5/10 EOM, and the invoice is for $5,600. Payment is made on August 10. How much should be remitted?

37. An invoice for $3,290, dated April 26, covering merchandise received May 19, carries terms of 8/10 EOM, ROG. It is paid on June 10.

    a. How much should have been remitted?

    b. What would have been remitted had ROG not been included? Why?

38. Goods that are invoiced on July 26 are received on August 10. Indicate the final discount date and the final date for net payment if terms are:

	Final discount date	Final net payment date
3/10 EOM	_____	_____
2/10, net 30	_____	_____
1/20–30X	_____	_____
8/10 EOM as of Sept. 1	_____	_____
8/10 EOM, ROG	_____	_____

39. On June 24, a buyer received a purchase that amounted to a total list price of $16,000. This merchandise had a trade discount of 37.5%. The buyer wanted to negotiate with the supplier the last date possible to take a cash discount. The invoice on this purchase was dated June 22. Determine the various cash payment dates for the buyer under the following purchase terms:

    a. 2/10, n/30.

    b. 2/10, n/30 ROG.

    c. 2/10, n/30 EOM.

    d. 2/10–60X, anticipation allowed.

40. On June 10, the buyer for Charm Stores placed an order for 24 dozen turtleneck tops, costing $81 per dozen, with AOK Inc. The vendor offered the terms of 8/10 EOM, ROG, anticipation allowed, FOB store.

    a. Complete the accompanying purchase order indicating a delivery date of November 10, complete.

    b. What amount should be remitted if the shipment was received October 26 and paid on November 10?

Figure 3. Purchase Order for Charm Stores

CHARM STORES				**INVOICE INSTRUCTIONS**		
3025 PALM CANYON DRIVE				ORIGINAL INVOICE MUST ACCOMPANY THE MERCHANDISE FOR ALL SHIPMENTS.		
PALM SPRINGS, CA. 92264				FOR LOCAL SHIPMENTS DELIVERED TO OUR PLATFORMS:		

INVOICE INSTRUCTIONS
ORIGINAL INVOICE MUST ACCOMPANY THE MERCHANDISE FOR ALL SHIPMENTS.
FOR LOCAL SHIPMENTS DELIVERED TO OUR PLATFORMS:
¥ Driver present invoice with merchandise.
LOCAL SHIPMENTS DELIVERED TO U.S. PACKING AND SHIPPING CO.
FOR { ALL PARCEL POST AND RAILWAY EXPRESS SHIPMENTS
ALL OTHER OUT-OF-TOWN SHIPMENTS
¥ Enclose invoice in an envelope glued to outside of the lead carton.
For Out-of-Town where the above instructions cannot be followed, Mail Original Invoice to:

And also Enclose PACKING SLIP in an envelope glued to outside of lead carton.

FIRM	AOK Inc.
STREET	1300 Broadway
CITY	New York, New York 1000

ORDER NUMBER

Serial	Store	Dept.
2 4 6	8 2	4

Order Number, Weight and Pkg. No. MUST be shown on all packages and invoices or shipment is subject to refusal.

SHIP VIA:
❏ TRUCK
❏ FRT.
❏ P.P.
❏ R.E.A

DATE WRITTEN	TO BE SHIPPED FROM	DELIVERY DUE	F.O.B.	Charges on Shipments bought F.O.B. XXXX XXXXXX our premises must be prepaid.	FREIGHT ALLOWED	TERMS
						Dating is From Date of Receipt of Goods

CLASS.	HOUSE & STYLE OR LOT NO.	DESCRIPTION	S	M	L	XL					QUAN.	DOZEN COST	TOTAL COST	
CT	5107	LS. Cotton Turtleneck									24 doz.	81 00		
		Camel	12	24	24	12								
		Navy	12	24	24	12								
		Wine	12	12	12	12								
		Black	12	24	36	24								

41. Merchandise amounting to $6,800 was shipped on March 23 and was received the same day. Terms were 7/10 EOM and anticipation was permitted. The bill was paid on April 10. How much should have been remitted?

42. The following goods, shipped on June 7 and received on July 2, are:

    - 50 occasional tables at $75 list price.

    - 200 folding chairs at $20 list price.

    Trade discounts are 40% and 5%, with terms of 5/10 ROG, and anticipation is permitted. What amount must be remitted if the bill is paid on July 12?

43. An invoice for $4,500 is dated and received on March 15, along with the merchandise it covers. Terms are 1/10 EOM, ROG, anticipation permitted. If the bill is paid on March 25, how much should be remitted?

44. An invoice is dated and received on April 6, which carries terms of 2/10, net 30. Anticipation is permitted. It is paid on April 16. What is the discount taken?

45. An invoice dated August 28 carrying terms of 4/10–90X is paid on October 8. Anticipation is permitted. If the billed amount is $875, what should be the remittance?

46. An invoice for $1,800 dated August 10 is paid on August 20. Terms are 5/10, net 30. Anticipation is not permitted. What is the loaded cost when the buyer requested an 8% cash discount?

47. An invoice was received by Grandma's Closet in the amount of $2,100, with terms of 2/10–30X, n/90. If the invoice is dated April 20, what payment would be made on April 30? If the buyer desired a 6% cash discount, what is the loaded cost?

48. Calculate the payment that should be made on August 26 by Tom's Swift Shop for merchandise amounting to $5,600. The invoice is dated August 16 and terms are 8/10–60X, anticipation allowed.

49. Marie's Book Shop received an invoice dated March 26 for books amounting to $2,500, with terms of 2/10 EOM, anticipation permitted. Indicate the amount to be remitted if payment is made on April 10.

UNIT I.III
Evaluating a Buyer

Management evaluates the performance of a buyer on objective results. The common measurements used, expressed in figures, are:

1. Sales Results: Measured in dollars and indicates how well the merchandise purchased has been accepted, priced, and sold. This is reflected in the net sales achieved. Increase is the major consideration. Buyers are expected to achieve planned sales goals based on reasonable appraisal of both outside and inside conditions and trends. In addition, sales can be measured by units, or by number of sales transactions and sales per square foot of selling space.

2. Inventory Results: Refers to the amount of merchandise in stock as shown by stock turn (sales for that period divided by the average stock for that period). This goal is set by management and compared to industry standards. It indicates the use of capital investment. The control of merchandise shrinkage or shortage is another criterion of the buyer's performance.

3. Margin Results: Achieved by pricing merchandise at a profitable initial markup (aggregate original retail prices minus aggregate invoice costs) and realizing a planned gross margin (final selling price minus cost of goods sold, including cash discounts and alteration costs). This occurs after performing the specialized task of selecting vendors and negotiating costs and other terms of sale that are included in the total cost of merchandise delivered and sold, when subtracted from the net sales achieved.

4. Net Operating Profit Results (gross margin minus all expenses chargeable to the selling department): Evaluated properly at the level when management has chosen an expense plan that designates expenses, which can be attributable to the department's operation and are subtracted from the gross margin results.

The mathematics required to achieve these desired results will be studied in appropriate units of study that pertain to each topic. Once studied and mastered in application, success cannot be far away.

In addition to these criteria expressed by figures, buyers can be assessed on their daily buying, pricing, and stock control activities when improvement is shown over a period of time, resulting in developments that generate increased profits.

50. An invoice for a shipment of luggage is dated September 27 and is paid on October 25. The trade discount is 45% and 5%, with terms of 2/10 EOM, anticipation permitted, FOB retailer's warehouse. There is a quantity discount of 1% on initial orders of $6,000 or more. What amount should be remitted to the vendor if the bill was for:

Quantity	Luggage item	List price
50	Two suiter	$45
120	Overnighter	25
70	Dress bag	30
90	Vacationer	60

51. A bill for $6,000 is dated November 8 for merchandise that is to arrive on November 25. What is the last date for taking the discount if terms are 7/10 ROG?

52. An invoice for $2,300 has terms of 2/10–30X, net 60, FOB factory, anticipation permitted. The vendor prepaid the shipping charges of $34. The invoice was dated August 29 and was paid on September 24. How much should the vendor have received?

53. The infants' and nursery department receives an invoice for merchandise with a list price value of $10,750. It is dated January 28 and is paid on February 25. Terms are 2/10 EOM, FOB store, with trade discounts of 40% and 10%. Anticipation is not forbidden. The manufacturer prepaid the freight of $125.

    a. What is the last date on which a discount may be taken?

    b. What is the last date for payment without penalty?

    c. What amount should be remitted under the conditions given in this problem?

54. An athletic wear buyer receives a shipment of 30 dozen pairs of 50/50 sweatpants costing $9 each. The invoice is dated April 26 and terms are 6/10 EOM, FOB factory. Anticipation is not permitted. Shipping charges of $92 are prepaid by the vendor.

    a. What is the last possible date that a discount may be taken?

    b. If the bill was paid on May 11, how much was remitted to the vendor?

55. What amount must be remitted on an invoice for $3,200 that is dated April 26 and paid on May 10? Terms are 8/10 EOM, anticipation permitted.

56. Research and Discussion: If you were a small, independent dress manufacturer in a very competitive market, what terms of sale would you offer to your customers? Explain your reasoning.

57. Research and Discussion: Your department receives a bill dated July 16, which is paid July 26. Which set of terms, 5/10–30X or 7/10, net 30, anticipation permitted for both, would you choose as the most advantageous to your department? Explain your choice with supporting calculations.

58. Research and Discussion: If you were an owner/buyer for a medium-size specialty shop, would you always take advantage of the anticipation option when offered? Why or why not? Explain your answer.

59. For the Fall season, a gift boutique received an invoice dated April 23. In negotiating terms of purchase with the resource, a series discount of 35%, 25%, and terms of 2/10, n/30 ROG were agreed upon. The retail value of the merchandise received in the store on April 28 was $1,800. How much should have been remitted to the resource if the bill was paid on May 6?

60. Jean's Fashion placed an order for 12 dozen silk scarves that cost $120 per dozen, with freight charges of $18. The terms negotiated on this purchase were 2/10–30X, n/60 EOM, FOB store, anticipation permitted. If the invoice is dated June 10, determine the payment to be made to the manufacturer on July 10.

61. On June 10, the juniors' sportswear buyer for a large department store placed an order with a resource who offered terms of 8/10, n/30 EOM, FOB warehouse, freight prepaid. Determine the required payment if the date of the invoice was August 10, the amount of the invoice was $8,700, and the bill was paid August 18.

CASE STUDY 1
TERMS OF SALE

Mr. Williams, the silverware buyer for a specialty store located in San Francisco, decides to review his vendor analysis report before making his forthcoming season's purchases. The report shows that among the top six resources, there are three relatively strong and three relatively weak suppliers in relation to the gross margin each generated. Mr. Williams realizes that some important aspects of his job as buyer are negotiating trade discounts, quantity discounts, cash discounts, and dating, as well as transportation charges. Because any and/or all of these factors can increase the essential gross margin figure, he examines copies of past orders to determine the terms of sale on previous purchases. He discovers that some suppliers granted all his requests pertaining to discount and dating elements, certain vendors negotiated these factors only after an initial order was placed, and a considerable number allowed only the absolute minimum discount that prevailed in the market.

Because business conditions have been less than favorable, Mr. Williams feels that the success of the next season depends not only on his ability to select the most desirable items from his key resources, but also to negotiate with those vendors who offer the most advantageous terms of sale, in order to help maintain or improve the gross margin performance.

The first classification he shops in the market is sterling flatware. He had, and continues to have, strong sales in one well-advertised national brand that is distributed and can be bought directly from the manufacturer or from a jobber (i.e., middleperson). Customarily, Mr. Williams places his order for these goods with the manufacturer because he is able to view the complete line of patterns and buy any quantity he needs. Additionally, he has developed a rapport with one of the salespeople who has served him. This salesperson would rush special orders, call Mr. Williams about special promotions, etc. Consequently, during market week, Mr. Williams visits the manufacturer's showroom, shops the entire line, gets delivery dates, and inquires about the current terms of sale, which are:

- Trade discounts from list price: 40%, less 25%.

- Quantity discounts offered: None.

- Cash discount: 2/10, n/30.

- FOB: Factory/shipping charges, running 0.5%.

When Mr. Williams returns to the store, he studies his open-to-buy for this category and decides to purchase:

- 15 sets of Pattern A: List price $175 for each 5-piece place setting, 40-piece service.

- 10 sets of Pattern B: List price $200 for each 5-piece place setting, 40-piece service.

- 8 sets of Pattern C: List price $225 for each 5-piece place setting, 40-piece service.

He is interrupted in his calculations by his assistant, who informs him that the salesperson of an out-of-town jobber would like to speak with him. This particular supplier has tried for several seasons to get the store as an account. In the past, Mr. Williams had used local jobbers, often for immediate shipment of various items when his stock would become "low" on fast-moving items, but he had not done business before with this particular firm. Mr. Williams invites the salesperson into his office and, during their conversation, Mr. Williams senses the salesperson's eagerness to open an account with him now. He deduces this because of all the concessions the salesperson is willing to offer the store. Because this jobber carries the same brand of silverware Mr. Williams has just seen at the manufacturer's showroom, he asks the prices, terms, etc. They are:

- Trade discount from list price: 40%, less 20%, less 5%.

- Quantity discount: An additional 1% for orders over $10,000; 1.5% for orders over $15,000; and 2% for orders over $20,000.

- Cash discount: 2/10–60X, anticipation allowed.

- FOB store.

With which resource should Mr. Williams place his order—the manufacturer, the jobber, or both? Justify your choice mathematically.

CASE STUDY 2
RESOURCES INFLUENCED BY TERMS OF SALE

Mr. Lawrence is the owner of a three-store shoe chain called TRED-RITE. The merchandise featured in these stores, which are located in small strip malls, could be described as fashion forward at moderate to high prices. The strength of his operation is the services offered to the customers combined with merchandise that has a unique twist.

Mr. Lawrence has developed an extensive mailing list over the fifteen years of the store's existence. Periodically throughout the year he sends out a direct-mail brochure, which has successfully produced more business because of the items featured.

In April, as he covers the market for the Fall season, he is on the lookout for THE promotional item to be selected and promoted in this year's Christmas mailing piece.

He finally decides on a very trendy, attractive slipper that can be worn outdoors. It is a lamb-lined scuff with a leather suede upper, made in China. The slipper has a one-inch platform with a hard sole, available in this season's four most desirable fashion colors. It would be priced at $55 and represents exceptional value. This item is being offered by X-Cel Co., an importer from which Mr. Lawrence has bought consistently because this resource has had superior sales performance. Their deliveries and terms have been exactly as negotiated, and their offerings are synonymous with good value. The X-Cel Co. has quoted on this particular item a landed cost of $30 per pair, requiring a minimum order of 3,000 pair, with terms of n/30, FOB store. The date of mailing this Christmas brochure is set for October 15, and X-Cel Co. has agreed on an October 1 complete delivery date. Mr. Lawrence is confident about the item, but he questions his stores' capacity to meet the demand of this quantity in a relatively short selling period.

Mr. Lawrence saw in the market a similar, though not identical, branded slipper manufactured by a medium-size local factory, quoted with a cost of $31.50. This resource does not require a minimum quantity, yet guarantees shipment of sufficient quantities as needed (by the response to the brochure), with prompt delivery throughout the holiday season and the life of the "mailer." The terms for this resource are 5/10 EOM, anticipation allowed, FOB store. This resource will set a delivery date of September 26 and, should Mr. Lawrence write the order for 3,000 pairs, will ship half the order by September 26 and then the balance by November 1.

With which resource should Mr. Lawrence negotiate? Would the terms offered by each vendor affect the profitability of this purchase? How? Explain mathematically.

RETAIL PRICING AND REPRICING OF MERCHANDISE

UNIT 2

"Ideas are a dime a dozen.
People who put them into action are priceless."

2002 GEMS OF EDUCATIONAL WIT & HUMOR (PARKER PUBLISHING 1994)

OBJECTIVES

- Identification of activities that retailers can use to maximize profits.

- Understanding of price lining, pricing strategy, and identification of the types of price zones.

- Recognition and identification of the three basic pricing elements and how they relate to one another.

- Calculation of markup as dollar amounts and percentages for individual items and groups of items.

- Establishment of retail prices.

- Ascertainment of the types of price adjustments and confirmation of their importance as merchandising decisions.

- Calculation of markdowns as dollar amounts and percentages.

- Delineation of the procedures for making price changes.

- Recognition of the impact of pricing and repricing decisions on profit.

KEY TERMS

additional markup	markup	price lining
cost complement	markup cancellation	price range
employee discount	markup percentage	price zone
gross markdown	net markdown	promotional price zone
markdown	point-of-sale markdown	retail price
markdown cancellation	prestige price zone	retail reductions
markdown percentage	price line	volume price zone

Key Concept Formulas

Cost

Cost = Retail − $ Markup

$$\text{Cost \%} = \frac{\text{\$ Cost}}{\text{\$ Retail}} \times 100$$

Cost = Retail × (100% − Markup %)

Markdown

$ Markdown = Original or present retail − New retail

$ Markdown = Percentage off × Present retail price

Total $ markdown = First total $ markdown + Second total $ markdown

Planned $ markdowns = Net sales × Markdown %

$$\text{Markdown \%} = \frac{\text{\$ Markdown}}{\text{Net sales}} \times 100$$

$$\text{Markdown \%} = \frac{\text{\$ Markdown}}{\text{Total dollar sales of group's final selling prices}} \times 100$$

Markdown cancellation = Higher retail − Markdown price

Net markdown = Gross markdown − Markdown cancellation

Markup

$ Markup = Retail − Cost

$$\text{Markup \% on retail} = \frac{\text{\$ Markup}}{\text{\$ Retail}} \times 100$$

$$\text{Markup \% on cost} = \frac{\text{\$ Markup}}{\text{Cost}} \times 100$$

$$\text{Retail markup \% on entire purchase} = \frac{\text{Total \$ markup}}{\text{Total retail}} \times 100$$

Retail

$$\text{Retail} = \frac{\text{Cost}}{(100\% - \text{Markup \%})}$$

Retail = Cost + $ Markup

Every business aims to yield the largest possible total profit. One way a retail merchandiser attempts to secure maximum profits is through the skillful pricing of goods offered for sale. Price is a strong motivation in consumer buying habits. It is a competitive weapon and, very frequently, it is the only way to attract customer patronage when merchandise assortments are comparable, if not identical. Because many factors influence pricing, it can be considered an art as well as a science.

In large industrial organizations, the actual pricing decisions are generally the responsibility of management. In large retail stores, the actual pricing of merchandise is determined by individual departmental buyers or a comparable person designated by the particular organizational structure. Top management, however, does formulate the basic price policies of the store, such as the implementation of a policy of underselling the competition by 10% on all items. Although the retailer establishes the price of individual items as they are offered for sale, ultimately the total of all purchases must realize maximum profits. In the final analysis, the volume of sales as an aggregate figure must be great enough to cover not only the costs of merchandise sold, but also to provide a profit. Pricing, therefore, is an integral part of merchandising that requires training and skill.

UNIT II.I
Retail Pricing

Pricing refers to **price lining**, which is the practice of predetermining the retail prices at which an assortment of merchandise will be carried. A retail buyer selects and offers to the consumer a merchandise assortment at a specific price point, or **price line**, such as $15, $20, and so on.

THE STRUCTURING OF PRICE LINES

A buyer creates a stock assortment by considering what price lines to carry and the depth of assortment offered at the various price points. The number of price lines, and those particular price lines in the assortments, can help reflect the desired character that management wishes to project. The emphasis of a stock by price lines depends on the composition of the consumer segment that management wishes to attract. Usually there is a price structure around which buying for a specific retail establishment is concentrated. For example, a sportswear department stocks tops to retail for $35; this price line may cover a variety of types, fabrics, and sizes. The buyer, with the proper source of information, knows that this particular store's customers will pay $35 for a top.

The sportswear department, however, may stock a variety of tops that retail from $8 to $50. This is called the **price range**, which refers to the spread from the lowest to the highest price line carried. Most customers generally prefer to concentrate their purchases either at one price line or at several that are relatively close to one another. **Price zone** refers to a series of price lines that are likely to appeal to one group of the store's customers. When more than two price lines are stocked, a price zone situation exists. The price zones can be referred to as **volume price zone**, **promotional price zone**, and **prestige price zone**. Figure 4 illustrates three possible price zones for a price range from $15 to $100.

In general, the promotional price zone refers to the lower price lines carried; the volume price zone is the middle price lines, where the largest percentage of sales occur;

Figure 4. Price Line Structure Promotional Chart

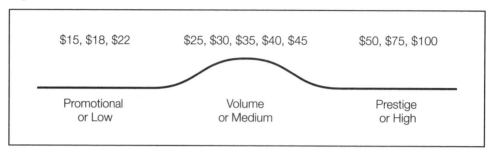

$15, $18, $22 $25, $30, $35, $40, $45 $50, $75, $100

Promotional   Volume   Prestige
or Low   or Medium   or High

and the prestige price zone refers to the highest price lines carried in a department, which "tone up" the assortment. This distribution curve typically occurs within a price range, regardless of the price lines.

In economics, the central idea is use, which is closely associated with the idea of choice and value. Without going into the realm of the psychology of the concept, it is easy to understand that before anything is consumed, somebody must choose to use it. The choices made determine the relative value. Price reflects these uses and choices. Some of the influences on the pricing strategies within the merchandising framework are store type and policy—for example, department stores versus "off-price" stores, and the choice of fashion versus staple goods in addition to customer demand as it relates to the supply-demand theory and competition.

The mathematical skill of the buyer helps to produce an assortment balanced in variety, breadth, and depth by retail price lines, while satisfactory costs are obtained that will eventually yield a profit on the goods purchased. The success of optimizing the sale of merchandise depends on sound pricing and repricing principles. It is one of the customer selection factors that affects the ultimate sale or rejection of merchandise. Although pricing goods for resale is the sole responsibility of the buyer, limitations are set by management on the buyer's freedom in order to cover costs and expenses, while ensuring a desired profit margin. The policies used to price merchandise throughout the organization can also reflect the store image that is chosen to lure the appropriate customer to the "right" store. Retailers who project a prestigious image featuring high-quality merchandise and exclusivity will focus on prestige high-priced lines. Competitive pricing will be used by some when they concentrate on easily identifiable brand goods and want to offer comparable merchandise; discount or "off-price" retailers will resort to pricing merchandise lower than normal to reflect consumer savings. However, all retailers on occasion may offer merchandise at lower prices than normal for promotional purposes. Optimizing pricing by only 10% may result in optimizing gross margin by 100%.

SETTING INDIVIDUAL RETAIL PRICES AND/OR PRICE LINES

The pricing of individual items and the establishment of price lines also require experience and skill. When pricing merchandise as it is bought, a buyer must always consider its salability in terms of its retail price, remembering that the aggregate of all prices must be high enough to cover merchandise costs, operating expenses, a fair profit return, possible reductions, shortages, and discounts to employees. Variations in pricing occur because there are some noncontrollable factors that influence pricing decisions, such as the volatility of ready-to-wear. The basic factors influencing the setting of the retail price that a buyer must consider in pricing are:

- Wholesale costs.

- Competition.

- Price maintenance policies of manufacturers, such as "suggested" retail prices.

- Handling and selling costs.

- Store policies, such as "off-price" policy.

- Nature of the goods, such as markdown risk in fashion goods.

- Correlation among departments.

- Supply and demand factors.

ADVANTAGES OF PRICE LINING STRATEGY

The practice of offering merchandise for sale at a limited number of predetermined price points creates several merchandising problems, but the practice is prevalent because the advantages are numerous and significant. The advantages of price lining are that it:

- Simplifies customer choice, which facilitates selling.

- Enables the store to offer wide assortments at best-selling price lines.

- Simplifies buying by limiting the range of wholesale costs.

- Reduces the size of stock, resulting in more favorable stock turnover and decreased markdowns.

- Simplifies stock control.

- Decreases marking costs.

- Provides a basis for stock-sales control of customer preferences by price.

PRICE LINE REPORTS

Reports by price line make possible an analysis of an entire department's sales trends. The control over planning and purchasing a stock that reflects customer demand is improved by knowledge of net sales. The information regarding stock-on-hand, outstanding orders, receipts, transfers, and markdowns, as well as the stock-sales ratio for each group, aids present and future buying decisions.

Figure 5 shows a typical report of price line by classifications and presents a complete selling history by dollars and units of merchandise by classifications or groupings. Only two price lines are included here due to space. The practice problem following this section shows the value and application of this report analysis.

THE RELATIONSHIP OF THE BASIC PRICING FACTORS

Merchandising, or the act of buying and selling, is performed by the retailer, who selects and buys merchandise that is offered for resale to the consumer. To make a profit, the retail merchandiser must set the proper price on the merchandise. Although the profitable pricing of selected individual items cannot always be done by applying a mathematical formula, the three basic elements involved in the pricing of all goods are the cost of the merchandise, the **retail price**, and the difference in value between them, which is referred to as **markup** (MU). Markup is the amount that is added to the cost price of merchandise to arrive at a retail price. This amount must be large enough to cover the cost of the merchandise, the expenses incurred to sell it, and the markdowns, shortages, and employee discounts, which reduce the value of total purchases as well as profit. Finally, it must also generate profit for the retailer. The aim of proper pricing can be expressed by the following:

Cost of goods   Expenses

+   Markup $\left\{\vphantom{\begin{array}{c}a\\b\\c\end{array}}\right.$ Markdowns, shortages, and employee discounts

=   Retail price

If one knows any two of the basic pricing factors (cost of goods and markup), the third (retail price) can be calculated both in dollar amounts and/or in percentage relationships. The following formulas show the relationship, in dollars, of the three basic pricing elements.

Calculating Retail When Cost and Dollar Markup Are Known

CONCEPT | Retail = Cost + $ Markup

PROBLEM | A retailer buys a crop top for $10 and has a markup of $8. What is the retail price?

Figure 5. Price Line Report by Classification

(1) Code No.	(2) Code Description	(3) Store	(4a) This Week Ending 02/07	(4b) One Week Ago Ending 01/31	(4c) 2 Weeks Ago Ending 01/24	(4d) Last 4 Weeks Ending 01/10	(4e) Season to Date 02/07	(5) On Hand Units	(6) On Order Units	(7a) MTD Receiving	(7b) MTD Transfer	(7c) MTD Markdown $	(7c) MTD Markdown %	(7d) MTD Net Sales $	(7d) MTD Net Sales %	(7e) Inventory Stock Sales $	(7e) Stock Sales Ratio	(7f) Open Order	(7g) Inventory + On Order	Code No.
96	JEANS $15.01 – $20.00	01					48	51	120											96
		05					34	15	84											
		08					31	13	48											
		10					13	1	48											
		14					26	24	48											
		15					25	25	60											
	TOTAL UNITS						177	129	408											
96	TOTAL DOLLARS						3142	2310	6528											
96	JEANS $20.01 – $29.00	01	4	1		5	5	5–												96
		05	3			3	3	3–												
		08	2	1		3	3	3–												
		10	4	1		5	5	5–												
		14	2	1		3	3	3–												
		15	1	3		4	4	4–												
	TOTAL UNITS		16	7		23	23	23–												
96	TOTAL DOLLARS		464	203		667	667	667–												
96	JEANS PRICE LINE–ALL	01	6	3	1	11	391	199	120					1	30	28	20	19	47	96
		05	3		3	8	325	66	84					1	19	8	9	13	21	
		08	2	5	1	8	259	111	48					1	12	14	24	8	21	
		10	4	2	3	12	188	14	48					1	25	1	1	8	9	
		14		2	6	9	238	100	48						7	14	41	8	21	
		15	2	4	1	11	285	76	60						7	11	32	10	20	
	TOTAL UNITS		17	16	15	59	1686	566	408											
96	TOTAL DOLLARS		468	320	188	1099	23005	7656	6528					5	100	75	16	65	140	
90	CLASS TOTALS PRICE LINE–ALL	01	108	154	302	884	7673	2394	1192					11	28	264	24	140	404	90
		05	67	131	93	362	3475	1636	958	16				8	20	172	22	109	281	
		08	30	121	67	258	3054	1136	906					3	7	112	41	107	219	
		10	65	118	65	317	2680	1072	708	12				7	18	107	15	79	186	
		14	49	56	72	225	2609	1162	796					5	12	114	24	91	205	
		15	69	92	86	327	3610	1319	792	14				6	16	135	22	87	222	
	TOTAL UNITS		388	672	685	2373	23101	8719	5352											
90	TOTAL DOLLARS		3965	6019	5385	20605	239725	84680	77191	42				40	100	905	23	612	1516	
99	INVALID CODES PRICE LINE–ALL	01		1	1	1	3	52	530		29					62–		80	18	99
		05	1–	1–	2	3–	33–	84	378						13	5–	62	58	53	
		08				1–	31–	35	378									58	59	
		10		3		4	20–	53	378						24		2	58	58	
		14	1–	1–	1–	3–	84	70–	378						63	10–	25	58	48	
		15		1–		2	19–	29	378							7–		58	51	
	TOTAL UNITS		2–	1	2		16–	183	2420											
99	TOTAL DOLLARS		62–	10–	37–	330–	4875–	3751	37204		29	638–		1–	100	84–	133	372	288	

1 = Code Number: Designates code within a classification. Example: Code 96.

2 = Code Description: Description of codes separated by price lines. Example: Jeans are separated as $15.01–$20.00. Totals include:

  a = By Code: Example: Under STD (season-to-date) for all price lines in the code both by units and dollars, 1,686 total units, $23,005 total dollars.

  b = By Classification: Example: Under STD (season-to-date), all codes and all price lines, both in units and dollars, 23,101 total units, $239,725 total dollars.

  c = By Department: All classifications, codes, and price lines both in units and dollars. (Not shown.)

3 = Store: Designates by store, each store. Example: 01.

4 = Net Sales Units: Permits analysis of unit sales. This category is divided into the following sections:

  a = This Week Ending: Net units sold for the week ending indicated. Example: 02/07.

  b = One Week Ago Ending: Net units sold for the week previous to the date of this report. Example: 01/31.

  c = Two Weeks Ago Ending: Shows the net sales for the week, two weeks previous to the date of this report. Example: 01/24.

  d = Last Four Weeks Ending: An accumulated statistic of net units sold over the total last four weeks. Example: 01/10.

  e = Season to Date: A cumulative statistic of units and/or dollars from the beginning of the season's accounting period to present date. Example: 02/07.

5 = On-Hand Units: Net units on hand as of the date of the report. Example: Code 96, Store 01—51 units.

6 = On Order Units: Numbers that are shown are obtained from an order file of the purchase order. Example: Store 01—Jeans $15.01—$20—120 units.

7 = Dollars to the Nearest Hundred: Financial figures that reflect the actual value of the indicated transactions. This category is divided into the following sections:

  a = MTD Receiving: Net receipt to inventory, month-to-date.

  b = MTD Transfers: Cumulative transfers between stores during the current month.

  c = MTD Markdown: Cumulative markdowns processed for the current month in both dollars and as percentages.

  d = MTD Net Sales: Cumulative dollar sales for the current month, by price line for each store, plus the percentage of the total company's business equaling 100% for each total.

  e = Inventory: The stock-sales ratio is calculated by Stock-sales ratio = Current dollar inventory ÷ Net sales previous week. This can be looked upon as "weeks supply." Example: 20 stock-sales ratio means if a particular price line continues to sell at the rate of last week's sales, and nothing new is received, it will sell out in 20 weeks.

  f = Open Order: Dollar value of the outstanding orders.

  g = Inventory and On Order: Total liability calculated by adding the on hand to the on order figures.

SOLUTION

$$\begin{array}{lcl} \text{Cost} & = & \$10 \\ + \quad \text{\$ Markup} & = & + \quad 8 \\ \hline \textbf{Retail price} & = & \$18 \end{array}$$

Calculating Dollar Markup When Retail and Cost Are Known

CONCEPT

$ Markup   =   Retail   –   Cost

PROBLEM

A retailer buys a crop top for $10 and decides to price it for $18. What is the dollar markup on this item?

SOLUTION

$$\begin{array}{lcl} \text{Retail} & = & \$18 \\ - \quad \text{Cost} & = & - \quad 10 \\ \hline \textbf{\$ Markup} & = & \$8 \end{array}$$

Calculating Cost When Retail and Dollar Markup Are Known

CONCEPT

Cost   =   Retail   – $ Markup

PROBLEM

What is the cost of an item that retails for $18 and has a dollar markup of $8?

SOLUTION

$$\begin{array}{lcl} \text{Retail} & = & \$18 \\ - \quad \text{\$ Markup} & = & - \quad 8 \\ \hline \textbf{Cost} & = & \$10 \end{array}$$

Although retailers pay for and sell merchandise in dollars, knowing the relationship of the three basic pricing elements (i.e., retail, cost, markup) in both percentages and dollars is useful to the merchandiser. Frequently, the retailer thinks in terms of dollars only, as for example, "My customers prefer crop tops that retail for eighteen to twenty-five dollars." Similarly, a resource might quote the cost of an item to a retailer at $10 each. In other cases, the retailer is concerned about achieving a 44.4% markup on an item that retails for $18 and costs $10. If this markup percentage is perceived as low, it may determine whether a particular item will be purchased. Furthermore, sometimes the buyer thinks simultaneously in terms of dollars and percentages. For example, in determining the dollar cost of an article to be purchased, a buyer must balance the retail price the customer is willing to pay with the particular markup percentage required by management.

Calculating Cost and Markup Percentages When Dollar Cost and Retail Are Known

To fully understand the relationship among the three basic elements in terms of percentages, it should be known that the retail of the basic equation is always 100%, and the dollar cost and markup can be converted from dollars to percentages by expressing each as a part of the retail.

CONCEPT

$$\text{Cost \%} = \frac{\$\text{ Cost}}{\$\text{ Retail}} \times 100$$

$$\text{Markup \%} = \frac{\$\text{ Markup}}{\$\text{ Retail}} \times 100$$

PROBLEM

What is the cost percentage and the markup percentage of a crop top that costs $10 and retails for $18?

SOLUTION

$$\text{Cost \%} = \frac{\$10\text{ Cost}}{\$18\text{ Retail}} \times 100$$

Cost % = 55.6%

Markup % = $8 Markup   or   ($18 Retail − $10 Cost)

$$= \frac{\$8\text{ Markup}}{\$18\text{ Retail}} \times 100$$

Markup % = 44.4%

Therefore:

	Dollars		Percentages	
Retail	$18	=	100.0%	
− Cost	− 10	=	− 55.6%	($10 ÷ $18)
Markup	= $8	=	44.4%	($8 ÷ $18)

The markup percentage is commonly called the **cost complement**.

Price Line Reports Practice Problem

1. Answer the following questions based on the data in Figure 5.

   a. What is the price line with Code 96 that generates the major unit and dollar sales?

   b. Which store has the best performance for Class Totals, Code 96? How many units were sold STD (season to date)?

   c. Which two stores contributed 49% of the MTD (month to date) sale in Code 96 Jeans?

   d. In the Jeans $15.01–$20.00 price lines, which store requires a "rush" delivery of its order so that it can stay "in business" with this price line in this classification? How many units does this store have on hand?

   e. Consider the Inventory and On Order figures for 96 Class Totals—Price Line—All. Which two stores require adjustments to an order because of the relation between their stock-sales and their MTD net sales percentage? What adjustments should be made?

f. For each store, calculate the percent increase or decrease in sales from the previous week to the current week. Which store has shown the largest increase?

g. What reasons might explain a decline in sales from one week to the next?

h. Since January 24, which stores show a continuous decline in sales of this merchandise classification?

i. Why must changes be made in merchandising strategies at these stores?

j. What changes in merchandising strategies would you suggest?

Retail Pricing Practice Problems

2. A merchant buys a sweatshirt for $15 and has a dollar markup of $14.95. What is the retail price?

3. The toddlers' department buyer purchases some wool robes that cost $30 each and prices them at $65 each. What is the dollar markup on this item?

4. What is the cost of a set of golf clubs that retail for $250 and has a markup of $157?

5. What is the markup percentage on a jacket that costs $49.75 and retails for $125?

6. What is the cost percentage for a sweater that retails for $38 and has a 55% markup?

UNIT II.II
BASIC MARKUP EQUATIONS
USED IN BUYING DECISIONS

Markup, as defined in this text, applies to an individual item, a group of items, or the entire merchandise stock of a department or a store, and it can be expressed in either dollars or percentages. For comparison and analysis, it is the markup percentage (rather than the dollar amount) that is significant. To understand the effect of markup on buying decisions, it helps to know the basic markup equations and their relationship to other pricing factors.

BASIC MARKUP PERCENTAGE EQUATIONS

Markup percentages can be computed as a percentage of the retail or cost price. Because the retail method of inventory is prevalent in large stores, it is more common to calculate the markup percentage on the retail price. The cost method of calculating markup, considered relatively old-fashioned, may still be used by some retailers.

Calculating Markup Percentage on Retail
Using the Retail Method of Inventory

$$\text{Markup \% on retail} = \frac{\$ \text{ Markup}}{\$ \text{ Retail}} \times 100$$

CONCEPT

What is the markup percentage on an item when the markup is $8 and the retail is $18?

PROBLEM

$$\text{Markup \% on retail} = \frac{\$8 \text{ Markup}}{\$18 \text{ Retail}} \times 100$$
$$= 44.4\%$$

SOLUTION

Calculating Markup Percentage on Cost

$$\text{Markup \% on cost} = \frac{\$ \text{ Markup}}{\text{Cost}} \times 100$$

CONCEPT

What is the markup percentage on cost when the markup is $8 and the cost is $10?

PROBLEM

SOLUTION

$$\text{Markup \% on cost} = \frac{\$8 \text{ Markup}}{\$10 \text{ Cost}} \times 100$$

$$= 80\%$$

(Note: Markup percentage calculated on cost is higher than markup percentage on retail.)

Generally, the retail calculation of markup is more acceptable because retailers also figure expenses and profits as a percentage of retail sales. Thus, they tend to consider price lines, stocks, and customer demands in retail values when making plans, and the calculation of markup on retail price is consistent with this approach. In this book, discussions and problems on markup will use the retail basis for all further calculations.

The retailer faces numerous purchase-planning and merchandise-pricing problems when buying goods for resale. To achieve maximum profits, the same estimated initial (original) markup percentage is not applied to all purchases. The astute merchandiser sets an ultimate goal but realizes that unexpected situations may cause deviations as goods are sold to individual purchasers. Therefore, manipulation of the markup and sales volume will ultimately provide the largest possible dollar profit. Calculations of the various buying and pricing situations that may occur in merchandising are expressed in formulas that must be understood by all retail merchandisers.

Calculating Markup Percentage When Individual Cost and Individual Retail Are Known

CONCEPT

$$\text{Markup \% on retail} = \frac{\$ \text{ Markup}}{\$ \text{ Retail}} \times 100$$

PROBLEM

What is the markup percentage on an item that costs $6.50 and is priced at $12.75?

SOLUTION

Given:

Retail	=	$12.75
− Cost	=	$6.50
Markup	=	$6.25

$$\text{Markup \%} = \frac{\$6.25 \text{ Markup}}{\$12.75 \text{ Retail}} \times 100$$

Retail markup % = 49%

When the individual cost and the individual retail do not change, but the number of purchased pieces varies, the markup percentage is the same whether it is calculated for one piece or for the entire quantity purchased. The following calculations illustrate this principle:

What is the markup percentage on a purchase of 12 pieces that cost $6.50 each and are retailed at $12.75 each?

Individual retail	=	$12.75
Individual cost	=	− 6.50
Markup	=	$6.25
Markup %	=	$\dfrac{\$6.25\ \text{Markup}}{\$12.75\ \text{Retail}} \times 100$
Retail markup % **on individual item**	=	49%

While:

	Unit retail	Volume	Total retail
Retail	$12.75	12	$153.00
Cost	$6.50	12	$78.00
$ Markup on total			$75.00
Retail markup %			49%

Total retail	=	$153 (12 pieces × $12.75)
− Total cost	=	− 78 (12 pieces × $6.50)
$ Markup on entire purchase	=	$75
Markup %	=	$\dfrac{\$75\ \text{Markup}}{\$153\ \text{Retail}} \times 100$
Retail markup % on entire purchase	=	49%

As a buyer evaluates a particular item, the markup percentage on the individual piece will generally be used to determine its salability. Once an order is placed, however, the **markup percentage** will be calculated on the basis of the entire quantity to be purchased.

Calculating Markup Percentage on a Group of Items with Varying Costs or Retail Prices, i.e., Order Writing

In the final analysis, purchases are evaluated on an overall basis. The following variations on markup formulas illustrate this concept in that the markup percentage is calculated on the total amounts ordered, rather than on an individual basis, so that the total purchase can be evaluated.

CONCEPT

$$\text{Retail markup \% on entire purchase} = \frac{\text{Total \$ markup}}{\text{Total retail}} \times 100$$

Calculating the Markup Percentage When Writing Orders Placed for a Variety of Items and Prices

Currently, some stores are using computer-generated purchase-order systems and automated replenishment systems. Although the mechanics of order writing can vary, determining the markup percentage on the entire purchase always requires a calculation of the total cost and total retail to determine the overall percentage on the purchase.

PROBLEM

A buyer ordered 10 raincoats at a cost of $59.75 each to retail for $100 each, and 6 jackets costing $79.75 each to retail for $150 each. What is the markup percentage on this entire purchase?

SOLUTION:
Spreadsheet format

	Unit retail	Volume	Total retail	Unit cost	Volume	Total cost	$ Markup	Markup %
Raincoats	$100.00	10	$1,000.00	$59.75	10	$597.50		
Jackets	$150.00	6	$900.00	$79.75	6	$478.50		
Total			$1,900.00			$1,076.00	$824.00	43.4%

Total retail

10 raincoats × $100	=	$1,000.00	
6 jackets × $150	=	+ 900.00	
Total retail		$1,900.00	$1,900.00

− Total cost

10 raincoats × $59.75	=	$597.50	
6 jackets × 79.75	=	+ 478.50	
Total cost		$1,076.00	− $1,076.00

$ Markup on entire purchase = $824.00

Markup % $= \dfrac{\$824.00 \text{ Total markup}}{\$1900 \text{ Total retail}} \times 100$

**Retail markup %
on entire purchase** = 43.4%

Calculating Markup Percentage with Varying Retail Prices of Either a Classification or a Group That Has the Same Cost

A buyer bought 150 handbags that cost $22.50 each. The buyer then retailed Group A, 50 pieces, for $40 each, Group B, 75 pieces, for $48 each, and the balance, Group C, for $55 each. What is the markup percentage on this purchase?

	Unit retail	Volume	Total retail	Unit cost	Total cost	$ Markup	Markup %
Group A	$40.00	50	$2,000.00	$22.50	$1,125.00	$875.00	43.8%
Group B	$48.00	75	$3,600.00	$22.50	$1,687.50	$1,912.50	53.1%
Group C	$55.00	25	$1,375.00	$22.50	$562.50	$812.50	59.1%
Total		150	$6,975.00		$3,375.00	$3,600.00	51.6%

	Volume	Unit retail		Total retail	
Group A, 50 pieces	×	$40	=	$2,000	
Group B, 75 pieces	×	$48	=	$3,600	
Group C, 25 pieces	×	$55	=	$1,375	
Total retail				$6,975	$6,975
− Total cost					
150 pieces × $22.50			=	$3,375	
Total cost					− $3,375
$ Markup on entire purchase			=		$3,600

Markup % $= \dfrac{\$3,600\ \text{Total markup}}{\$6,975\ \text{Total retail}} \times 100$

**Retail markup %
on entire purchase** $=$ 51.6%

Calculating Markup Percentage on Merchandise with Varying Costs at the Same Retail Price

A jewelry buyer has an unadvertised promotion on rings at a special price of $25 each. The group consists of 75 pieces that cost:

15 pieces at $10.00 each

40 pieces at $12.50 each

20 pieces at $16.00 each

What is the markup percentage on this group?

	Unit retail	Volume	Total retail	Unit cost	Total cost	$ Markup	Markup %
Group A	$25.00	15	$375.00	$10.00	$150.00	$225.00	60.0%
Group B	$25.00	40	$1,000.00	$12.50	$500.00	$500.00	50.0%
Group C	$25.00	20	$500.00	$16.00	$320.00	$180.00	36.0%
Total			$1,875.00		$970.00	$905.00	48.3%

Total retail

75 pieces × $25	=	$1,875	
Total retail	=		$1,875
− Total cost			
15 pieces × $10.00	=	$150	
40 pieces × $12.50	=	500	
20 pieces × $16.00	=	+ 320	
Total cost		970	− $970
Total $ markup on entire group	=	$905	

$$\text{Markup \%} = \frac{\$905 \text{ Total markup}}{\$1,875 \text{ Total retail}} \times 100$$

**Retail markup %
on entire purchase** = 48.3%

BASIC DOLLAR MARKUP CALCULATIONS
USED IN BUYING DECISIONS

Calculating Retail When Cost and Desired Markup Percentage Are Known

Although cost prices can be quoted by individual prices or by-the-dozen prices, in pricing an item for retail, the merchandiser "thinks" in terms of unit retail and therefore uses the cost per piece as a basis for calculating the retail per piece.

$$\text{Retail} = \frac{\text{Cost}}{(100\% - \text{Markup \%})}$$

A manufacturer quotes a cost of $42 per dozen for a visor; the markup that the buyer wants is 51.7%. At what retail price should the item be marked to obtain the desired markup?

Given: Cost	=	$42 per dozen
	=	$42 ÷ 12
	=	$3.50 per piece
Retail	=	$\dfrac{\$3.50 \text{ (Cost per piece)}}{100\% - 51.7\%}$
	=	$\dfrac{\$3.50}{0.483}$
Retail	=	**$7.25**

Calculating Cost When Retail and Markup Percentage Are Known

In maintaining established price lines, a retailer who knows the required markup must be able to determine the maximum affordable price to pay for an item so that it can be sold profitably.

CONCEPT

Cost = Retail × (100% – Markup %)

PROBLEM

A children's underwear buyer plans to retail pajamas for $10.95 with a 48% markup. What is the maximum price the buyer can pay for the pajamas to be sold at this price line?

SOLUTION

Given: Retail	=	$10.95
Cost	=	$10.95 (Retail) × (100% – 48%)
	=	$10.95 × 52% (Cost complement %)
Cost	=	**$5.69**

THE RELATIONSHIP OF
THE BASIC PRICING FACTORS TO PROFIT

Retail stores buy and sell. All of the buying and selling activity is in terms of price. There is great interest in the relationship between the buying price and the selling price because the difference between these two largely determines profit. The size of this margin between the cost and the selling price, referred to as **markup**, not only has to include markdowns, shortages, expenses, and profit, but also affects the amount of gross margin achieved. Management generally plans a reasonable, realistic figure to meet this objective, but it must be controlled and monitored constantly, like "locking the barn before the horse is stolen."

Fundamentally, there are two elements in this scenario: the cost of the goods and the selling price of these goods. The cost of the merchandise bought is a stationary factor, because after this is negotiated it rarely changes. It is constant. Therefore, in an intensely competitive retail climate, it is more important than ever to "buy right." It has been said that "merchandise well bought is half sold." Private branding becomes more prevalent, and emphasis must be placed on a thorough and complete knowledge of domestic and foreign market conditions and offerings. The retail prices, governed by price lining principles, store policies, etc., that are initially placed on merchandise offered for sale is the variable factor. The pricing of merchandise must be a consideration at the time of purchase, whether the merchandise is bought as an individual item or to build an assortment. Pricing will influence the purchase or rejection of merchandise. In fashion goods versus staple goods, pricing will be further influenced by the risk factor of acceptability, in addition to other pertinent considerations. The manipulation of selling prices requires skill and experience for its impact on profit to be recognized. Any change from the initial retail price will automatically change the markup achieved; therefore, these changes, generally downward, must also be planned and controlled in order to achieve the gross margin necessary for a profitable operation.

Markup Practice Problems

7. Fill in the blank spaces for each of the exercises below. (Note: Several of the examples may be done without written calculations.)

	Retail	Cost	$ MU	MU %
a.	$5.00	$2.70		
b.	$14.95	$7.50		
c.	$200.00		$90.00	
d.	$1.75	$9.60/dozen		
e.	$29.95	$14.50		
f.	$10.00	$60.00/dozen		
g.		$15.00 each		48%
h.		$42.50 each		46.6%
i.		$106.00/dozen		45%
j.		$15.00/dozen		47.5%
k.	$100.00			49%
l.	$80.00			50%
m.		$16.00	$14.00	
n.		$55.00	$45.00	
o.	$75.00			52%
p.	$3.98			37.8%
q.		$21.60/dozen		46.5%
r.	$9.95	$72.00/dozen		
s.	$465.00	$235.00		
t.	$590.00	$310.00	$280.00	

8. A buyer purchases ballet dresses at $42.50 each.

    a. At what price must these dresses be marked to achieve a 52% markup?

    b. At what actual customary price line are the dresses most likely to be marked?

    c. What would be the percentage of markup if the dresses were priced at $79.50?

9. A buyer purchased:

- 500 nylon windbreakers costing $12 each, to sell at $22 each.
- 700 sweatpants costing $9 each, to sell at $17.50 each.
- 300 acrylic sweaters costing $16 each, to sell at $30 each.

What is the markup percentage for this order?

10. Apply the following "typical" departmental markups to find the cost of an item that retails for $49.95 in each department:

   a. Girls' (4–6X) department: 59%.

   b. Electrical appliances: 27.8%.

   c. Juniors' sportswear: 55.8%.

   d. Gifts and clocks: 56.2%.

   What would cause the wide range of markup percentages among the various products?

11. A buyer of men's furnishings purchased a manufacturer's closeout and paid $96 per dozen for wool-blend knit neckties. If the desired markup was 58%, what was the exact retail per tie? What price line would the buyer probably use in ticketing the ties for the selling floor?

12. A buyer is interested in a group of tweed jackets costing $35 each. If the required markup is 53.6%, what would be the minimum retail price for each jacket? If the buyer had previously bought these jackets at $39.75 and retailed them for $79.50, what was this previous markup percentage?

13. For a holiday catalog, a buyer makes a special purchase of infant knit shirts that cost:

    - 40 dozen at $60/dozen.

    - 20 dozen at $72/dozen.

    - 18 dozen at $66/dozen.

    If the shirts all retail at the same unit price of $11, what markup percentage will be yielded?

14. The accessory buyer buys straw visors at $45 per dozen and sells them at $7.50 each. What markup percentage has been achieved?

15. A toy buyer planned a special sale of dolls to retail at $25 each. If the overall markup on the purchase was 46%, what was the cost per doll?

16. Men's walking shorts that cost $264/dozen require a markup of 50%. What should be the retail price of each pair?

17. A suit that costs $67.50 has a markup of 62.5%. What should be the retail price of each suit?

18. A buyer purchased 50 assorted leather attaché cases that cost $79.50 each and subsequently merchandised them as follows:

    • 25 pieces to retail for $175 each.

    • 10 pieces to retail for $150 each.

    • 15 pieces to retail for $125 each.

    Find the markup percentage on this purchase.

19. An outerwear buyer arranges a special purchase from a manufacturer who offers a group of 150 plastic raincoats (with varying costs) at one low price of $25 each. The buyer decides to price this purchase as follows:

    • 50 pieces to retail at $35.95 each.

    • 50 pieces to retail at $45.00 each.

    • 50 pieces to retail at $55.00 each.

    What markup percentage is realized on this purchase?

20. A special promotion, consisting of 10 dozen novelty sweaters, is purchased at the cost of $240 per dozen. Determine the retail selling price of each sweater if the buyer wants a 52% markup.

21. After its arrival in the store, the buyer (in Problem 20) reviewed the shipment of sweaters and decided to include this purchase in a store flyer featuring a group of sweaters retailing for $42 each. What markup percentage was achieved on this particular purchase?

22. If the shoe buyer wants to buy some leather sandals to retail for $49.50 per pair and needs to obtain a markup of 53.4%, what is the most that these sandals can cost?

23. Calculate the markup percentage on the following order placed by the handbag department:

    - 3½ dozen costing $180 per dozen, to retail for $32.50 each.

    - 15 pieces costing $37.50 each, to retail for $79 each.

24. The jewelry buyer wants to spend $15,000 at retail. The department maintains a 56.7% markup. The buyer needs a minimum of 600 pairs of earrings to cover each branch with an adequate assortment.

    a. What should be the retail price per pair?

    b. What should be the cost per pair?

25. The sportswear buyer wants to spend $84,000 at retail. Orders for $18,500, at cost, have already been placed. If the planned markup percentage to be achieved is 52.5%, how much, in dollars, does the buyer have left to spend at cost?

26. Calculate the amount of this order.

   a. Style #300: 25 leather attaché cases costing $79.50 each, retailing for $169.99.

   b. Style #401: 10 leather folders costing $55 each, retailing for $125 each.

   c. Style #411: 15 leather briefcases costing $69.50 each, retailing for $150 each.

27. Calculate the amount of this order. As the men's raincoat buyer, a manufacturer offers you a group of 225 pieces at one low price of $50 each. You decide to price this group as follows:

   a. Style #132: 25 pieces, retailing for $75 each.

   b. Style #145: 50 pieces, retailing for $90 each.

   c. Style #160: 50 pieces, retailing for $125 each.

   d. Style #165: 100 pieces, retailing for $138 each.

28. Calculate the amount of this order. You purchase the following from a glove resource:

    a. Style #321: 20 dozen children's wool gloves costing $66 per dozen.

    b. Style #492: 30 dozen men's wool gloves costing $72 per dozen.

    c. Style #563: 10 dozen women's wool novelty gloves costing $78 per dozen.

You decide to price them all at the same retail price of $12 per pair.

UNIT II.III
REPRICING OF MERCHANDISE

The dynamic nature of merchandising makes the repricing of goods in retailing universal. Price adjustments are made to either increase or decrease the original retail price placed on merchandise. These changes in prices must be properly recorded to:

- Achieve an accurate book inventory figure used in the retail method of inventory.

- Plan initial (original) markup goals when pricing goods.

- Control and manage the amount received in an attempt to merchandise at a profit.

The repricing of goods for sale is constant, the causes are numerous, and the skill required is considerable. It is rare that a retailer makes an upward adjustment to the retail price, and often a buyer is forced to make a downward retail price change on a significant portion of sales. In a profit and loss statement, the downward differences frequently have a group heading of retail reductions that include:

- Markdowns.

- Employee discounts.

- Shortages.

Although all retail reductions have an impact on markup, they are, for the most part, considered a necessity. Their study is of major importance, for only with complete understanding of their use can the retailer turn them into a dynamic and advantageous merchandising tool.

MARKDOWNS

The most common and important type of price adjustment is technically called **markdown** (MD). It is the lowering or reducing of the original or previous retail price on one item or a group of items. For example, a sweater that was retailed for $25 when it was received in the store was reduced to $18 because it became soiled. This price adjustment is called a markdown because the retail value of the merchandise was lowered. The difference between the new selling price ($18) and the former price ($25) is $7. The amount by which the retail value has been lowered is called the markdown and is the meaningful figure to the merchandiser. The merchandiser expresses markdowns as a percentage of net sales of all goods during a period, month, or year. Frequently, the merchandiser needs to calculate the markdown percentage that is necessary to sell a group of items. When this occurs, the markdown is still expressed as a percentage of the net sales figure.

Markdowns are an important tool in merchandising. They are recognized as a means of promoting and increasing sales volume, yet they have an impact on gross margin and profit and therefore must be controlled. Markdowns vary depending on the type of merchandise and conditions. In order to use them advantageously, there must be an analysis of the purpose of the markdown, the causes, the timing, and the repricing principles.

The Purpose of Markdowns

Markdowns are "a cure, not a curse." This merchandising tool can be used to good advantage if the retailer realizes the objectives of markdowns. The major aims of price reductions are:

- To stimulate the sale of merchandise to which customers are not responding satisfactorily.
- To attract customers to stores by offering "bargains."
- To meet competitive prices.
- To provide open-to-buy money to purchase new merchandise.
- To create special "promotions," or sales (e.g., birthday sales).
- To clear fashion merchandise that has a short life cycle.
- To clear slow-moving lines.

Causes of Markdowns

By analyzing all the possible causes of markdowns, a merchandiser can make an effort to minimize them. The most common causes (not in order of importance) are listed below:

- Buying errors, which include:
  - Overbuying in quantities.
  - Buying of wrong sizes because of unbalanced buying, or accepting of merchandise that is sized contrary to order.
  - Buying of poor styles, quality, materials, and colors.
  - Poor timing in ordering goods.
  - Receiving and accepting merchandise that has been shipped late.
- Pricing errors, which include:
  - Poor timing of markdowns.
  - Setting the initial price too high.
  - Not being competitive in price for same goods.
  - Deferring markdowns too long.
  - Calculated risks of carrying "prestige" merchandise.
  - Unbalanced buying, or accepting of merchandise that is sized contrary to order.

- Selling errors, which include:
  - Poor stock keeping.
  - Careless handling that results in soiled and damaged goods.
  - Failure to display merchandise properly or advantageously.
  - Uninformed salespeople.
- Special sales from stock, which include:
  - Off-price promotions.
  - Multiple sales (e.g., 3 for $1.00).
  - Broken assortments, remnants, and so on.
  - Necessary price adjustments.
  - Remainders from special sales.

Timing of Markdowns

Accurate timing of markdowns can help reduce the amount of the markdown needed to sell the merchandise. It is suggested that merchandise be analyzed and reduced when:

- Merchandise becomes "slow selling."
- The customer demand is sufficient to sell the merchandise with a minimum price reduction.
- The consumer's interest in the merchandise in stock diminishes because of the appearance of a new fashion or product, or of a lower price.

The Amount of the Markdown

Judgment is required to determine the price at which items can be cleared quickly. The pricing of goods is a major factor in the control of markdowns. It is difficult to generalize on the amount of the markdown to be taken because the "right" price depends on:

- The reasons for the reduction.
- The nature of the merchandise.
- The time of the selling season (the proper moment during the selling season).
- The quantity on hand.
- The original (initial) markup.

Because the purpose of a markdown is to sell the merchandise quickly, the size of the markdown must be large enough to produce the desired results. Some rules to be considered in repricing are:

- The first markdown should be sharp enough to move a considerable amount of the goods.

- The markdown should be sufficiently large to attract customers who rejected the merchandise at its original price.

- The price may be reduced sufficiently to appeal to the next price zone customer.

- Markdowns should not be so large as to invite customer suspicion.

- Small markdowns are ineffective.

- Small, successive markdowns may increase the total loss.

MARKDOWN CALCULATIONS

Calculating the Dollar Markdown

To find the dollar amount of markdown taken when there is a group of items, it is customary to first determine the difference per piece between the present and new retail prices, and then to determine the total cost of the markdown.

On an Individual Item

A cashmere pullover that was slightly soiled was reduced from $198 to $169. What is the dollar markdown?

	Original or present retail	$198
−	New retail	− 169
	$ markdown	$29

On a Group of Items

A buyer reduces 93 calculators from $15 to $10. What is the total markdown in dollars?

PROBLEM

	Original or present retail	$15
−	New retail	− 10
	$ markdown	$5 per piece
	Total $ markdown	= $5 markdown × 93 pieces
	Total $ markdown	= $465

SOLUTION

Using Percentage "Off" Method

However, the retailer frequently advertises markdowns as a percentage off the current retail price; for example, "25% off the selling price."

CONCEPT	$ Markdown = Percentage off × Present retail price

PROBLEM	A store advertises 25% off on a group of 50 chairs currently retailed at $100 each. What is the total dollar markdown?

SOLUTION

Percentage off	=	25% × $100 Retail
$ Markdown	=	$25 per chair
Total $ markdown	=	$25 markdown × 50 pieces
Total $ markdown	=	$1,250

Calculating the Total Dollar Markdown When a Second Markdown Is Taken

Even with the markdown, not all merchandise will sell. Therefore, after a reasonable period of time, an additional reduction must be made to move the remaining goods of that style and/or group.

CONCEPT	Total $ markdown = First total $ markdown + Second total $ markdown

PROBLEM	The men's clothing buyer had a group of 50 jackets priced at $225 each that were selling very slowly. To stimulate sales of these jackets, the buyer reduced the price of jackets in that group to $175. At this price, 40 pieces were sold in a short time. At a later date, the remaining pieces became shopworn and needed a further reduction to clear them from stock. The buyer reduced them to $100 each, and at that price they all sold out. What was the total dollar markdown taken?

SOLUTION:
Spreadsheet format

	Original price	Markdown price	Markdown per piece	Number of items	Dollar markdown
1st markdown	$225.00	$175.00	$50.00	50	$2,500.00
2nd markdown	$175.00	$100.00	$75.00	10	$750.00
Total markdown					$3,250.00

First Markdown on Group

Original retail price		$225	
– First markdown price	–	175	
Amount of markdown per piece	=	$50	
× Number of jackets	×	50	
First $ markdown	=	$2,500	$2,500

PLUS

Second Markdown on Group

First markdown price		$175	
– Second markdown price	–	100	
Amount of markdown per piece	=	$75	
× Number of jackets	×	10	
Second $ markdown	=	$750	+ 750
Total $ markdown on this group	=		$3,250

SOLUTION: Arithmetically (right margin)

Calculating the Planned Dollar Markdown
When the Markdown Percentage and Net Sales Are Known

Once an estimated net sales figure for an accounting period has been projected and the markdown percentage allowed is known, the total amount of markdown in dollars can be determined. Because markdowns are taken in dollars off the retail price, a buyer's thinking and decisions in merchandising markdowns alternates, according to circumstances, from percentages to dollars and vice versa.

Planned $ markdowns = Net sales × Markdown %

CONCEPT (right margin)

The sales in the men's footwear department were planned for $560,000, and the markdown percentage was estimated at 5%. Find the dollar amount of markdowns that would be permitted.

PROBLEM (right margin)

Total planned $ markdowns = $560,000 Net sales × 5% Estimated markdown %

Total planned $ markdown = $28,000

SOLUTION (right margin)

Calculating the Markdown Percentage

Markdowns taken are expressed as a percentage of the net sales for an accounting period. It is important to control and plan markdowns within a store. **Markdown percentages** can be calculated for an entire department, as shown in the following calculations:

CONCEPT

$$\text{Markdown \%} = \frac{\$\,\text{Markdown}}{\text{Net sales}} \times 100$$

PROBLEM

In March, Department #33 had net sales of $5,000. The markdowns taken for March totaled $500. What was the markdown percentage for March?

SOLUTION

$$\textbf{Markdown \%} = \frac{\$500\ \text{Markdown}}{\$5,000\ \text{Net sales}} \times 100$$

$$= 10\%$$

Also, markdown percentages can be used to evaluate a group of items and/or a vendor. The following shows this type of calculation:

CONCEPT

$$\text{Markdown \%} = \frac{\$\,\text{Markdown}}{\text{Total \$ sales of group's final selling prices}} \times 100$$

PROBLEM

A buyer had a special selling price group of 100 faux snakeskin belts marked at $16 each. At the end of the season, the 15 pieces that were unsold were reduced to $10 each and sold out immediately. What is the markdown percentage on this purchase?

SOLUTION:
Spreadsheet format

	Original price	Selling price	Markdown per unit	Number of items	Dollar markdown	Retail sales	Markdown %
Faux snakeskin belts	$16	$16	$0	85		$1,360	
1st markdown	$16	$10	$6	15	$90	$150	
Total					$90	$1,510	5.96%

Step 1: Determine markdown per piece.

$16 to $10   = $6 each

Step 2: Determine markdown amount.

15 Pieces reduced   =   15 Pieces × $6   = $90 Markdown

Step 3: Determine final selling price sales of group.

85 Pieces × $16   = $1,360

15 Pieces × $10   =   + 150

Sales of group   = $1,510

Markdown %   = $$\frac{\$90 \text{ Markdown}}{\$1,510 \text{ Sales of group}} \times 100$$

Markdown %   =   5.96% or 6%

Calculating Markdown Cancellations

It is easier to describe a markdown cancellation than to define it. When the markdown price is raised to a higher retail price, it is considered a cancellation of a markdown. Cancellations may occur after special sales from stock, if the remaining merchandise is repriced upward. The restoration of a markdown price to the former retail is a **markdown cancellation**. The calculation is included to indicate the arithmetic and mechanics involved in reviving the selling price upward.

Currently, markdown cancellations are much less common because most large stores electronically program temporary markdowns into the cash register. This means of recording the markdown as the reduced offering when an item is being sold is called a **point-of-sale (POS) markdown**. It eliminates the need to mark the goods with the reduced price, and, subsequently, to remark the goods to the original price. Figure 6 shows a sales slip recording the purchase of a pair of comfort shoes selling for $52, less 30%. The $15.60 is an example of a POS markdown.

Figure 6. POS Markdown Receipt   **Figure 7.** POS Credit Slip

Figure 7 is a credit slip indicating the return of "sale" merchandise and shows how the $15.60 markdown taken at the time of purchase was canceled. The amount of markdown taken on this simple transaction is zero because the $15.60 markdown recorded by the cash register on the purchase was neutralized by the return of the goods.

For those firms that are not yet using the POS system of recording and canceling markdowns, the following material, though not popular, is included to show the basic principles for the manual procedure. (Note: There are no review problems that illustrate this material.) Currently, it is common that the sales slip records the selling prices only, or it may include the total savings (markdown amount).

CONCEPT | Markdown cancellation   =   Higher retail   –   Markdown price

After a one-day sale, a buyer marked up the remaining 12 pieces to the original price of $50, which had been reduced to $43 for the special event. What was the amount of the markdown cancellation?

Markdown cancellation	=	$50	Higher retail
	–	43	Markdown price
	=	$7	Difference per piece
	=	12 Pieces ×	$7 Difference
Markdown cancellation	=	$84	

Calculating Net Markdown

When a reduction in price is made originally, it is called the **gross markdown**. The difference between gross markdown and markdown cancellation is called the **net markdown** figure, or the amount of the permanent markdown.

Net markdown   =   Gross markdown   –   Markdown cancellation

A buyer reduces each of the 75 pieces from $50 to $43 for a one-day sale. After the sale, the remaining 28 pieces were marked up to the original price and were sold out at that price.

What was the gross markdown in dollars?

What was the markdown cancellation?

Find the net markdown in dollars.

	Original price	New price	Change per piece	Number of pieces	$ Markdown
Original MD	$50	$43	$7	75	$525 Gross
MD cancellation	$43	$50	$7	28	$196 Cancellation
Net MD					$329 Net

Determine gross markdown.

Individual markdown	=	$50	–	$43
or markdown per piece	=	$7 per piece		
	=	75 Pieces	×	$7 Markdown
Gross markdown	=	$525		

Determine markdown cancellation.

Markdown cancellation	=	$43 to $50		
	=	$7 per piece		
	=	28 Pieces	×	$7 Markdown cancellation
Markdown cancellation	=	$196		

Determine net markdown.

Gross markdown	=	$525
– Markdown cancellation	=	– 196
Net markdown	=	$329

EMPLOYEE DISCOUNTS

It is common practice for a retail store to give its employees a reduction off a retail price. This type of retail reduction is called an **employee discount**. As noted previously, this is another type of price adjustment that must be recorded, because it lowers the value of merchandise. This reduction is generally stated as a percentage off the retail price (e.g., a 20% discount). It must be recorded by the statistical department of the accounting division for accuracy of the book inventory figure under the retail method of inventory. The cumulative amount of employees' discounts is usually shown on the profit and loss statement under the general heading of "**retail reductions**."

PROBLEM

Store X grants its employees a 20% discount on all merchandise purchased. If a salesperson buys an item that retails for $16.95, what is the employee discount in dollars? What is the amount paid for the item?

Retail price of item	=	$16.95			
Discount allowed	=	20%			
	=	$16.95	×	20%	
Employee discount	=	$3.39			
Employee's price	=	$16.95	–	$3.39	
	=	$13.56			
or	=	$16.95	–	(0.20	×	16.95)
	=	$13.56			

ADDITIONAL MARKUP

An **additional markup** is a type of price adjustment that raises the price of merchandise already in stock. It increases the original retail price placed on the merchandise. It is taken after, and in addition to, the original (initial) markup. Although it is not a common type of adjustment, a provision must be made when an upward change of the retail prices of existing inventories is necessary. For example, an upward change of wholesale costs might necessitate the immediate upward revision of retail prices on existing inventory.

MARKUP CANCELLATION

Markup cancellation is a downward price adjustment that offsets an original inflated markup to a markup that is more normal. It is used to adjust the markup on a purchase in accordance with the original intent and is not used to manipulate stock values. Currently, it is controlled by law, which dictates the time period allowed from receipt to reduction of the purchase, as well as the size of the markup resulting from this practice. It is justified when quoting "comparable value" prices used in promoting goods. For example, a resource offers a retailer gloves at $7, which is lower than the normal cost of $10. This item may be presently in stock and retailing for $22. During the permitted time, the gloves costing $7, which originally retailed at $22, are reduced to $14. This lowered price appears to the public as a markdown, yet results in a markup that is close to normal. The $8 difference between $22 and $14 is the markup cancellation.

PRICE CHANGE PROCEDURES

An efficient system of reporting and recording price changes is important for the following three reasons:

- Facilitation of the review of price adjustments.

- Accurate calculation of inventory records.

- Identification of shortages.

Figure 8 illustrates a computer printout of a buyer-authorized price change. It instructs the individual stores to change the retails on certain merchandise, where to change them (i.e., store location), if the change is permanent or temporary, what the new retails should be, and the reason for repricing. Presently, most systems do not require that the store count the merchandise, only remark it, because, financially, the perpetual inventory system has already made the adjustment.

Figure 8. Price Change

Run Date: 02/28/13	Price Change					Report No: Page: 12		
Run Time: 22:29:30								
BUYER 02				DEPT NO: 02				
P/C NO: 2331916		P/C TYPE: 01 MARKDOWN-PERMANENT, TOTAL STYLE			ORIGINATING LOCATION: 02 ENTRY DATE: 02-27-13			
EFFECTIVE DATE: 03/04/13					REASON: 02 REPRICING CLEARANCE			
DOCUMENT NO:								

APPLICABLE LOCATIONS: 01 02 03 05 07 08 09 11 12 13 14 15 16 17 18 19 20 21 23 24 25 26
SPECIAL INSTRUCTIONS: REPRICING

CLASS	VENDOR	STYLE	UPC	OLD RETAIL	NEW RETAIL	CURR TKT RETAIL	NEW TKT RETAIL	DESCRIPTION
41	1	6028	400100964255	11.00	7.00	11.00	7.00 ( )	LG CIRCULAR STRETC
41	1	6140	400101350996	6.00	4.00	6.00	4.00 ( )	CHANNEL CIRCLE STR
41	1	6143	400101365136	6.00	4.00	6.00	4.00 ( )	STRETCH MATTE META
41	1	9106	400101338239	11.00	7.00	11.00	7.00 ( )	½" MESH
41	1	9107	400101109839	14.00	9.00	14.00	9.00 ( )	MESH BELTS
41	1	9115	400101338246	13.00	9.00	13.00	9.00 ( )	ROLLED MESH
41	28	1602	400101479789	10.00	7.00	10.00	7.00 ( )	STUD BELT
41	28	1730	400101479796	10.00	7.00	10.00	7.00 ( )	STUD BELT
41	117	1305	400101271024	9.00	6.00	9.00	6.00 ( )	1¼" W/SILVER 3
41	117	1359	400101207726	5.00	3.00	5.00	3.00 ( )	¾" CROCO SILVER

THE RELATIONSHIP OF REPRICING TO PROFIT

Every price change has an impact on gross margin and net profits. Because the elimination of price adjustments in retailing is impossible, stores must classify each type of adjustment separately so that they can be analyzed, planned, and controlled. Markdowns, the major type of price changes, reduce the retail price, causing a decrease in gross margin that is further reflected in a decrease and/or elimination of profit. With certain merchandise or classifications, the markdown risk is frequently anticipated. It is offset by planning a higher initial (original) markup. Unfortunately, profit cannot always be preplanned because there are business forces that do not permit easy solutions to such problems (e.g., nonacceptance of a newly introduced fashion or style, change in competition, etc.). However, it is important for the retailer to realize the effect of price adjustments on gross margin and profit, as illustrated by the following example:

	Initial retail value of new purchase	$105,000	=		100.0%
−	Cost of goods sold	− 49,980	=	−	47.6%
	Gross margin	$55,020	=		52.4%
−	Operating expenses	− 45,990	=	−	43.8%
	Net profit	$9,030	=		8.6%

The total retail reductions for the period are $5,000:

	Net sales	$100,000	=		100.0%
−	Cost of goods sold	− 49,980	=	−	50.0%
	Gross margin	$50,020	=		50.0%
−	Operating expenses	− 45,990	=	−	46.0%
	Net profit	$4,030	=		4.0%

29. The merchandise manager of the Fashion-Rite stores approved the following reductions. Complete the price change form for the reductions taken.

In Department 32, a group of 75 wool sweaters, Style #203, Vendor #16, priced at $55 each, were selling slowly. Because it was late in the season, the buyer felt a markdown was needed to stimulate sales of these sweaters and reduced them to $42 each. In addition, 50 cotton sweaters, Vendor #203, Style #20, priced at $38, were reduced to $25. What was the total dollar markdown amount?

30. On Columbus Day, the suit buyer in Department 25 offered 30% off for an unadvertised special. On that special sale day, 50 suits, Style #1000, Vendor #39, originally priced at $100 each, were sold. Calculate the total dollar markdown taken.

31. The children's buyer (Department 49) had a group of 150 ski jackets, Style #2000, Vendor #87, priced at $75 each. The weather was warm, and sales on this particular style were poor. After 25 pieces sold, the buyer decided to reduce them to $68. At this price, 90 pieces sold. The remaining pieces were broken in size and color, so the buyer decided to clear them from stock and further reduced them to $58. What was the total dollar markdown taken?

32. The juniors' sportswear buyer planned sales for the month amounting to $700,000. The markdown percentage was estimated at 12%. How much dollar markdown could be taken?

33. A children's buyer took markdowns in the month of July totaling $2,000. During this month, the net sales for the department were $18,000. If the original markdown plan for this month called for 14% markdowns, was the actual markdown over or under the original plan, and by how much in dollars?

34. For the month of November, a suit buyer took markdowns totaling $1,600. During this month, the net sales for the department amounted to $50,000. What was the markdown percentage for this month?

35. In the month of July, a domestics buyer took markdowns totaling $1,800. During this month, the net sales for the department were $25,000. If the original markdown plan for this month called for 8% markdowns, was the actual markdown over or under the original plan, and by how much in dollars? What was the actual markdown percentage?

36. The seasonal plan for a shoe department shows sales of $153,000, with planned markdowns of 6.4%.

    a. What is the planned dollar amount of markdowns?

    b. If the actual markdowns are $7,200, how does the real percentage compare with the plan? Is the actual percentage more or less than planned? By how much?

37. A buyer reduced 75 jackets from $39.50 to $32.95 for a sale. A short while after the sale, the remaining 30 jackets were reduced further to $27. At that price, they all sold out. Find the total markdown amount taken.

38. A coat department had sales of $60,000 for the month of November. During the month, the buyer reduced 50 coats from $60 to $40 and another 100 coats from $80 to $60.

    a. What was the total dollar markdown for the month?

    b. Find the markdown percentage for the month.

39. A buyer had 400 pocket calculators in stock at $25 each. They were on sale for $18 each for a one-day special event. At the end of the day, 210 remained unsold and were sold eventually at their original price.

    a. What was the total markdown in dollars?

    b. What was the markdown percentage on this purchase?

40. A retailer purchased some terry slippers from a new resource. In evaluating the purchase, the records indicated that the total purchase of 360 pairs of slippers originally retailed for $9.50 per pair. At this price, 290 pairs were sold. The first markdown to $7 resulted in the sale of another 50 pairs. A second markdown to $5 was required on the balance of the merchandise to sell the remaining broken sizes. What were the retailer's total reductions in dollars?

41. For Columbus Day, the buyer advertised all suede coats at 35% off. The records indicated sales of:

    • 50 pieces with original retail of $275 each.

    • 30 pieces with original retail of $195 each.

    • 10 pieces with original retail of $150 each.

    a. What was the total markdown in dollars?

    b. If sales for October were planned at $80,270, with estimated markdowns of 9%, did the buyer have more markdown money to spend for the month? If so, how much? If not, why not?

42. If the markdowns in Problem 41 were the only ones taken for the month, what was the markdown percentage for the month of October?

43. A buyer bought 300 leather belts that were retailed at $18 each. At the end of the season, 25 unsold belts were cleared at $10 each and sold immediately. What was the markdown percentage on this purchase?

44. The lingerie department's estimated sales for the entire Spring season were $750,000, with anticipated markdowns of 11.5%. At the end of the season, the buyer had taken $67,500 in markdowns. Were the actual dollar markdowns taken more or less than planned? Compare the estimated markdowns to the actual markdowns in both dollars and percentage.

45. A buyer wants to sell sleds at $39.95 each. The markup is 48.5%. How much can the buyer afford to pay for each sled?

46. If a manufacturer suggests a retail price of $12.50 for a line of tote bags costing $84.00 per dozen, what is the suggested markup percentage?

47. A manufacturer offered woven belts at $54 per dozen. If a buyer were to take a 47.5% markup, at what retail price would each belt sell?

48. A buyer purchased 1,500 pairs of men's lounging pajamas at $10 each for a Father's Day sale. The advertised price was $20 retail, and 1,000 pairs were sold at this price. After Father's Day, the remaining pieces of this special purchase were integrated into stock at $25 each. Between July 1 and September 1, all but 50 pairs were sold at this price. The remainder was then cut to $12 each, and all sold at that price except 10 pairs that were too damaged and soiled to sell at any price, and therefore were reduced to zero value. What is the markup percentage on this purchase?

49. Find the markup percentage on the following handbag purchases:

- 36 bags costing $22, with a retail of $45.

- 24 bags costing $28, with a retail of $55.

- 12 bags costing $41, with a retail of $75.

- 12 bags costing $53, with a retail of $95.

50. Down quilts costing $82 per unit were promoted at an advertised retail price of $160 each. Of the 800 pieces purchased, 600 sold at full price, and another 140 sold at a one-day special midseason sale at $125 each. An additional 35 were cleared at $90 in the markdown corner. The 25 soiled counter samples were salvaged. What markup percentage was yielded on this purchase?

51. A purchase of 350 exercise bikes was made at a cost of $106 each and was unit priced at $200. They sold well at the regular price for a time, but ultimately the last 45 pieces were reduced and sold at $155 each.

a. What was the markup percentage on this purchase when the order was written?

b. What was the markdown percentage on the sale of the 350 machines?

52. A job lot of 650 formal bow ties costs $1,950. If 400 are priced at $6 and the remainder at $7.50, what markup percentage is achieved?

53. A junior sportswear department took the following markdowns for August:

    - 160 tops from $28 to $21.

    - 230 tops from $25 to $17.

    - 170 tops from $20 to $14.

    Gross sales for the month in this department were $76,500, and customer returns totaled 6%. What were the departmental markdown percentages for the month?

54. For a Veterans Day sale, a buyer reduced 95 jackets from $95 to $69 each. The following day, the buyer reduced 59 additional coats from $125 to $95. What was the total dollar markdown taken?

55. A buyer had 96 suitcases in stock at a retail price of $85 each. For a special sale, they were marked down to $55. The markdowns for this month were planned at 6%, with sales for the month estimated at $90,000. After this event, did the buyer have more markdown money to spend? If so, how much more? If not, why not?

56. A lamp retailing for $97 was advertised at 30% off. What was the new selling price of the lamp after the markdown was taken?

57. In May, markdowns taken in a children's department were:

    - 60 jackets from $18 to $15.

    - 30 sweatshirts from $15 to $12.

    - 70 T-shirts from $10 to $7.

    Gross sales for the month in this department were $85,000, and customer returns totaled 6%. What was the departmental markdown percentage for the month?

58. The seasonal plan for a swimwear department showed planned sales of $650,000 and planned markdowns of 18%.

    a. What was the amount of planned markdown dollars?

    b. If the markdowns amounted to $120,000, was the actual markdown percentage more or less than the planned percentage and by how much?

59. For Valentine's Day, the candy department buyer purchased a special offering of 150 heart-shaped boxes of candy that cost $6 each. There were two assortments, and the buyer decided to retail 75 boxes at $15 each and 75 boxes at $10 each. On February 15, the remaining $15 assortments were reduced to $9, taking total markdowns of $144, and the balance of the $10 assortments were reduced to $6 each, with these markdowns amounting to $72. Six of the $15 hearts that did not sell at $9 were reduced to $5 and were cleared out. Four of the $10 hearts were reduced to $3 and sold out at that price. The net sales of the department for February were $9,750.

    a. Determine the markup percentage on the original order.

    b. What was the markdown percentage on this purchase?

    c. What was the markdown percentage for the month if these were the only markdowns taken?

    d. What was the markup percentage achieved on this purchase?

60. Discussion Problem: "Markdowns are a normal and positive element of merchandise planning. The markdown factor may be used advantageously by a buyer in an effective departmental operation." What factors should be carefully scrutinized and why?

CASE STUDY 1
PRICING IN MERCHANDISING

At the end of October, a key resource offered a department store buyer a group of acrylic knit tops that are promotionally priced at $96 per dozen. The resource, who owns 60 dozen pieces, quoted this low price providing the purchaser bought the entire group. These tops are comparable in quality and styling to similar merchandise purchased from this vendor at $144 per dozen that sold well at $25 each earlier in the season with the normal department markup. The group now being offered by the resource consists of three different styles currently in demand. Group A has 30 dozen pieces, Group B consists of 20 dozen pieces, and Group C is 10 dozen pieces. As a combined offering, the sizes are well balanced and the colors are "fashion" for this season. Group A is a "staple" in styling, Group B reflects this season's "hot seller," and Group C is considered "avant-garde" in both color and silhouette. Because sales are sluggish, the buyer wants to stimulate selling for Election Day by retailing these tops with only a 50% markup. By taking a lower-than-normal markup, the buyer hopes this purchase will result in additional sales and be a total "sellout."

As the buyer reviews the stock condition of the department, it seems the inventory is higher than planned, and the report shows that:

a. 55% of the inventory is current and salable.

b. 150 pieces remain from a recent promotion, currently priced at $19 each, and are broken in size and color.

c. A group of 75 pieces, all one style, priced at $22.50 each, are selling very slowly.

d. 15 pieces are badly soiled and are marked $25 each.

The buyer also noted that there is $1,000 of markdown money available in November.

The buyer feels the purchase would ultimately be advantageous because increased departmental activity will lead to improved sales. To ensure this high-volume day, the proper pricing of this purchase, plus an accurate count of the current inventory, is essential.

To make the correct decisions, the following questions must be answered:

a. If this group purchase was to be retailed at the normal markup, what would be the retail per piece? What degree of excitement would this produce by quoting a higher "comparable value"?

b. Determine the markup percentage achieved if the three groups are retailed as follows:

    i. Group A at $16 each.

    ii. Group B at $18 each.

    iii. Group C at $20 each.

The last group seems to represent particularly good value.

a. Should the available November markdown money ($1,000) be used now to clear the present inventory by reducing all three groups to $16 and using their comparable value prices? Or should the buyer defer these reductions (which seem inevitable) until the storewide clearance in December?

Decide what course of action the buyer should pursue and mathematically justify your suggestions as you apply the principles of pricing and repricing.

CASE STUDY 2
THE JUSTIFICATION OF THE PRICING STRATEGY

You are a glove buyer for a major specialty store. On November 1, one of your occasionally used importers offers immediate delivery on a group of men's kidskin gloves made in the Philippines that are 100% wool-lined. The vendor offers 1,200 dozen pairs of gloves at $228 per dozen if the entire quantity is purchased. If not, the cost is $264 per dozen. To properly assess this offering, you must consider the factors that will be helpful in making the appropriate decision. They are:

   a. There is only one style in this group, but it is similar to a fast-selling style at a higher price line from another resource.

   b. The size range is complete and the staple seasonal colors are represented.

   c. This classification (men's leather gloves) has enjoyed stronger sales this season than in previous years. The "healthy" position of this classification is such that this offering could contribute to an unexpected sales increase for the entire department.

   d. An analysis of the selling reports and the "on order" of this category shows that the condition of the present inventory is inadequate to cover the conservative, realistic anticipated sales for November and December.

   e. Currently the market is not flooded with desirable merchandise.

Because of the strong sales of this classification and the market conditions, the buyer would like to take advantage of this offering and use a strategy in pricing this group that will generate a markup above the required departmental 52.5% to afford a successful post-Christmas clearance sale. The buyer begins to make more basic calculations and considerations that will justify the final course of action to be taken.

Plan 1. If the normal departmental 52.5% markup were applied in pricing this group, what would be the retail price per pair at a cost of $228 per dozen?

Usually the gloves that cost $264 per dozen carry a 50% markup. Using this as a guideline, what would be the retail price per pair?

Plan 2. What would be the markup realized if the entire group was purchased and integrated into the $44 price line?

Plan 3. There is a GIFT FOR CHRISTMAS ad planned for December 1 that features women's fine Italian kidskin leather gloves priced at $39. This merchandise represents exceptionally good value and quality. Should the men's gloves be combined with this particular promotion?

Plan 4. Immediately upon delivery, should the buyer integrate half of the entire amount of gloves into the $44 price line assortment, and include the balance in the December 1 ad?

State the possible negative and/or positive results for each suggested option. Recommend or develop a pricing strategy and justify your recommendations mathematically.

BASIC MARKUP EQUATIONS USED IN MERCHANDISING DECISIONS

UNIT 3

"Strategy without tactics is the slowest route to victory. Tactics without strategy is the noise before defeat."

SUN TZU, ANCIENT CHINESE MILITARIST, PHILOSOPHER, AND STRATEGIST, AND AUTHOR OF *THE ART OF WAR* (CIRCA 500 B.C.)

OBJECTIVES

- Identification of the types of markups and the use of each in making merchandise decisions.

- Calculation of initial markups, cumulative markups, and maintained markups.

- Recognition of the need to balance markups among different items of merchandise.

- Balance of markups for diverse situations.

- Recognition and understanding of both the dollar amounts and percentages of markup needed to evaluate the impact of merchandising decisions.

KEY TERMS

average cost

average retail

averaging or balancing markups

billed cost

cumulative markup

final selling price

gross margin

initial or original markup

initial or original retail

maintained markup

retail reductions

vendor analysis

KEY CONCEPT FORMULAS

Initial markup %

$$\text{Initial markup \%} = \frac{\text{Gross margin \% + Retail reductions \%}}{\text{100\% + Retail reductions \%}}$$

$$\text{Initial markup \%} = \frac{\text{\$ Gross margin + \$ Retail reductions}}{\text{\$ Sales + \$ Retail reductions}} \times 100$$

$$\text{Initial markup \%} = \frac{\text{Gross margin + Alteration costs} - \text{Cash discount earned + Retail reduction}}{\text{Sales (100\%) + Retail reductions \%}}$$

Cumulative markup % $= \dfrac{\text{\$ Cumulative markup}}{\text{\$ Cumulative retail}} \times 100$

Gross margin %

$$\text{Gross margin \%} = \frac{\text{Net sales} - \text{Total cost of goods sold}}{\text{Net sales}} \times 100$$

$$\text{Gross margin \%} = \frac{\text{Maintained markup + Cash discounts} - \text{Alteration costs}}{\text{Net sales}} \times 100$$

Maintained markup %

$$\text{Maintained markup \%} = \frac{\text{Net sales} - \text{Gross cost of goods sold}}{\text{Net sales}} \times 100$$

$$\text{Maintained markup \%} = \frac{\text{Gross margin} - \text{Cash discounts + Alteration costs}}{\text{Net sales}} \times 100$$

$$\text{Maintained markup \%} = \text{Initial MU \%} - \text{Retail reduction \%} \times (100\% - \text{Initial MU \%})$$

$$\text{Purchase balance} = \frac{\text{Total planned}}{\text{(pieces, retail, cost, or markup \%)}} - \text{Purchases to date}$$

Retail reduction % $= \dfrac{\text{Initial markup \%} - \text{Maintained markup \%}}{\text{Sales (100\%)} - \text{Initial markup \%}}$

Unit III examines the significance of pricing and repricing, as well as factors that influence the retailer when setting retail prices. Thus, the retail prices of merchandise should be based on the markup deemed appropriate by the merchandiser. Markup, which is simply the difference between retail prices placed on merchandise and the cost of this merchandise, has an effect on the:

- Sales volume it can generate.

- Markdowns it can cause.

- Gross margin it can achieve.

- Profits it can produce.

As a result, markup must be estimated, always controlled, and, if necessary, adjusted. Because basic markup calculations in both dollars and percentages are used in buying decisions as they relate to a single item or a group of items, the buyer responsible for a particular department is involved with the markups planned and obtained. These markups are constantly monitored because the desired gross margin depends on how successfully they are achieved.

To better understand the various markups indigenous to the retailing business, the term "retail price" must be clarified. The first price placed on merchandise for resale is the **initial** or **original retail**. The price received when an item sells (which may be different) is the **final selling price**. The original, initial, or first retail placed on merchandise is the price the retailer hopes to realize, and the final selling price is the price actually received for the merchandise. (For example, a raincoat costing $55 is retailed at $120 when received in the store, but eventually sells for only $100.) The initial retail price is often higher than the price at which the merchandise ultimately sells, because price reductions may be necessary before the goods are sold.

UNIT III.I
TYPES OF MARKUPS

INITIAL MARKUP CONCEPTS

Initial markup, also known as "**mark on**" or "**original markup**," is the difference between the **billed cost** of merchandise and the original or first retail price placed on a given item or group of items. When freight charges are known, they are added to the billed cost when calculating initial markup. Certain vital factors and common practices must be considered in determining the initial markup; the following considerations cannot be ignored:

- Plan in advance an **initial markup** on merchandise when it is received in the store to ensure a favorable gross margin figure that will cover expenses and provide a reasonable profit.

- Forecast an initial markup percentage that will be required on all the merchandise handled during a particular period (e.g., a six-month season), because it is virtually impossible to have available all the data necessary for the calculation of each purchase.

- Recognize that the gross margin figure can fluctuate because it is the result of many merchandising decisions.

- Understand that the initial markup placed on new purchases will be reduced by markdowns, shortages, and employee discounts.

- Be aware of and act on cash discounts offered to retailers in the purchase of goods, as well as estimated alteration costs.

For a department, an **initial markup** planned on a seasonal and/or annual basis can be expressed in either dollar figures or percentages, and is usually calculated for both. In most large retail stores, the buyer and/or divisional merchandise manager (under the guidance and supervision of the control division) establishes this initial markup as a guide to check against aggregate markups obtained in pricing new merchandise purchases. In addition, it is essential to know that the initial markup planned for a season must take into consideration the markups on the new purchases and the effect they have on the markup of the merchandise inherited from the last season, because the gross margin figure for the period depends on the markups achieved on all the inventory available for sale. Thus, in planning an initial markup, probable expenses, the profit goal, probable reductions, estimated alteration costs, and anticipated sales must be projected first.

An initial markup is expressed as a percentage of the aggregate original retail price placed on the merchandise, not on the price at which the merchandise sold. The price at which the merchandise sold is expressed as sales plus reductions. For example, if sales are planned at $1,000,000 and all retail reductions at $150,000, the goods that eventually sell at $1,000,000 must be introduced into stock at $1,150,000, with the desired markup expressed as a percentage of this total. This seasonal planned markup percentage can be calculated, and the concept can be expressed by a formula.

Establishing an Initial Markup

To better appreciate the establishment of an initial markup, examine the methods commonly used to institute a seasonal markup, and the calculations (in both dollars and percentages) as they appear in the chart and steps below. (The figures listed in the chart are for illustration only; they do not represent actual retail figures.)

GIVEN		Dollars	Percentages
	Planned sales	$1,000,000	100.0%
	Estimated expenses	393,000	39.3
	Price reductions	150,000	15.0
	Profit	50,000	5.0

METHOD

Step 1: Forecast the total sales for the season or the year ($1,000,000).

Step 2: Estimate the required expenses ($393,000) and price reductions ($150,000) needed to reach the sales plan.

Step 3: Set a profit goal—operating profit or department contribution ($50,000).

Step 4: Add the estimated expenses ($393,000) to the price reductions ($150,000) and profit ($50,000) to determine the dollar markup ($593,000).

	Dollars	Percentages
Estimated expenses	$393,000	39.3%
+ Price reductions	+ 150,000	+ 15.0
+ Profit	+ 50,000	+ 5.0
Dollar markup	= $593,000	= 59.3%

Step 5: Determine the original retail price ($1,150,000) by adding the planned reductions ($150,000) to the planned sales ($1,000,000).

	Dollars	Percentages
Planned sales	$1,000,000	100.0%
+ Price reductions	+ 150,000	+ 15.0
Original retail price	= $1,150,000	= 115.0%

Step 6: Compute the markup percentage (51.6%) by dividing the dollar markup ($593,000) found in step 4 by the original price ($1,150,000).

	Dollars	Percentages
Markup	$593,000	59.3%
÷ Original retail price	÷ 1,150,000	÷ 115.0
Initial markup %	= 51.6%	= 51.6%

CALCULATING THE INITIAL MARKUP

The formula for calculating an initial markup percentage on goods purchased shows the amount of markup necessary to achieve a desired profit. As already discussed, this markup should cover expenses, reductions, and profits. These projections can be based on past results or calculated mathematically on the basis of anticipated sales, reductions, and expenses. The equation to determine an initial markup percentage can spell out each factor (i.e., expenses + profits + markdowns + stock shortages + employee discounts), or it can be simplified (i.e., expenses + profits = **gross margin** [net sales minus cost of goods], and markdowns + stock shortages + employee discounts = **retail reductions**). Because gross margin and retail reduction figures are more significant in planning than the analysis of expenses, shortages, and other factors, the second, simplified equation is more often used.

Finding Initial Markup Percentage When Gross Margin Percentage and Retail Reduction Percentage Are Known

CONCEPT

$$\text{Initial markup \%} = \frac{\text{Gross margin \%} + \text{Retail reductions \%}}{100\% + \text{Retail reductions \%}}$$

PROBLEM

A store has a gross margin of 42.3% (39.3% expenses + 3% profit) and retail reductions (markdowns, shortages, and employee discounts) of 15%. What is the initial markup percentage?

SOLUTION

$$\text{Initial markup \%} = \frac{\underset{\text{(39.3\% Expenses} + 3\% \text{ Profit)}}{42.3\% \text{ GM}} + \underset{\text{(markdowns, shortages, employee discounts)}}{15\% \text{ Retail reductions}}}{100\% \text{ Sales} + 15\% \text{ Retail reductions}}$$

$$= \frac{57.3\%}{115\%}$$

Initial markup % = 49.8%

Finding Initial Markup Percentage When Gross Margin and Retail Reductions in Dollars Are Known

CONCEPT

$$\text{Initial markup \%} = \frac{\$ \text{ Gross margin} + \$ \text{ Retail reductions}}{\$ \text{ Sales} + \$ \text{ Retail reductions}} \times 100$$

PROBLEM

A store plans sales of $1,000,000 and retail reductions of $150,000, and it requires a gross margin of $423,000 (i.e., expenses $393,000, profit $30,000). What should be the initial markup percentage?

SOLUTION

$$\text{Initial markup \%} = \frac{\$423,000 \text{ (GM)} + \underset{\text{(Retail reductions)}}{\$150,000}}{\$1,000,000 \text{ Sales} + \underset{\text{(Retail reductions)}}{\$150,000}} \times 100$$

$$= \frac{\$573,000}{\$1,150,000}$$

Initial markup % = 49.8%

Finding Initial Markup Percentage When Cash Discounts and Alteration Costs Are Known

As shown in Unit I, the cost of goods sold is adjusted by alteration and workroom costs and cash discounts. Therefore, these factors (if and when they exist) are essential in calculating retail markups. Because markup covers alteration and workroom costs, these factors are added to gross margin. Because cash discounts reduce the cost of goods sold, which affects the final markup obtained, they are subtracted from gross margin.

CONCEPT

$$\text{Initial markup \%} = \frac{\text{Gross margin} + \text{Alteration costs} - \text{Cash discount earned} + \text{Retail reduction}}{\text{Sales (100\%)} + \text{Retail reductions \%}}$$

PROBLEM

The desired gross margin of a store is 42.3%, and the retail reductions are 15%; the cash discounts earned are 3%, and the alteration costs are 2%.

SOLUTION

$$\text{Initial markup \%} = \frac{\text{42.3\% Gross margin} + \text{2\% Alteration costs} - \text{3\% Cash discounts} + \text{15\% Retail reductions}}{\text{100\% (Sales)} + \text{15\% Retail reductions}}$$

$$= \frac{56.3\%}{115.0\%}$$

$$= 48.96\%$$

Initial markup % = **49%**

CUMULATIVE MARKUP

Although an initial markup may be calculated for individual items, the initial markup on merchandise received is more commonly reported for season-to-date, or for the year. Over any such extended period, an initial markup is called "cumulative markup," which is the markup percentage figure generally used by retailers to compare merchandising performance and information with other stores. **Cumulative markup** is the markup percentage achieved on all goods available for sale from the beginning of a given period. It is an average markup because it is the markup percentage obtained on the accumulated inventory at the beginning of the given period, plus the markup of all the new purchases received season-to-date. The cumulative markup in dollars equals the difference between the invoiced cost of the merchandise (including transportation) before cash discounts have been adjusted and the cumulative original retail prices of all merchandise handled (opening inventory + net purchases) during a given period of time. Markdowns do not enter into the calculation of the cumulative markup percentage. The concept is simply stated by saying:

CONCEPT

$$\text{Cumulative markup \%} = \frac{\text{\$ Cumulative markup}}{\text{\$ Cumulative retail}} \times 100$$

PROBLEM

On February 1, a boys' clothing department has an opening inventory of $200,000 at retail with markup of 49.0%. On July 31, the new purchases season-to-date (STD) amounted to $1,350,000 at retail with a 49.9% markup. Find the cumulative markup percentage achieved.

SOLUTION

The given information is in bold, and the other items are calculated from the basic markup formulas. Each calculation is identified with the steps of the procedure.

	Cost	Retail (R)	MU %
Opening inventory	$102,000	**$200,000**	**49.0%**
+ Purchases STD	+ 676,350	**+ 1,350,000**	**49.9%**
Total merchandise handled	$778,350	$1,550,000	49.8%

Step 1: Find the cost value of the retail opening inventory.

Cost	=	R × (100% – MU %)
	=	**$200,000** × (100% – **49%**)
	=	**$200,000** × 51%
Cost	=	$102,000

Step 2: Find the total cost value of all purchases season-to-date.

Cost	=	R × (100% – MU%)
	=	**$1,350,000** × (100% – **49.9%**)
	=	**$1,350,000** × 50.1%
Cost	=	$676,350

Step 3: Find the total retail value of total merchandise handled.

Total retail value	=	$200,000 + $1,350,000
Total retail value	=	$1,550,000

Step 4: Find the total cost value of total merchandise handled.

SOLUTION
continued

Total cost value	=	$102,000 + $676,350
Total cost value	=	$778,350

Step 5: Find the cumulative markup on total merchandise handled.

Cumulative retail (Step 3)	=	$1,550,000
Cumulative cost (Step 4)	=	– 778,350
Cumulative markup (Step 5)	=	$771,650

$$\text{Cumulative markup \%} = \frac{\$771{,}650 \text{ Cumulative markup}}{\$1{,}550{,}000 \text{ Cumulative retail}} \times 100$$

Cumulative markup %	=	49.8%

The new purchases required a 49.9% markup to achieve a 49.8% cumulative markup, because the merchandise of the opening inventory came into the period with only a 49% markup.

At this point, it must be understood that both the initial and cumulative markup are on merchandise purchased. Initial markup percentage refers to those markups obtained when pricing new merchandise purchases. Cumulative markup percentage is the amount of markup on all the merchandise available for sale, whether it is new purchases or stock-on-hand at the beginning of the period. The cumulative markup percentage is the initial markup percentage calculated from the beginning of the season to any given later date (e.g., the end of the season or year).

MAINTAINED MARKUP

A maintained markup that is controlled helps merchandizers to analyze results to date, and is ultimately the determination of a gross margin figure.

Before maintained markup is explained, it is essential to know that although gross margin and a maintained markup are related, they are not identical. Gross margin is the difference between net sales and the cost of merchandise sold, adjusted by subtracting cash discounts and adding alteration and workroom costs (i.e., total cost of merchandise sold). **Maintained markup** (MMU) is the difference between net sales and the cost of merchandise sold without the credits of cash discounts and without the addition of alteration and workroom costs (i.e., gross cost of merchandise sold). If these differences are not considered in calculations, the gross margin and maintained markup figures will be the same. For both, the net sales figure reflects the final selling prices received for the goods sold and the margin actually realized when the goods are sold. They are both markups on sales. The relationship between gross margin and maintained markup is revealed clearly in the following example:

	Net sales	$1,000,000
	Cost of goods sold	$220,000
+	New purchases	+ 645,000
+	Inward freight	+ 14,000
	Total merchandise handled	$879,000
−	Closing inventory	− 280,000
	Gross cost of merchandise	$599,000
−	Cash discounts earned	− 32,000
	Net cost of merchandise sold	$567,000
+	Alteration/workroom costs	+ 10,000
	Total cost of merchandise sold	= $577,000
	Gross margin	= $423,000

CONCEPT

$$\text{Gross margin \%} = \frac{\text{Net sales} - \text{Total cost of goods sold}}{\text{Net sales}} \times 100$$

$$= \$1{,}000{,}000 \text{ (Sales)} - \$577{,}000 \text{ (Total cost of goods sold)}$$

$$= \$423{,}000 \text{ Gross margin}$$

$$= \frac{\$423{,}000 \text{ Gross margin}}{\$1{,}000{,}000 \text{ Net sales}} \times 100$$

Gross margin % = 42.3%

While

CONCEPT

$$\text{Maintained markup \%} = \frac{\text{Net sales} - \text{Gross cost of goods sold}}{\text{Net sales}} \times 100$$

$$= \frac{\$1{,}000{,}000 \text{ Net sales} - \$599{,}000 \text{ (Gross cost of goods)}}{\$1{,}000{,}000 \text{ Net sales}}$$

$$= \frac{\$401{,}000 \text{ Maintained margin}}{\$1{,}000{,}000 \text{ Net sales}} \times 100$$

Maintained markup % = 40.1%

Because the difference between gross margin and maintained markup is the amount of cash discounts and alteration and workroom costs, this relationship can also be expressed (using the same figure) as the following concept.

$$\text{Gross margin \%} = \frac{\text{Maintained markup } + \text{ Cash discounts } - \text{ Alteration costs}}{\text{Net sales}} \times 100$$

$$= \frac{\$401{,}000 \text{ MMU } + \dfrac{\$32{,}000}{\text{Cash discounts}} - \dfrac{\$10{,}000}{\text{Alteration costs}}}{\$1{,}000{,}000 \text{ Sales}}$$

$$= \frac{\$423{,}000}{\$1{,}000{,}000} \times 100$$

$$\textbf{Gross margin \%} = 42.3\%$$

While

$$\text{Maintained markup \%} = \frac{\text{Gross margin } - \text{ Cash discounts } + \text{ Alteration costs}}{\text{Net sales}} \times 100$$

$$= \frac{\dfrac{\$423{,}000}{\text{Gross margin}} - \dfrac{\$32{,}000}{\text{Cash discounts}} + \dfrac{\$10{,}000}{\text{Alteration costs}}}{\$1{,}000{,}000 \text{ Sales}}$$

$$= \frac{\$401{,}000}{\$1{,}000{,}000} \times 100$$

$$\textbf{Maintained markup \%} = 40.1\%$$

Maintained markup is the markup actually achieved on the sale of the merchandise and is generally calculated for a department or, when desired, for a **vendor analysis,** which is an investigation of the profitability of each vendor's products sold by a retailer. It is not customary to plan a maintained markup, because it is the result of merchandising activities. The initial markup must be planned in advance so that the desired final or maintained markup goal is achieved. In addition, maintained markup must be large enough to cover expenses and provide a profit, while, as previously explained, the initial markup must be high enough to anticipate and also cover all possible retail reductions (i.e., markdowns, shortages, and employee discounts). However, once the initial markup and retail reductions are planned, the probable maintained markup can be projected.

Finding Maintained Markup Percentage When Initial Markup Percentage and Retail Reductions Percentage Are Known

CONCEPT	$\dfrac{\text{Maintained}}{\text{markup \%}}$ = Initial MU % − Retail reduction % × (100% − Initial MU %)

PROBLEM

A department planned an initial markup of 49.8% and retail reductions of 15%. What is the maintained markup?

SOLUTION

Maintained markup % = 49.8% − 15% × (100% − 49.8%)

= 49.8% − 15% × 50.2%

= 49.8% − 7.53%

Maintained markup % = 42.27% or 42.3%

Finding Retail Reductions Percentage When Initial Markup Percentage and Maintained Markup Percentage Are Known

CONCEPT	Retail reduction % = $\dfrac{\text{Initial markup \%} - \text{Maintained markup \%}}{\text{Sales (100\%)} - \text{Initial markup \%}}$

PROBLEM

The department planned an initial markup of 49.8% and wanted to achieve a maintained markup of 42.3%. What should be the amount of retail reductions?

SOLUTION

Reduction % = $\dfrac{49.8\% \text{ Initial MU} - 42.27\% \text{ MMU}}{\text{Sales (100\%)} - 49.8\% \text{ Initial MU}}$

= $\dfrac{7.53\%}{50.2\%}$

Reduction % = 15.0%

The same factors have been used deliberately to show the calculations of both initial and maintained markups, so that the relationship can be fully appreciated. The maintained markup concepts can also be expressed in dollars, and the procedure for calculation is identical. A particular merchandising situation, however, may require the focus to be on dollars rather than percentages (e.g., merchandising fast-turnover goods).

Initial Markup Concepts
Practice Problems

1. A lingerie buyer determines that the department has net sales of $750,000, expenses of $315,000, and total reductions of $75,000. This buyer also wants to attain a net contribution of 4.5%. Find the initial markup percentage.

2. A department shows a gross margin of 41% (37.9% expenses + 3.1% profit) and lists retail reductions (i.e., markdowns, shortages, and employee discounts) of 13%. What is the initial markup percentage?

3. A chain of specialty shops plans sales of $1,500,000 and retail reductions of $260,000. It needs a gross margin of $605,000 (i.e., expenses $550,000, profit $55,000). What should be the initial markup percentage?

4. In a small leather goods department, the markdowns, including employee discounts, were 18.7%, stock shortage was 3.8%, and the gross margin was 46.6%. Determine the initial markup percentage.

5. A retailer in a boutique jewelry store has estimated expenses of 39%, markdowns at 15%, and stock shortage at 6.3%. A profit of 4% is desired. Calculate the initial markup percentage required.

6. The intimate apparel buyer wants to determine an initial markup percentage for the robe classification. The buyer knows that the gross margin is 44%, markdowns are at 31.4%, and shortages are at 0.6%. Calculate the initial markup percentage.

7. A gross margin of 49.4% is targeted by a gift department. Retail reductions are 16% and cash discounts are 4%, with alteration costs of 1%. Find the initial markup percentage.

8. A buyer plans, for the period, net sales of $1,500,000, with a 49% gross margin. The acceptable markdowns are 12%, with employee discounts at 1%, and planned shortages of 2.5%. Cash discounts to be earned are estimated at 6%, and alteration costs are 0.5%. What initial markup percentage is needed to achieve the desired results?

9. Determine the initial markup percentage from the following data:

Gross margin	=	46.8%
Markdowns	=	10.0%
Employee discounts	=	1.5%
Cash discounts to be earned	=	5.0%
Alteration costs	=	0.5%

10. The petite sportswear buyer plans seasonal net sales of $2,000,000, with a gross margin of 48%, markdowns (including employee discounts) estimated at 32.9%, planned shortages at 2.1%, cash discounts to be earned planned at 6%, and alteration costs at 1%. Calculate the planned initial markup percentage.

Cumulative Markup Practice Problems

11. A sleepwear buyer has an opening stock figure of $180,000 at retail, which carries a 52% markup. On March 31, new purchases since the start of the period were $990,000 at retail, carrying a 54% markup. Find the cumulative markup percentage on merchandise handled in this department to date.

12. The slipper department showed an opening inventory of $80,000 at retail, with a markup of 48%. The purchases for that month amounted to $30,000 at cost, which were marked in at 52%. The initial markup planned for this department was 50.5%.

    a. Determine the season-to-date cumulative markup percentage for the department.

    b. Was the department markup achieved on target? If not, what factors caused a deviation?

13. A belt department had an opening inventory of $95,000 at retail, with a 55.8% markup. Purchases during November were $64,000 at cost, and $142,000 at retail. Determine:

  a. The cumulative markup percentage.

  b. The markup percentage on the new purchases.

14. During the Fall season, a retailer determined that in order to meet the next season's planned sales, the total amount of merchandise required next season was $360,000 at retail, with an initial markup goal of 52%. At the beginning of the next season, the merchandise on hand (opening inventory) came to $80,000 at retail, with a cumulative markup of 49% on these goods. For the coming season, what initial markup percentage does the buyer need to achieve on any new purchases?

15. In preparation for a foreign buying trip, a buyer determines that a 55.4% markup is required on purchases that will amount to $560,000 at retail. While on this trip, the following purchases are made:

	Cost	Retail
Resource A	$20,000	$45,000
Resource B	$50,000	$125,000
Resource C	$70,000	$170,000

What markup percentage is needed on the balance of the purchases?

Maintained Markup Practice Problems

16. A men's shop with an initial markup of 53% had markdowns of 12%, employee discounts of 2.5%, and shortages of 1.5%. What was the maintained markup percentage?

17. A sporting goods store has an initial markup of 44.5%. The expenses are 31%, markdowns are 12%, cost of assembling bicycles, etc. (i.e., workroom costs), are 6%, and shortages are 1%. What was the maintained markup percentage?

18. The Closet Shop had the following operational results:

Net sales	=	$125,000
Billed cost of new purchases	=	$64,000
Inward freight	=	$1,000
Alteration costs	=	$2,000
Cash discounts	=	$7,000

Find:

    a. The maintained markup in dollars and percentages.

    b. The gross margin in dollars and percentages.

19. The jewelry department has an initial markup of 55.6%, with total retail reductions of 15%. There are no alteration costs or cash discounts. What is the maintained markup percentage and the gross margin percentage?

20. A children's store has sales of $500,000, with markdowns of 14.5% and shortages of 2%. The initial markup was 51.7%. What was the maintained markup percentage?

21. The T-shirt department buyer determined that the department's initial markup should be 51.5%. The buyer also wanted to attain a maintained markup of 45%. Under this plan, what retail reductions (in percentages) would be allowed?

22. A boutique had planned a gross margin of 49%, with total retail reductions of 18%. At the end of the period, the maintained markup attained was actually 48.8%.

    a. Find the initial markup percentage needed to achieve the planned gross margin of 49%, with total retail reductions of 18%.

    b. Find the actual amount of markdowns (in percentages) taken.

    c. Prove your calculations and explain your findings. What may have caused the maintained markup percentage to vary from the planned gross margin target?

UNIT III.II
AVERAGING OR BALANCING MARKUP

A buyer's skill is truly tested by the ability not only to buy "the right goods, at the right time, in the right amounts," but also to achieve a predetermined markup percentage over a season or year. Failure to reach this goal can have an adverse effect on profits, and sometimes can determine whether or not a profit is generated at all. Ultimately, as short-term buying decisions are made, the merchandiser must know how any deviations from the markup objective will affect the long-term performance.

In the actual pricing of goods in retailing, it is seldom possible to obtain the same markup on all lines of merchandise, all classifications, all price lines, or all items carried within a particular department. In the real world of retailing, deviations from the planned seasonal markup will occur. These differences can be the result of competition, variations in special promotional merchandise offered by resources, special buying arrangements, private brands, imports, and other factors that depend on the buyer's judgment. Thus, to realize the planned markup necessary for a profitable operation, below-average markups should be balanced by above-average markups. **Averaging markups** means adjusting the proportions of goods purchased at different markups to achieve the desired aggregate markup, either for an individual purchase or for a certain period. In merchandising the purchases, the buyer builds a "cushion" or lowers the markup, depending on the situation. This practice is prevalent in the fashion and fashion-related industries.

There are diverse pricing policies that are determined by an industry or by the specific retailer. Some of these factors are odd pricing (e.g., $89.99 instead of $90); multiple-unit pricing (e.g., one for $3.25, two for $6); loss leaders, in which an item is sold below the retailer's cost; high-low pricing, in which high everyday prices are combined with "specials"; or low leader pricing on featured items advertised weekly. Each retailer must evaluate the usefulness of each type of pricing service. The appropriate cumulative markup originates from effective averaging of many purchases.

When solving problems that illustrate how markups are averaged or balanced, it is helpful to remember that:

- On a day-to-day basis, buyers strive to achieve a projected markup by the averaging process.

- Appropriate cumulative markups result from the effective averaging of many purchases, and the effects of this averaging on the entire inventory.

- Basic markup equations are applied to given information to calculate the figures required for solutions.

- Solutions can be calculated readily when:

  - It is understood what information is missing.

  - The given information is determined.

  - The calculations required for the solution (based on the given information) are identified.

The next section's problems and solutions employ the above principles in two ways; that is, the steps necessary for the calculations are listed in sequence, and the results of these calculations are arranged in a diagram. It should be understood that an average markup is always determined by working with a total cost figure and a total retail figure. Spreadsheets simplify the calculating of averages.

AVERAGING COSTS WHEN RETAIL AND MARKUP PERCENTAGE ARE KNOWN

Determining the **average cost**, a merchandising technique, involves one retail price with two or more costs. It is common to have one retail line that consists of merchandise with varying wholesale costs. The merchandiser must be able to calculate the proportion of merchandise at different cost amounts that can carry the same retail price and still achieve the desired markup percentage. To understand this, it is essential to realize that the merchandiser is attempting to proportion the varying costs to achieve the desired markup percentage, because the aggregate results are the buyer's major concern.

PROBLEM

For a special sale, a men's sportswear buyer plans to promote a $25 vest. Consequently, the buyer purchases 500 vests and wants to achieve a 52% markup. An order for 100 vests that cost $10.75 each is also placed by this same buyer. What will be the average cost of the remaining pieces?

SOLUTION:
Spreadsheet format

Given information is in bold, and the other items are calculated.

	# Vests	Unit price	Total retail	MU %	Unit cost	Total cost
Special sale	**500**	**$25.00**	$12,500.00	**52%**		$6,000.00
Purchased	**100**				**$10.75**	$1,075.00
Balance	400				$12.32	$4,925.00

Given information is in bold, and the other items are calculated from the basic mark-up formulas. Each calculation is identified with the steps of the procedure.

Step 1: Find the total planned retail.

500 Pieces × **$25 Retail** = $12,500 (Total planned retail)

Step 2: Find the total cost of total planned retail using a planned markup percentage.

Total cost = R × (100% – MU %)

= $12,500 × (100% – 52%)

= $12,500 × 48%

Total cost = $6,000

Step 3: Find the cost of purchases to date.

100 Pieces × **$10.75** = $1,075 (Cost of purchases to date)

Step 4: Find the purchase balance in units and dollars.

Purchase balance = Total planned figures – Purchases to date

= (500 Pieces cost $6,000) – (100 Pieces cost $1,075)

= (400 Pieces cost $4,925)

	Total pieces	Total $ cost	Total $ retail	MU %
Total plan	500 (1)	$6,000 (2)	$12,000	52%
– Purchases to date	– 100 (3)	– 1,075 (3)		
Purchase balance	400 (4)	$4,925 (4)		

Step 5: Find the average cost of purchase balance.

Average cost of purchase balance = $ Cost on balance

Purchase balance   *Number of units*

= $4,925 (Purchase balance cost)   400 Pieces (Purchase balance pieces)

= $12.31 each is the average cost of the remaining pieces

AVERAGING RETAIL(S) WHEN COSTS AND MARKUP PERCENTAGE ARE KNOWN

In merchandising, a buyer must be able to manipulate markups, because purchases may be made that have two or more costs, and the buyer may want to determine an **average retail** that will achieve the desired markup percentage. Furthermore, the buyer may make purchases that not only have two or more costs, but also two or more retails. These situations require the proper proportion of varying retails to achieve the planned markup percentage, because a buyer is always concerned with the aggregate results. The following problems illustrate the averaging processes.

PROBLEM

At the end of the season, a swimwear manufacturer offered a retailer 50 two-piece solid-color suits that cost $16.75 each, 75 nylon tank suits that cost $12.75 each, and 40 one-piece skirted suits that cost $14.75 each. The average retail price on each unit was based on the buyer's goal of obtaining a 49% markup on this purchase. What would be the average retail price of each swimsuit?

SOLUTION:
Spreadsheet format

Given information is in bold, and the other items are calculated from the basic mark-up formulas.

Swimsuits	# Suits	Unit cost	Total cost	MU %	Total $ retail	Average retail per piece
Two-piece solid	**50**	**$16.75**	$837.50			
Nylon tank suits	**75**	**$12.75**	$956.25			
One-piece skirted	**40**	**$14.75**	$590.00			
Total	165		$2,383.75	**49%**	$4,674.02	$28.33

SOLUTION:
Arithmetically

Given information is in bold, and the other items are calculated from the basic mark-up formulas. Each calculation is identified with the steps of the procedure.

Step 1: Find the total cost and total units of purchase.

	50 Two-piece solid suits @ **$16.75**	=		$837.50
+	**75** Nylon tank suits @ **$12.75**	=	+	956.25
+	**40** One-piece suits @ **$14.75**	=	+	590.00
	165 Total suits	=		$2,383.75 Total cost

Step 2: Find the total retail from the planned markup percentage.

$$\text{Total retail} = \frac{\text{Cost}}{(100\% - 49\%)}$$

$$= \frac{\$2,383.75}{51\%}$$

Total retail = $4,674.02

	Total pieces	Total $ cost	Total $ retail	MU %
Total plan	165 (1)	$2,383.75 (1)	$4,674.02 (2)	49%

Step 3: Find the average retail for each piece.

$$\text{Average retail} = \frac{\text{Total retail}}{\text{Total units purchased}}$$

$$= \frac{\$4,674.02 \ (\text{Total retail})}{165 \text{ pieces (Total units purchased)}}$$

Average retail = $28.33

PROBLEM

The men's apparel buyer bought 50 corduroy sport jackets that cost $32.75 each and 80 wool sport jackets that cost $42.75 each. An overall markup of 52.5% is needed. If the buyer retails the corduroy sport jackets at $65.00 each, what must be the average retail price for each wool sport jacket to achieve the planned markup percentage?

SOLUTION: *Spreadsheet format*

Given information is in bold, and the other items are calculated from the basic markup formulas.

	# Jackets	Unit cost	Total cost	MU %	Unit retail	Total retail
Corduroy jackets	**50**	**$32.75**	$1,637.50		**$65.00**	$3,250.00
Wool jackets	**80**	**$42.75**	$3,420.00		$92.47	$7,397.37
Total	130		$5,057.50	**52.5%**		$10,647.37

SOLUTION: *Arithmetically*

Given information is in bold, and the other items are calculated from the basic markup formulas. Each calculation is identified with the steps of the procedure.

Step 1: Find the total cost and total units.

50 Corduroy sport jackets @ **$32.75**	=	$1,637.50
+ **80** Wool sport jackets @ **$42.75**	=	$3,420.00
130 Corduroy and wool sport jackets	=	$5,057.50

Step 2: Find the total retail from the planned markup percentage.

$$\text{Total retail} = \frac{\text{Cost}}{(100\% - 52.5\%)}$$

$$= \frac{\$5,057.50}{(100\% - 52.5\%)}$$

$$= \frac{\$5,057.50}{47.5\%}$$

$$\text{Total retail} = \$10,647.37$$

SOLUTION
continued

Step 3: Find the total on the established retail price.

50 Corduroy sport jackets × **$65 each** = $3,250

Step 4: Find the purchase balance in units and dollars.

Purchase balance = Total planned figures − Total established retail figures

= 130 Pieces @ $10,647.37 (Total $ retail)

− 50 Pieces @ $3,250.00 (Established retail)

80 Pieces $7,397.37

	Total pieces	Total $ cost	Total $ retail	MU %
Total plan	130 (1)	$5,057.50 (1)	$10,647.37 (2)	52.5%
− Established retail	− 50 (3)		− $3,250.00 (3)	
Purchase balance	80 (4)		$7,397.37 (4)	

Step 5: Find the average retail of the purchase balance.

$$\text{Average retail of purchase balance} = \frac{\text{Purchase balance \$ retail}}{\text{Purchase balance number of units}}$$

$$= \frac{\$7,397.27}{80 \text{ Pieces}}$$

Average retail for each remaining piece = $92.47

AVERAGING MARKUP PERCENTAGE WHEN RETAIL AND PLANNED MARKUP PERCENTAGE ARE KNOWN

Realistically, a profit goal can be realized only when a buyer is able to determine the markup percentage that must be obtained on present or future purchases to balance out the markup percentage that has already been achieved on past purchases. This involves the proportioning of markup percentages on goods so that the aggregate results produce the desired, planned markup percentage.

PROBLEM

A coat buyer plans to buy $5,000 (retail) worth of merchandise. This same buyer requires a 49% MU. The first purchase is 50 coats costing $31.75, with a planned retail of $55. What MU percentage should the buyer obtain on the balance to attain the planned MU goal of 49%?

SOLUTION:
Spreadsheet format

Given information is in bold and the other items are calculated from the basic markup formulas.

	# Coats	Unit cost	Total cost	MU %	Unit retail	Total retail	Markup
1st purchase	**50**	**$31.75**	$1,587.50	**49%**	**$55.00**	$2,750	$1,162.50
Balance			$962.50	57.2%		$2,250	$1,287.50
Total			$2,550.00			**$5,000**	

SOLUTION:
Arithmetically

Given information is in bold, and the other items are calculated from the basic markup formulas; each calculation is identified with the steps of the procedure.

Step 1: Find the total cost of the total planned retail from the planned markup percentage.

Total cost   = R × (100% − MU %)

                 = **$5,000** × (100% − **49%**)

                 = $5,000 × 51%

Total cost of purchase   = $2,550

Step 2: Find the total cost and retail of purchases to date.

50 Coats @ **$31.75**   =   **$1,587.50** Total cost of purchases to date

50 Coats @ **$55.00**   =   **$2,750.00** Total retail of purchases to date

Step 3: Find purchase balance at cost and retail.

Purchase balance $=$ Total planned retail and cost $-$ Retail and cost of purchases to date

$\quad = \dfrac{\$2,550}{\text{(Planned total cost)}} - \dfrac{\$1,587.50}{\text{(Cost of purchases to date)}}$

$\quad = \dfrac{\$962.50}{\text{(Cost of purchase balance)}}$

$\quad = \dfrac{\textbf{\$5,000}}{\text{(Planned total retail)}} - \dfrac{\$2,750}{\text{(Total retail purchases to date)}}$

Total retail of purchases balance $\quad = \quad \$2,250$

	Total $ cost	Total $ retail	MU %
Total plan	$2,250	$5,000	49%
– Purchase to date	– 1587.50 (2)	– 2,750.00 (2)	
Purchase balance	$962.50 (3)	$2,250.00 (3)	

Step 4: Find the markup percentage on purchase balance.

Dollar markup $=$ R $-$ C

$\quad = \$2,250 \text{ (Purchase balance retail)} - \$962.50 \text{ (Purchase balance cost)}$

$\quad = \$1,287.50 \text{ (Markup on purchase balance)}$

Markup % $\quad = \dfrac{\$ \text{ MU}}{\text{R}} \times 100$

$\quad = \dfrac{\$1,287.50 \text{ (Markup on purchase balance)}}{\$2,250 \text{ (Retail on purchase balance)}} \times 100$

Markup % $\quad = 57.2\%$

23. A buyer plans to purchase 120 dozen pairs of socks for a pre-Christmas sale. The unit retail price is planned at $17.50, and the markup goal for the purchase is 48%. Forty dozen pairs are purchased at the Slimline Company showroom, at $110 per dozen.

    a. What is the most the buyer can pay for the balance of the total purchase?

    b. What will be the average cost per dozen for the socks (80 dozen) yet to be purchased?

24. A separates buyer—who operates on a 51% markup—needs 300 skirts to retail at $32 each and 180 sweater vests to retail at $25 each. If this buyer pays $11.75 for each sweater vest, how much can be spent for each skirt, without deviating from the target markup percentage?

25. A buyer who needs $10,000 worth of merchandise at retail for a house-wares department has written orders for $2,875.50 at cost. The planned departmental markup percentage is 53.5%. How much (in dollars) is left to spend at cost?

26. A December promotion of 1,500 crystal bud vases to retail at $40 each is planned. The buyer requires a 48.5% average markup and has made an initial purchase consisting of 1,200 units costing $23 each. What is the cost to be paid on each remaining unit? Comment on the buyer's "predicament" if you detect one.

27. A buyer for the exclusive Britique Shop purchased 100 cashmere pull-over sweaters at $41 each and priced them at $90 retail. Also planned is a purchase of 72 Shetland/mohair-blend bulk-knit pullovers to retail at $50 each. Departmental goal markup is 51.8%. How much can be paid for each Shetland/mohair pullover?

Average Retail Practice Problems

28. A buyer purchases a job lot of 400 pairs of men's jeans, 280 pairs costing $14 each and 120 pairs costing $9 each. If a 51% markup is targeted, what would be the average unit retail price on the lot?

29. A buyer purchased 120 maillot swimsuits at $32 cost and placed a $65 retail on them. Sixty string bikinis are also purchased at $14 each. What would be the retail price on the bikinis if a 50% markup is desired on the combined purchase?

Average Markup Percentage Practice Problems

30. A buyer plans to purchase jackets at a 48% markup with a retail value of $18,500. If the buyer acquires 100 jackets at $69.75 each and retails them at $125 each, what markup percentage must now be obtained on the balance of the purchases in order to achieve the desired markup percentage?

31. A buyer, who needs $23,000 worth of goods at retail for May, has a planned markup of 49.5%. On May 10, the orders to date total $5,500 at cost and $9,800 at retail. What markup percentage must now be obtained on the balance of the purchases for May to achieve the planned markup percentage for the month?

32. The men's outerwear buyer, who needs a 51% average markup for this department, is planning to buy $9,500 worth of merchandise at retail for the month of January. To date, 100 imported rain jackets costing $21.75 each have been purchased, with a plan to retail them at 48% markup. What markup percentage is needed on the balance of the purchase to attain the average markup percentage?

33. A suit buyer who plans sales of $75,000 at retail during April has an average markup goal of 49%. An order is placed with the B&C Sportswear Company for April delivery in the amount of $5,975 at cost and $11,000 at retail. What markup must be made on the balance of the April purchases to achieve the planned markup?

34. A housewares buyer plans a $15,000 promotion of decorative stepstools to retail at $25 each at a 48% markup. A local manufacturer supplies 500 stools for $14 each. What markup percentage must be obtained on the remainder of the planned purchase to reach the markup goal?

UNIT III.III
LIMITATIONS OF THE MARKUP
PERCENTAGE AS A GUIDE TO PROFITS

From the discussions on markup and its relationship to profit, it is understood that markup can be calculated in both dollars and percentages. A markup percentage is a useful guideline in establishing a markup high enough to cover expenses, provide for reductions, and still realize a profit.

In the calculation of all types of markup, the focal point is generally on the markup percentage because it is particularly meaningful for analysis and comparison. However, under certain conditions, attention must be given to the dollar markup. Expenses are paid in dollars and profit is invested, reinvested, or taken to the bank in dollars. During periods of declining sales, a markup percentage initially deemed appropriate may be insufficient for a profit because a certain markup percentage is based on a specific estimated sales figure. There is a correlation between these two figures. For example, a buyer achieves sales of $300,000 and attains the required initial markup of 52% that would be large enough to cover expenses of $136,000 and markdowns of $12,000, and allow a profit of $8,000. In dollars and percentages this calculation would be:

	Dollars	Percentages
Sales	$300,000	100%
− Cost of goods sold	− 144,000	− 48%
Initial markup	= $156,000	52%
Expenses $136,000 Markdowns + $12,000 }	− 148,000	− 49.3%
Total profit	$8,000	2.7%

If sales declined 10% to $270,000, the 52% markup may not yield a profit. As sales decline, the fixed nature of expenses will not decline proportionately to the sales, if at all, and it is not always possible to lower markdown reductions, which may increase to stimulate lagging sales. This type of situation can result in a loss despite the establishment of what seemed a satisfactory markup percentage. The results are illustrated in the following example:

With the same 52% markup, only $140,400 would be available to cover the expenses of $136,000 and the markdowns of $12,000.

	Dollars	Percentages
Sales	$270,000	100%
− Cost of goods sold	− 129,600	− 48%
Initial markup	= $140,400	52%
Expenses $136,000 Markdowns + $12,000 }	− 148,000	− 54.8%
	− $7,600 (Loss)	2.8%

Conversely, as sales increase, the markup percentage can decline even though the dollar markup is maintained at an adequate level. The astute retailer recognizes that the dollar markup figure cannot be ignored while attempting to achieve a fixed markup percentage.

Practice Problems for Review

35. Determine the initial markup for a designer boutique that has the following projections for the next season:

Planned sales	=	$4,000,000
Markdowns	=	$600,000
Expenses	=	38%
Cash discounts	=	4%
Shortages	=	$20,000
Profit	=	5%

36. What is the cumulative markup to date for an accessories department whose figures are:

	Cost	Retail
Opening inventory	$360,000	$780,000
Purchases resource X	$60,700	$120,500
Purchases resource Y	$120,000	$245,000
Purchases resource Z	$150,000	$325,000

37. A shoe department with an initial markup of 53.2% had total retail reductions of 12%. What maintained markup was achieved in this department?

38. A men's outerwear department, with an initial markup of 54%, needs to maintain a markup of 48%. How much can be allowed for reductions?

39. Determine if the maintained markup of 48% would be obtained using the reduction percentage calculated in Problem 38.

40. The owner of a children's store wishes to increase annual profits (which were 2.5% of net sales) from $5,000 to $15,000. The operating expenses are anticipated to increase from 30% to 32% because of increased promotional events. The total retail reductions are planned at 15.5%, the same as last year, and there are no cash discounts or alteration costs.

   a. What was last year's initial markup percentage?

   b. To achieve the owner's increased profit on the same sales volume, what initial markup should be planned for this year?

41. A buyer wishes to buy 3,500 novelty scarves for a special import promotion. The item is to retail at $16.95 each with a planned markup of 54%. If the cost for each of 2,100 scarves is $8.75, how much may be paid for each scarf not yet purchased?

42. A luggage buyer plans a European buying trip to purchase $250,000 (cost value) of assorted travel packs. On the first stop in London, orders are placed for $92,000 (at cost) for an assortment of leather luggage, which will be priced at $180,000 retail. If the average markup is targeted at 52%, what markup percentage should now be taken on the balance of the European orders?

43. A men's buyer purchases a closeout of 1,500 velour shirts offered at $9.85 each and 950 knit shirts at $5.80 each. The planned markup on the purchase is 49.5%. If a unit retail of $17.95 is placed on the velour shirts, what is the lowest possible retail price at which the knit shirts may be marked to remain within the markup framework indicated?

44. A buyer, who has a departmental markup of 49%, wants $40,000 (retail) worth of men's casual shirts for next season. An order for turtlenecks is placed in the amount of $6,400 at cost and $11,000 at retail. What markup percentage must now be achieved on the balance of the purchases?

45. A lingerie department made a special purchase of 100 dozen nylon briefs costing $36/dozen, 75 dozen stretch bras costing $54/dozen, and 12 dozen teddies at $84/dozen. If the briefs are retailed at $6 each, and the bras at $9 each, at what retail price should the teddies be marked to attain a 53% markup?

46. The buyer of decorative pillows needs a markup of 50% and plans to purchase $5,000 worth of goods (retail value) during the month of November. At the middle of the month, the total of the invoices for the purchases to date (at both cost and retail) for the month to date amount to $2,000 at cost and $3,700 at retail. What markup in dollars and percentage must be obtained on the balance of the purchases?

47. A buyer needs 5,000 umbrellas for the 37th annual storewide "April Showers" promotional event, to retail at $14 each. The planned markup is 49%. If 3,500 units are bought at one resource for $7.70 each, how much can the buyer afford to pay for each of the remaining 1,500 units?

48. A children's apparel buyer is offered a lot of denim jackets consisting of 125 toddler boys' jackets at $20 each and 160 toddler girls' jackets at $23 each. All the jackets will be sold at the same retail price. If the buyer is to make a 54% markup on the entire transaction, at what price must each jacket be retailed?

49. A men's accessories buyer purchases 10,000 neckties from a manufacturer, who is relocating, at the low cost price of $10 per tie. Noticing that the ties are of two types, 6,200 solids and 3,800 stripes, the buyer decides to attempt some creative merchandising. If each solid tie is retailed at $18, what retail price should be placed on each striped tie if an average markup of 51% is desired?

50. An outerwear buyer confirms an order reading as follows:

     • 145 tailored raincoats costing $47 each.

     • 75 three-quarter-length rain jackets costing $26 each.

     If a retail price of $85 is placed on the tailored coats, and a markup average of 48% is sought, what retail price must the rain jackets carry?

51. The boys' wear buyer purchases 20 dozen pairs of jeans at $108/dozen and 15 dozen flannel shirts at $96/dozen. The departmental markup is planned at 52%. If the jeans are priced at $18, what price must be put on the shirts to reach goal markup?

52. A buyer purchases a closeout of 1,000 fleece coats at a cost of $46 each, which are divided into two groups: 425 belted coats and 575 unbelted. If the desired average markup is 49%, what retail price should be placed on each of the unbelted coats if the belted ones are priced at $95 each?

53. A junior sportswear department shows an opening stock figure of $540,000 at retail, owned at a 48% markup. To date, since the last stock determination, new purchases were $1,700,000 at retail, with a 50% markup. Find the cumulative markup percentage on total merchandise handled in this department to date.

54. The gross margin in a handbag department is 42.7% (40% expenses + 2.7% profit), which shows reductions (total of markdowns, shortages, and employee discounts) of 14.5%. State the initial markup percentage.

55. The planned gross margin in a young-men's sportswear department is 46%, with reductions of 15%, cash discounts earned equaling 6%, and alteration costs amounting to 2%. What is the initial markup percentage?

56. A men's apparel department planned an initial markup of 49% and reductions of 16%. Find the maintained markup.

57. For a Columbus Day event, a buyer plans to purchase 250 knit dresses to retail for $75 each. A 47% markup is needed on the total purchase. From one of the buyer's best resources, 110 dresses were purchased that cost $33.75 each. The buyer knows, however, that the costs will have to be averaged on the balance of other purchases from alternate resources in order to achieve a 47% markup on the entire group.

   a. What must be the average cost per dress on the balance of the purchases if the buyer is to attain the planned markup percentage?

   b. What markup percentage did the buyer attain on the first purchase of 110 dresses?

   c. What markup percentage did the buyer have to get on the balance of the purchases to realize the overall needed markup?

58. For the month of July, a sporting goods department had net sales of $250,000. The billed cost of the goods, including transportation, was $120,000. Cash discounts amounted to $9,600 and there were alteration costs of $400. Calculate (in dollars):

   a. The maintained markup.

   b. The gross margin.

CASE STUDY 1
ACHIEVING A PREDETERMINED MARKUP

Miss Jay Tee is the shoe buyer for a fashion specialty store located in the trendy "Near North Side" of Chicago. It is October 1, and she is scheduled for a European buying trip on October 25, during which she will place orders for Spring delivery. Her Spring six-month plans are complete and have been approved by management.

Before leaving on her buying trip, she reviews her current operational figures to evaluate her position for the forthcoming last quarter of the year (i.e., November, December, January). They are:

- Merchandise on hand (BOM, or beginning of the month) November 1: $1,300,000 with a 51.5% cumulative markup.

- Closing inventory (BOM) February 1: $400,000.

Planned sales:	November	December	January	Total sales
	$500,000	$550,000	$250,000	$1,300,000

- Planned markdown to be taken in November, December, January: $80,000, or 6.2%.

- Estimated shortages for this period: 2.0%.

- Gross margin (no cash discounts or alteration costs): 48.1%.

Based on this information, Miss Tee does some calculations and determines that she still has $506,000, at retail, to spend for this quarter.

It is customary for Miss Tee to devote several days at the beginning of her trip to scout the market to obtain extremely desirable current seasonal goods, available for immediate shipment, at advantageous prices that will stimulate pre-Christmas sales, and that will generate sales in the slow-selling month of January, traditionally associated with only clearance and/or highly competitively priced merchandise.

On October 25, she arrives in Florence, Italy, and as she covers the boot resources she finds there is an abundance of the current season's merchandise—available for immediate shipment—because of cancellations by importers and retailers. This situation has been caused by sluggish economic and business conditions. One of her best key resources has in stock 4,000 pairs of leather boots in this season's avant-garde styling with balanced sizes and colors. Fifty percent of the resource's offering are the same styles as 500 pairs currently in stock, selling reasonably well at $200 retail. Providing she agrees to buy the complete group, the final landed cost negotiated is $50 per pair. Despite the fact that she considers this merchandise to be superb value at this sensational cost, she is hesitant about buying such a large quantity so late in the selling season. However, she receives an e-mail from her assistant informing her that the boots are moving quickly and sales have increased due to very cold, wintery weather conditions. She decides to buy this offering before a competitor has an opportunity to do so. Her strategy considerations are:

- Retailing the group.

- Shipping for present selling.

- Integrating this purchase with present stock.

- Obtaining the necessary markup percentage.

She commits herself to the purchase, returns to her hotel, and diligently works to map out the delivery and pricing factors. Her first decision is to start shipping some of these goods so that they are available as soon as possible for November selling. Therefore, despite the expense, she immediately sends 1,000 pairs by air because it is fast and it serves her purpose. This mode of transportation increases the delivered cost of the 1,000 pairs from $50 to $55 a pair, and the retail is set at $150.

After making this decision, she turns her attention to the 500 pairs in stock currently selling at $200 a pair. Because markdown money is available, Miss Tee wants to begin to reduce the higher-priced boots while there is traffic. She can afford to reduce these 500 pairs from $200 to $150, taking a larger than usual first markdown, because the markup of the 1,000 pairs (that will sell simultaneously) is so above average.

On the balance of the 3,000 pairs, she divides half for December selling and retails them for $125. The remaining 1,500 pairs she reserves for her annual Blizzard Promotion scheduled in January. For this event, her boot sales rely solely on merchandise that creates "riots." She has not yet set a retail price on the 2,500 pairs for the January sale because she would like to price them at levels that are somewhat low, but that will not kill the required markup for the season. However, she calculates that a 54.4% markup is needed on the entire purchase so that her seasonal markup target will be met.

Prepare a merchandising plan for class discussion and, in doing so, consider the following:

- Do you agree with the merchandising techniques Miss Tee uses in this particular purchase? If so, why? If not, why? Justify your position mathematically.

- Advise Miss Tee of the retail price you would establish on the 1500 pairs of boots targeted for the January promotion, keeping in mind that all of her objectives should be satisfied.

CASE STUDY 2
ENSURING FAVORABLE MARKUP RESULTS

You have been hired by a group of investors to buy and merchandise accessories for their small chain (four stores) of infant apparel shops. This new classification is to complement and reflect their prestigious, unique merchandise assortments, which are targeted for the young, upper-income mother and/or grandparents looking for the "unusual." This new classification was introduced in the Fall/Winter period and was well received by their clientele. Although the projected sales goal was met, the profit performance was more than disappointing.

After analysis of each market segment and location, your focus will be on the combined merchandise selection factors that form the basis of your ultimate selections suitable for your particular customer group.

The pricing factor is one of the elements that is of major importance and is not only significant, but also observable. Because of the relationship of pricing to gross margin, management has planned and set certain gross margin guidelines and limitations to ensure that the store achieves a more satisfactory gross margin. These figures are to be achieved while accomplishing the projected sales. As an incentive, you have been promised an additional bonus if you provide gross margin results that are an improvement over the following expected guidelines:

Gross margin	47.4%	(43.4% expenses, 4% profit)
Sales	$600,000	
Markdowns	$660,000	(10%)
Shortages	$612,000	(2%)
Opening inventory	$150,000	
Closing inventory	$200,000	

You are confident that with appropriate planning and forecasting you will be able to attain the results management wants, and the phantom bonus mentioned could become a reality for you.

Situation 1. A key factor in gross margin control is the pricing of merchandise. Since management already established a 47.4% gross margin, will advance planning of an initial markup help ensure a favorable gross margin? Yes or no? Why? Should you be able to determine the gross margin or maintained markup having calculated the initial markup? What is to be gained by determining these two figures?

Situation 2. During the course of the season, you know the cumulative markup percentage is another important profit factor because it represents the markup on the merchandise on hand at the beginning of the season, as well as the purchases during this period. You notice that the opening inventory of $150,000 carried a 52.0%

markup. What, if any, effect will this have on the markup percentage required of the new purchases in order to achieve the cumulative markup of 53% for the season?

Situation 3. Although you will focus on obtaining the desired markup percentage, you will also have to pay attention to the dollar markup. Why? Because these (sales, markdowns, shortages) are projections (which could prove erroneous). Compute and compare how the dollar markup could give different results if the actual reductions increased to 13%. Should you aim for a higher initial markup in order to build a "cushion" to account for the unpredictable?

CASE STUDY 3
BALANCING MARKUP

In preparation for a buying trip, a buyer determined a 54% markup was required on all purchases, which amounted to $750,000 at retail. Upon completion of the trip, the buyer reviewed the orders placed. At the end of the season, a vendor analysis revealed the sales results shown below:

	Cost	Initial retail	Final retail
Resource A	$25,000	$50,000	$50,000
Resource B	40,000	85,000	83,000
Resource C	60,000	135,000	130,000
Resource D	55,000	135,000	135,000
Resource E	75,000	170,000	167,000
Resource F	90,000	175,000	165,000
Total	$345,000	$750,000	$730,000

Compute the following:

a. Initial markup percentage for each resource.

b. Final markup percentage achieved for each resource.

c. Compare the anticipated markup percentage of the entire purchase with the actual markup percentage achieved.

d. Which vendor(s) markup percentage performance was superior to the overall markup percentage and by how much?

THE RETAIL METHOD OF INVENTORY

UNIT 4

"What's measured improves."

PETER DRUCKER

OBJECTIVES

- Knowledge and understanding of the retail method of inventory.

- Differentiation between physical inventory and book inventory.

- Identification and description of information and procedures necessary to implement the retail method of inventory.

- Calculation of book inventory figures at cost.

- Recognition and identification of the causes of overages and shortages.

- Calculation of overages and shortages based on inventory figures.

- Evaluation of the advantages and limitations of the retail method of inventory.

KEY TERMS

book inventory	opening book inventory	retail method of inventory
charge-back to vendors	overage	return to vendor
closing book inventory	perpetual inventory	running book inventory
closing physical stock	physical inventory	shortage
debit memo form	price change form	transfer
	purchase record	

Key Concept Formulas

Book inventory

$$\begin{array}{c} \text{Book} \\ \text{inventory} \\ \text{at retail} \end{array} = \begin{array}{c} \text{Physical} \\ \text{inventory} \end{array} + \begin{array}{c} \text{Net retail} \\ \text{purchases} \\ \text{(Total merchandise handled)} \end{array} + \begin{array}{c} \text{Other} \\ \text{stock} \\ \text{additions} \end{array} - \begin{array}{c} \text{Net} \\ \text{sales} \end{array} - \begin{array}{c} \text{Markdown} \\ \text{differences} \end{array} - \begin{array}{c} \text{Other} \\ \text{deductions} \\ \text{from stock} \end{array}$$

$$\begin{array}{c} \text{Book} \\ \text{inventory} \\ \text{at cost} \end{array} = \begin{array}{c} \text{Opening} \\ \text{retail book} \\ \text{inventory} \end{array} \times \left(100\% - \begin{array}{c} \text{Cumulative} \\ \text{markup \%} \\ \text{achieved on} \\ \text{stock} \end{array} + \text{Purchases} \right)$$

Shortage or overage

$$\begin{array}{c} \text{Shortage} \\ \text{(or overage)} \end{array} = \text{Closing book inventory at retail} - \text{Physical inventory count}$$

$$\text{Shortage \%} = \frac{\text{\$ Shortage}}{\text{\$ Net sales}} \times 100$$

$$\text{Estimated dollar shortage} = \begin{array}{c} \text{Estimated shortage} \\ \text{percentage} \end{array} \times \text{Planned net sales}$$

To control and guide the operations of a retail organization, it is essential to keep records. Records are the working tools that provide information on the profitability of a business or for making everyday decisions (e.g., what types of merchandise are needed, when and how much is needed, etc.). Of particular concern to management and buyers is inventory control.

Successful merchandising requires that the size of stocks offered to the consumer be large enough to satisfy demand, but that the dollar investment be kept as low as possible. This can be accomplished only by having a frequent indication of stock-on-hand. The retail merchandiser who is concerned with the question "How much can I sell?" must know how much to buy to maintain this satisfactory relationship between the amount of sales volume and the size of stocks carried. Today, the increased use of computer information systems by department stores, small retail businesses, and most merchandising chains has a major impact on the management of merchandise inventories and other areas of record-keeping.

In large retail stores, it would be inconvenient and prohibitive in terms of cost to constantly determine the value of the amount of stock-on-hand by taking an actual count. However, because this balance of sales to stocks is vital, a system of accounting that determines the probable amount of stock-on-hand at any given time—

without physically counting the goods—has been devised. The retail method of inventory is a system of accounting that values merchandise at current retail prices, which can be converted by markup formula to cost value. Although the computer turns available information into electronic documents, for illustrative purposes in the study of the retail method of inventory, the actual types of records connected with this method are shown here in order to appreciate the data required by this accounting system. The information required is critical, not the means of collection.

The retail method of inventory is a method of averages, with the retail stock figure at the end of an accounting period providing the basis for determining the cost value of stock. The conversion of the closing inventory at retail to a cost figure is calculated by the determination of the cumulative markup percentage on the total merchandise handled as described in Unit III. To understand the retail method of inventory, it is vital to realize that it operates on the theory that the merchandise in stock is always representative of the total merchandise handled to date (i.e., stock plus new purchases). It allows an acceptable cost value of the book inventory to be established so that gross margin can be determined periodically.

It is common practice for large stores to "think at retail" because net sales (100%) are the primary basis for the analysis of all the relationships of expenses to sales and are the ultimate determining factors that show whether the merchandising endeavors result in a profit or a loss. Gross margin, which is the difference between the cost of goods sold and the income received from this merchandise (i.e., net sales) is also expressed as a percentage of net sales. Consequently, the danger of failing to make the correct percentage comparisons is eliminated, because these percentages are all calculated on the same base (i.e., net sales), which is a retail figure. The dollar value of the inventory owned must also be expressed as a retail figure to predetermine the desired relationship of these two factors (i.e., sales to stocks). In the process of buying and selling to yield a more satisfactory profit, retailers can compare and contrast their merchandising operations with that of other retailers. They compare such factors as net sales produced (a retail figure); the relationship of retail stock to net sales (figures used to attain the needed proportion); the pricing of merchandise expressed as a percentage based on the retail; and the percentage of reductions (figures needed to revise prices originally set on merchandise). Finally, when filing income taxes, insurance claims, and so on, the current retail price of the merchandise is the significant valuation.

These examples illustrate the importance of the maintenance of a perpetual retail inventory figure. Though inventory figures are not always perpetually derived, they can be obtained as often as is desirable, usually every week or month.

UNIT IV.I
EXPLANATION OF THE
RETAIL METHOD OF INVENTORY

The retail system of merchandise accounting permits the retailer to determine the value (at retail) of the stock-on-hand at frequent and periodic intervals without taking constant physical counts. However, it must be noted that periodic—generally semiannual—physical counts (i.e., inventories) are taken at the current retail prices of the merchandise on hand. To control stocks and determine the profitability of individual departments, the retail method of accounting is applied separately for each department. The retail method of inventory valuation involves:

- Taking a physical inventory count to determine the total retail value of a particular department.

- Determining the cumulative markup percentage on the total merchandise handled (sum of opening inventory plus the total purchases).

- Deriving the cost value of the closing inventory from the retail by using the cumulative markup percentage achieved on the total merchandise handled. Subsequently, this valuation is used to find the cost of goods sold to establish the gross margin.

This system requires the collection and analysis of data pertaining to any movement of merchandise from the time it is bought until it is sold to the consumer. The retail method of inventory requires maintaining a book inventory at retail, as well as other records that permit the calculation of the cost of total merchandise handled during the period. This, in turn, allows constant calculation of the gross margin amount, including the possible protection of profitability. All additions to and deductions from stock must be recorded in dollar values. The computation from "statistical records" or book figures of the amount of merchandise that should be on hand at retail is called a **book inventory**.

At the beginning of the accounting period under consideration, a **physical inventory** count is taken at the current retail price of the goods owned. It is common that when large stores take semiannual physical count of stocks and record the value at retail, that date of receipt of merchandise into stock is also recorded.

Figure 9 shows the diversity of the average number of physical inventories (of all product categories and departments) performed per store per year. Figure 10 illustrates the information generally recorded during a physical count. This form, as well as the subsequent forms used in this chapter, merely demonstrates what information is required by the retail method of inventory. Today's retailer, whether checking a price, handling a point-of-sales transaction, or tracking the receipt of inventory, relies on some type of data-collection technology to suit the needs of the company. The system of collecting the data may be different, but the data required will be identical.

Figure 9. Average Physical Inventories Performed

Average Physical Inventories Performed	Percent of Companies
1–3	60%
4–6	17%
7–9	4%
10–12	5%
13–15	1%
Over 15	6%
N/A	6%

Source: Tenth Annual Retail Horizons: Benchmarks for 2011, Forecasts for 2012 (KPMG/NRF Foundation)

Figure 10. Physical Inventory Count Sheet

When taking a physical inventory using this method, it is not necessary to list the cost price of each individual item. The physical count of each individual item, at the retail price stated on its ticket, is recorded, and the total retail figure (e.g., $100,000) is the actual amount of goods accounted for at the time the semiannual count is made. If warranted, this count can be made more often. This actual physical count figure is then used as the **closing physical stock** figure for that accounting period. If the physical inventory value is less than the book inventory, the difference is called a **shortage**. When the physical inventory value exceeds the book inventory, that difference is called an **overage**.

UNIT IV.II
GENERAL PROCEDURES FOR IMPLEMENTING THE RETAIL METHOD OF INVENTORY

FINDING AN OPENING BOOK INVENTORY FIGURE

When the "retail method" system is first installed, a complete physical count at retail (see Figure 10) is taken for each merchandising department. (Note: This physical count reflects the retail value of the inventory at aggregate retail prices.) The retail value of the goods counted is used as the **opening book inventory** figure. This is the same figure as the closing physical stock figure of the previous accounting period. Inventory counts continue to be taken semiannually at the current retail prices of the goods. (Remember, closing physical inventory at retail equals the opening book inventory at retail for the next period.)

MAINTAINING A PERPETUAL BOOK INVENTORY FIGURE

A book inventory indicates the amount of stock in dollars that has been determined from records, rather than from an actual count. During the time period between the semiannual physical counts just described, many other merchandising transactions occur:

- Goods are sold to customers.

- Merchandise is purchased and received from resources.

- Customers return merchandise.

- Merchandise is marked down.

- Goods are transferred to other departments in the same store for resale.

- Merchandise is transferred to other stores.

- Merchandise is returned to vendors occasionally.

Every such transaction, and any other kind of merchandise movement, is accompanied by paperwork in the form of sales checks, return-to-vendor forms, orders, and so on. The retail organization's statistical department or the accounting division records every transaction and adds to or reduces the "book stock" accordingly. For example, sales to customers or **transfers** to other departments reduce the "book stock" (also known as **perpetual** or **running book inventory**) by the dollar amount corresponding to the retail value of the goods sold or transferred. The records must be current and accurate so that a retail book inventory figure is always available during an accounting period. Any additions to or deductions from stock must be recorded as the current retail prices and reported to the statistical department. In other words, every change that affects the stock value must be recorded.

In a multistore operation, a constant inventory figure is maintained for a particular department in each store. This inventory figure is evaluated not only on an individual store basis, but also on a department's overall operation. The main reasons for calculating a physical book inventory are that:

- The determination of stock shortage whenever physical inventory is taken can prevent or lessen losses by taking prompt action.

- The accurate determination of stock-on-hand periodically maintains the proper relationship between sales and stock as merchandise purchases are controlled in ratio to ample stocks.

- The estimation of profits at any given time allows the timely correction of any adverse conditions.

- Possible insurance claims can be maximized by providing acceptable, accurate records of inventory validation.

The following is an example of a department for a branch store, which should serve to illustrate the "addition or deduction" of the value of the merchandise in stock. All these changes must be recorded to ensure accuracy.

EXAMPLE

Increase of retail value				*Decrease of retail value*		
	Purchases (total retail value of merchandise received)	$35,000		Net sales		$28,000
			+	Transfers out at retail	+	2,000
			+	Returns to vendor	+	3,000
+	Transfers in at retail	+ 5,000	+	Employee discounts	+	500
	Total stock additions	$40,000	+	Markdown differences	+	500
				Total stock deductions		$34,000

Calculating a Book Inventory Figure at Retail

A retail book inventory is determined by:

- Taking a periodic physical count at retail to determine a closing physical stock figure.

- Establishing the physical count amount as the opening retail book inventory.

- Adding all new purchases at retail to determine the total merchandise handled at retail.

- Subtracting all retail deductions (e.g., net sales, markdowns, etc.) from the retail total merchandise handled to find the **closing book inventory** at retail.

Book inventory at retail = Add the opening physical inventory figure to the net retail purchases (total merchandise handled) and any other stock additions; then (from the resultant sum) subtract net sales, markdown differences, and any other deductions from stock.

PROBLEM

On January 31, the physical count of the infants' department in Branch #15 revealed an inventory of $20,000. On February 1, the opening retail inventory of this department was $20,000. From February 1 to July 31 retail purchases amounting to $40,000 were received. The net sales for this period were $30,500, the markdowns taken were $2,300, employee discounts were $200, returns to vendors were $350, and transfers out were $750. What was the retail book inventory for this period under consideration?

SOLUTION

Opening book retail inventory (Feb. 1)			$20,000
+ Retail purchases (Feb. 1–July 31)		+	40,000
Total merchandise handled (Retail additions)			$60,000
Net sales	$30,500		
+ Markdown differences	+ 2,300		
+ Employee discounts	+ 200		
+ Returns to vendor	+ 350		
+ Transfers out	+ 750		
Total retail deductions	= $34,100	–	34,100
Retail book inventory		=	$25,900

Calculating a Book Inventory at Cost

A book inventory at cost is determined by:

CONCEPT

Step 1: Converting the opening retail book inventory to a cost inventory figure by using the cumulative markup percentage achieved on the stock plus purchases during the previous accounting period.

Step 2: Adding all new purchases at cost, plus freight (on cost only), to the cost opening inventory figure to determine the total merchandise handled at cost.

Step 3: Finding the cumulative percentage on total merchandise handled.

Step 4: Converting the closing book inventory at retail to a closing book inventory at cost, by using the cumulative markup percentage that has been calculated from the difference between the total merchandise handled at retail and the total merchandise handled at cost.

Calculate a book inventory at cost if the markup percentage on the previous season's inventory is 51% and the cost of the new purchases is $19,800. (The same figures are used as in the previous problem illustrating the determination of a book inventory figure at retail.)

Step 1: Convert opening book retail inventory to cost inventory figure, using the cumulative markup percentage achieved on stock plus purchases (total merchandise handled) for the previous accounting period.

$$\begin{aligned}
\text{Opening cost inventory} &= \underset{\text{(Opening retail book inventory)}}{\$20,000} \times (100\% - \text{Cumulative MU \%}) \\[1em]
&= \underset{\text{(Opening retail book inventory)}}{\$20,000} \times (100\% - 51\% \text{ Cumulative MU \%}) \\[1em]
&= \$20,000 \times 49\% \\[0.5em]
&= \$9,800
\end{aligned}$$

Step 2: Add all new purchases plus freight to opening inventory at cost. Given:

$19,800	(New purchases at cost)
+ 200	Freight
$20,000	New purchases including freight
+ 9,800	(Opening inventory at cost)
$29,800	Total merchandise handled at cost

Step 3: Find cumulative markup percentage on total merchandise handled.

	Cost	Retail
Opening inventory	$9,800	$20,000
+ Purchases	+ 20,000	+ 40,000
Total merchandise handled	$29,800	$60,000

$$\begin{aligned}
\text{Cumulative MU \%} &= \frac{\$60,000 \text{ Retail of total merchandise handled} - \$29,800 \text{ cost of total merchandise handled}}{\$60,000 \text{ Retail}} \\[1em]
&= \frac{\$30,200 \text{ MU}}{\$60,000 \text{ Retail}} \times 100
\end{aligned}$$

$$\text{Cumulative MU \%} = 50.3\%$$

Step 4: Convert closing book inventory at retail to closing book inventory at cost by using the cumulative markup percentage.

Closing book inventory at retail	=	$25,900
Closing book inventory at cost	=	$25,900 × (100% − 50.3%)
	=	$25,900 × 49.7%
	=	$12,872.30

FORMS USED IN THE RETAIL METHOD OF INVENTORY

Today a retailer's records are often supplemented and/or obtained through the store's (or organization's) computer system (e.g., POS markdowns). How the information is recorded is a matter of choice or monetary necessity, but the loss of records or the failure to record the proper information that shows the increase or decrease in the value of the stock will result in an inaccurate stock valuation of the book inventory. There are many forms to help the retailer accurately record this valuable information. Each form serves a particular function, but not all retailers use identical forms. The forms in this section illustrate and allow you to become familiar with the function of each record (some or all of which may be entirely part of a computerized operating system) required to appreciate or depreciate the value of a stock. Today, with the widespread use of automated merchandising systems, the information necessary to maintain an accurate recording of transactions is adopted and tailored to each retailer's needs.

Purchase Record

Figure 11 is a **purchase record**, which provides a record of the billed or invoiced costs, transportation charges, cash discounts, retail amounts, and the percentages of markup for each individual purchase. The names of the vendors, dates of invoices, and the invoice numbers are also entered. Each department checks this record periodically to ensure that the department is being charged or credited with merchandise either entering or leaving a department and that these amounts are only intended for that department. This report also shows the department classification, vendor, style, and price receipts in units for the total store as well as individual branches. The negative units represent returns to vendors or corrections. The purpose of the report is to allow buyers to examine receipts entered into the computer against copies of the purchase order. Discrepancies are then reported so that appropriate adjustments can be made.

Figure 11. Journal of Purchase Record

DIV 04

VENDOR NAME GREEN & CO.

ST	DEPT. NO.	VENDOR NO.	APRON NO.	INV. NO.	INV. DATE	REC. DATE	RETAIL	INV. AMT.	MU%	TRANS.	DISCOUNT	ANTIC.	VENDOR FRT.	NET
2	310100	616920	14020	004803	3/01/13	3/10	115	62.10	46.00	.00	1.86	.00	.00	60.24
8	310100	616920	48049	004805	3/08/13	3/10	126	69.10	45.16	.00	2.07	.00	.00	67.03
8	310100	616920	48049	004806	3/08/13	3/10	76	41.80	45.00	.00	1.25	.00	.00	40.55
8	310100	616920	48049	004807	3/08/13	3/10	773	395.05	48.89	.00	11.85	.00	.00	383.20
2	310100	616920	14936	004984	3/16/13	3/17	360	197.87	45.04	.00	5.94	.00	.00	191.93
2	310100	616920	14936	004985	3/16/13	3/17	619	387.23	37.44	.00	11.62	.00	.00	375.61
3	310100	616920	49226	005069	3/19/13	3/22	317	174.50	44.95	.00	5.24	.00	.00	169.26
3	310100	616920	49226	005070	3/19/13	3/22	417	229.54	44.95	.00	6.89	.00	.00	222.65
2	310100	616920	AJ742	074230 SU	4/05/13			.00		.00	17.65–	.00	.00	17.65
				TOTALS FOR VENDOR 616920			2,603	1,557.19		.00	29.07	.00	.00	1,528.12

UNIT 4: THE RETAIL METHOD OF INVENTORY | 171

Transfer of Goods

A **transfer** of merchandise involves the movement of goods. When the merchandise leaves a department, the transfer is out; conversely, when the merchandise is received, the transfer is in. When merchandise is transferred from one store to another (e.g., a branch), an Outstanding Transfer List Form is used to record the number of units transferred, unit cost, total cost, unit retail, and total retail. Merchandise may also be transferred from one department to another. This record is used to indicate the change of ownership of merchandise. Figure 12 (Outstanding Transfer List Form) illustrates the detailed information that an automated merchandising system can furnish on interstore transfers (e.g., reasons for transfers, size, color, etc.).

Figure 12. Outstanding Transfer List Form

*OUTSTANDING TRANSFER LIST AS OF OCT 08, 2013 DATE OCT 09, 2013 PAGE: 1												
								TIME 5:31 PM				
1) BY FROM STORE — WITH DETAILS												
FROM STORE	TO STORE	TRANSFER NUMBER	TYPE	TRANSFER DATE	SKU NO.	STYLE NO.	COL	SIZE	QTY	PRICE	RETAIL AMOUNT	COST AMOUNT	TRANSFER REASON
001	002	000002	1	OCT 08, 2013	0015149	SW10	030	XS	4	22.55	90.20	40.00	001 Slow Moving
					0015156	SW10	030	S	4	22.55	90.20	40.00	
					0015164	SW10	030	M	5	22.55	112.75	50.00	
					0015172	SW10	030	L	3	22.55	67.65	30.00	
					0015189	SW10	030	XL	2	22.55	45.10	20.00	
003	001	000001	1	OCT 07, 2013	0014555	200XT	020	R - 40	3	440.00	1,320.00	825.00	003 Fast Moving
					0014563	200XT	020	R - 42	3	440.00	1,320.00	825.00	
					0014571	200XT	020	R - 44	3	440.00	1,320.00	825.00	
					0014589	200XT	020	R - 46	3	440.00	1,320.00	825.00	
					0014662	200BK	020	T - 38	1	440.00	440.00	275.00	
					0014670	200BK	020	T - 40	1	440.00	440.00	275.00	
					0014688	200BK	020	T - 42	1	440.00	440.00	275.00	
					0014696	200BK	020	T - 44	1	440.00	440.00	275.00	
					0014704	200BK	020	T - 46	1	440.00	440.00	275.00	

Figure 13 (Shipment Summary) lists the amount of cartons received by number and their condition. The carrier and the store's designated person countersign receipt of goods.

Figure 13. Shipment Summary

SHIPMENT SUMMARY
Carrier Stop 5174000100

Expected : 80
Good : 81
Damaged : 0
Total Received : 81
Outbound : 0

RECEIVED   RECEIVED

Carton Number	Carton Condition	UPC/SKU	Damaged
517420471869	GOOD		
517420470798	GOOD		
517420471834	GOOD		
517420471654	GOOD		
517420469402	GOOD		
517420469375	GOOD		
517420466477	GOOD		
517420465036	GOOD		
517420467748	GOOD		
517420468473	GOOD		
517420462871	GOOD		
517420463742	GOOD		
517420463718	GOOD		
517420462894	GOOD		
517420466889	GOOD		
517420462994	GOOD		
517420462012	GOOD		
517420466556	GOOD		
517420463602	GOOD		
517420464100	GOOD		
517420466982	GOOD		
517420464261	GOOD		
517420455898	GOOD		
517420467245	GOOD		
517420464751	GOOD		
517420462991	GOOD		
517420462808	GOOD		
517420463340	GOOD		

SIGNATURES   SIGNATURES

(Store Associate)   (Driver)

**** PLEASE FILE SIGNED 'STORE COPY' IN CURRENT MONTH OF 6 MONTH RETENTION FILE. ****

Price Change Forms

All retail **price changes** that are required to merchandise must be recorded on **price change forms**. Among the changes necessary to record are:

- The number of units.

- The old retail price per unit.

- The new retail price per unit.

- The difference per unit.

- The total amount of difference.

Today it is common that temporary price changes (e.g., one-day sale items) are recorded by a cash register at the time of the purchase. As described in Unit II, this is called a point-of-sale markdown (POS). When a consumer pays for a purchase, the preprogrammed cash register records the new or lower retail, which corresponds exactly with the prescribed reduction posted on signs displayed with the merchandise. Only permanent reductions are recorded manually on forms illustrated by Figures 14 and 15. Figure 14 is a worksheet, which requires the listing of any or all price changes. Figure 15 shows the permanent or temporary price change information that has been entered onto a computer screen, and Figure 16 illustrates the form that is used by the individual branches. Figure 17 lists specific departments by classification, resource, description, current and new prices, and percentage off original price.

Figure 14. Buyers Price Change Worksheet

Figure 15. Computer Price Change Entry

DATE: OCT 09, 2013

PRICE CHANGE ENTRY

===

COMPANY 01 GROUP 0001 TYPE 1 FUNCTION 1 DATE 10/09/13 EFFECTIVE DATE FR: 10/10/13
                    (New)   (Price Change)   EFFECTIVE DATE TO: 12/31/13

1) AUTHORIZATION	:123456			
2) ENTRY TYPE	:1	MARKDOWN		
3) BUYER NO	:001	Michael Wood		
4) REASON	:001	Slow Moving		
5) EFF. DATE FROM	:10/10/13		6) EFF. DATE TO	:12/31/13
7) REGION FROM	:000		8) REGION TO	:000
9) STORE FROM	:000		10) STORE TO	:000
11) REM-1: Permanent price change			13) PRODUCE TICKETS (Y/N)	:Y
12) REM-2: effective for all stores			14) COUNT INVENTORY	:N

LINE	SEASON	DEPT	CLS	PR	LN COST	PT	COOR	GR	STYLE	CHANGE % AMT	TO RETAIL PRICE
001	FROM	L	01							10.00	
	TO	L	02								

EXCLUDE STYLES: 12056   12654   13101   141256

Figure 16. Branch Price Change

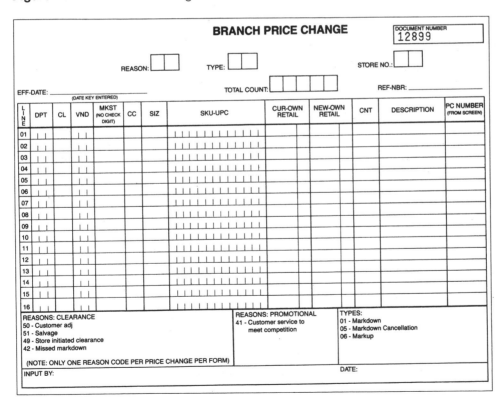

Figure 17. Specific Departments by Classification

STORE: 5147
DATE: 06/29/2013
503-RMPRCHA

SSI
PRICE CHANGE AUTHORIZATION
RED TICKET
EFFECTIVE DATE 07/05/2013

5174 BARKHAMSTED
5200 CHILDRENS

STORE GROUP DEPT	NAME	CLASS	BRAND	VPN	DESCRIPTION	COLOR	CURRENT PRICE	NEW PRICE	% OFF ORIG	TAKEN BY
5070	BOY'S 8–20 SEPARATES	ACTIVEWEAR	AMC KIDS	S6B8844	RVRS MESH SHORT	20 GREY	$7.19	$4.32	73	—
						400 BLUE	$16.00	$9.60	40	—
						410 NAVY	$16.00	$9.60	40	—
						600 RED	$16.00	$9.60	40	—
5070	BOY'S 8–20 SEPARATES	ACTIVEWEAR	AUTHENTIC GRAPH	S6B8158	MESH MUSCLE TEE	40 SILVER	$7.19	$4.32	73	—
5070	BOY'S 8–20 SEPARATES	DRESSWEAR	BRUNO BOYS	B122739	SM PLAID MICRO	410 NAVY	$16.00	$9.60	40	—
						300 GREEN	$24.00	$14.40	40	—
5070	BOY'S 8–20 SEPARATES	DRESSWEAR	BRUNO BOYS		STRIPE MICRO	450 LIGHT/PAST EL BLUE	$10.79	$6.48	73	—
				B124116		400 BLUE	$10.79	$6.48	73	—
5070	BOY'S 8–20 SEPARATES	DRESSWEAR	BRUNO BOYS	B124676	CHECK MICROFIBR	800 ORANGE	$24.00	$14.40	40	—
						300 GREEN	$24.00	$14.40	40	—
5070	BOY'S 8–20 SEPARATES	KNITS	DELTA	DG4848	HEAR NO EVIL TEE	BLACK	$14.00	$8.40	40	—
5070	BOY'S 8–20 SEPARATES	KNITS	DELTA	DG4855	GROUNDED FOR LIFE	HEATHER GREY	$14.00	$8.40	40	—
5070	BOY'S 8–20 SEPARATES	KNITS	DELTA	DG4862	SISTER FOR SALE TEE	400-ROYAL	$14.00	$8.40	40	—
5070	BOY'S 8–20 SEPARATES	PANTS	JAZZMAN SPORTSW	B3Q127	CAMDEN JEAN	400 BLUE	$13.19	$7.92	73	—
5070	BOY'S 8–20 SEPARATES	PANTS	LEE BOYS	5675344	BACKSTACK JEAN	410 NAVY	$29.99	$17.99	40	—
						400 BLUE	$30.00	$18.00	40	—
5071	BOY'S 8–20 COLLECTS.	LEVI	LEVI STRAUSS	309930819	PAINTER HUSKY	400 BLUE	$32.00	$19.20	40	—
5206	INFANT BOY APPAREL	PLAYWEAR	AMC KIDS	0318853156 B1707	STRPGIRFAPLQ CRP	400 BLUE	$12.00	$7.20	40	—
5206	INFANT BOY APPAREL	PLAYWEAR	AMC KIDS	S6B-1707	STRPFROGAPLQ CRP	400 BLUE	$12.00	$7.20	40	—
5209	INFANT GIRL APPAREL	PLAYWEAR	AMC KIDS	S6G-1705	PRNT FLRL CRPR	810 MEDIUM ORANGE	$12.00	$7.20	40	—

Charge-Back to Vendors

A **debit memo form**, shown in Figure 18, records the return of merchandise from the retailer to the vendor, which may occur for a variety of reasons. It displays the number of pieces or units, the name of the item, and both cost and retail prices. Typically, a worksheet, as illustrated by Figure 19, is used to record the **return to vendor** information before it is verified by the person packing the merchandise. This ensures that the actual debit memo is legible and correct.

Figure 18. Debit Memo

Figure 19. Return to Vendor Authorization and Worksheet

RETURN TO VENDOR AUTHORIZATION AND WORKSHEET   N⁰ 627893

Instructions: (Please print legibly)
                    Department Manager   DM No. _____ .

1) Dept. Mgr. prepares worksheet
2) Complete Worksheet including quantities and extensions
3) Completely prepare D.M. from information
   on Worksheet except for merchandise
   quantities, AND extensions.
   (D.M. Room will do this).
4) Do Not put in cost figures.

Dept._____ Store_____ Prepared by _____ Date _____

Mfr. Name _____ Freight paid by dept. _____ vendor _____
                                                                        CHECK ONE
Vendor No.   _____

Return arranged with _____ Sticker needed Yes _____ No _____

Special Instructions _____ Terms _____

Reason _____

CHARGE TO:					SEND TO:							
Name					Name							
Address					Address							
City State Zip					City State Zip							

Item / SKU No. *	Class	Style	Size	Color	Qty.	Units	Cost Unit	Ext.	Retail Unit	Ext.
Total										

ON DMS OVER $400 RETAIL

COMPLETE THE FOLLOWING:

ACCTS. PAYABLE AUTH. NO. _____

D.M. ROOM COMPLETES
D.M. # _____
Date _____
Total $ Amount _____
Packed by _____
Checked by _____

*IF BSR MERCHANDISE IS INVOLVED, INFORMATION MUST BE PROVIDED TO THE BSR OFFICE BY STYLE, SIZE AND COLOR.

17-930-061 (REV. 6/91)

Sales Reports

Today's automated business systems offer sophisticated reporting for processing and auditing sales. In addition to full accounting sales summaries, Figures 20 and 21 show information that can be provided to improve sales performance. Figure 20, Daily Exception Selling Price Report, highlights daily sales for items sold at prices other than current retail (e.g., markdown price). Salesperson performance is then analyzed by week with the use of a Sales and Productivity Report, as illustrated in Figure 21. Figure 22, Weekly Sales Challenge Recap, reports by department the actual and goal sales by units. Figure 23, District Flash Sales by Store, records for the week the daily dollar sales by individual store, recapping the performance and the changes in both dollars and percentages by week, month, and year to date. Figure 24, District Flash Sales by Group, offers the same information by merchandise grouping.

Figure 20. Daily Exception Selling Price Report

STORE NO.	SALES BILL NUMBER	CLERK	STYLE	SEASON	DESCRIPTION	COLOR	SIZE	QTY	PRICE PER UNIT CURRENT	PRICE PER UNIT ACTUAL	TOTAL EXTENDED DIFFERENCE	% M/DOWN
001	103256	0018	SW50A	M	Cotton V-Neck Sweater	030	- S	1	45.00	32.00	13.00	29
	103273	0026	SK1715	M	Cotton Pants	030	- L	2	64.00	50.00	28.00	22
					STORE DAILY TOTAL						41.00	24
002	204312	0042	SC1210	M	Wool Sweater	010	- M	1	95.00	75.00	20.00	21
	204317	0042	200XT	M	2 Pces Dress Suit	020	R - 40	1	440.00	390.00	50.00	11
					STORE DAILY TOTAL						70.00	13

DAILY EXCEPTION SELLING PRICE REPORT — DATE OCT 09, 2013 — PAGE: 1 — TIME 9.10 AM

DATE OF SALE: OCT 08, 2013

MINIMUM PRICE DIFFERENCE REQUIRED: 10.00%

APPROVED BY: _____

Figure 21. Sales and Productivity Report by Store by Salesperson

REGION: 001 EAST COAST
STORE: 001 BOSTON

SALESPERSON NO NAME	DOLLAR SALES	DOLLAR RETURNS	DOLLAR NET SALES	% STORE	UNITS SOLD	% STORE	UNITS/ SALE	DOLLARS/ SALE	AVG. SALE/ UNIT	GROSS PROFIT	EMPL. WAGES	HRS WORKED	% WAGES/ SALES	SALES/ HOUR	EMP $ PURCH
0018 George Brown															
THIS WEEK	4,200	76	4,124	35.0	84	40.0	2.3	113	49	2,288	600	40	14.6	103	0
THIS PERIOD	17,255	430	16,825	34.5	246	27.8	1.6	109	58	8,457	2,432	162	14.5	104	300
THIS YEAR	149,765	3,450	146,315	35.3	2,826	38.8	1.7	88	52	74,620	22,565	1500	15.4	98	1,450
0026 Mark Lewis															
THIS WEEK	3,155	65	3,090	26.2	59	28.1	1.7	88	52	1,623	495	40	16.0	77	105
THIS PERIOD	12,112	255	11,857	24.3	211	23.8	1.9	106	56	6,260	2,150	160	18.1	74	105
THIS YEAR	107,270	2,380	104,890	25.3	1,687	23.2	1.3	81	62	51,396	18,915	1525	18.0	69	600
TOTAL STORE															
THIS WEEK	12,465	216	12,249	100.0	210	100.0	2.1	122	58	5,980	1,702	180	13.9	68	352
THIS PERIOD	50,981	1,250	49,731	100.0	886	100.0	1.8	101	56	25,874	8,225	715	16.5	70	625
THIS YEAR	425,236	10,205	415,031	100.0	7,281	100.0	1.6	91	57	182,870	56,111	6864	13.5	60	3,584
TOTAL REGION															
THIS WEEK	45,243	752	44,491		983		1.6	72	45	21,885	6,583	692	14.8	64	1,125
THIS PERIOD	202,853	4,223	197,630		4,184		1.7	80	47	103,882	32,581	2835	16.5	70	2,152
THIS YEAR	1,602,356	42,347	1,560,009		31,483		1.4	70	50	678,401	223,004	27154	14.3	58	12,003
TOTAL COMPANY															
THIS WEEK	124,725	2,850	121,875		2,722		1.6	72	45	58,745	19,850	2102	16.3	58	3,002
THIS PERIOD	608,124	14,987	593,137		12,584		1.6	75	47	312,715	97,100	8525	16.4	70	6,100
THIS YEAR	4,707,453	108,401	4,599,052		91,123		1.4	71	51	2,001,453	658,343	80131	14.3	57	35,111

Figure 22. Weekly Sales Challenge Recap

DATE RUN 7/11/13			STORE 174	WEEK END 7/08/13		WEEKLY SALES CHALLENGE RECAP			PAGE 1	TIME RUN 11.27.21		CTL PAGE 1029	FORM # PSIR10

				SALES FOR WEEK				SALES MTD				SALES STD				SALES YTD				MTHS	PROJE CTED	SALES GOAL
ZONE	GRP	DPT	DESC	RESP	GOAL	ACTUAL	%LY	% GOAL	GOAL	ACTUAL	%LY	%GOAL	GOAL	ACTUAL	%LY	%GOAL	GOAL	ACTUAL	%LY	%GOAL	RESP	CURR MTH	NEXT MTH
3	5566	5567	Petites Active	C6	60	115		192	60	115		192	1354	1259		93.0	1354	1259		93.0	5	262	186
		5572	Pets. Classic Care	C6	466	346		74	466	346		74	13187	12017		91.1	13187	12017		91.1	5	2025	991
		5579	Petites Traditiona	C6	405	585		144	405	585		144	10178	11654		114.5	10178	11654		114.5	5	1760	1505
		5586	Womens Active	C6	17	100		588	17	100		588	362	1437		397.0	362	1437		397.0	5	75	105
		5587	Wans Classic Caree	C6	284	616		217	284	616		217	7871	10578		134.4	7871	10578		134.4	5	1237	1446
		5588	Wans Classic Casua	C6	327	485		148	327	485		148	5980	5602		93.7	5980	5602		93.7	5	1421	1131
		5590	Pets. Classic Casu	C6	395	609		154	395	609		154	9095	8459		93.0	9095	8459		93.0	5	1719	1716
		5591	Womens Traditional	C6	306	140		46	306	140		46	6716	5419		80.7	6716	5419		80.7	5	1332	700
		5755	Junior Plus	C6	186	68-		37	186	68		37	3254	2432		74.7	3254	2432		74.7	5	810	803
		SUB		C6	2446	3064		125	2446	3064		125	57997	58857		101.5	57997	58857		101.5	5	10641	8583
4	5110	5484	Wan's Opening Pric	C6	147	91		62	147	91		62	3659	3068		83.8	3659	3068		83.8	5	641	303
	5300	5300	Women's Fragrance	C6	287	79		28	287	79		28	8373	5104		61.0	8373	5104		61.0	5	1248	1069
		5304	Elizabeth Arden	C6	45	0			45	0			1420	521		36.7	1420	521		36.7	5	197	137
		5335	Men's Fragrance	C6	143	55		39	143	55		39	4143	1895		45.7	4143	1895		45.7	5	622	615
		5377	Cosmetic Accessori	C6	98	31		32	98	31		32	2159	1536		71.1	2159	1536		71.1	5	426	279
	5464	5464	Hndbgs, Sm Leather	C6	1180	0			1180	0			21809	12868		59.0	21809	12868		59.0	5	5131	3559
		5473	Costume Jewelry	C6	390	531		136	390	531		136	9753	12216		125.3	9753	12216		125.3	5	1697	791
		5482	Socks & Hosiery	C6	134	189		141	134	189		141	4485	4732		105.5	4485	4732		105.5	5	581	446
		5489	Wearable Accessori	C6	215	115		54	215	115		54	6109	4506		73.8	6109	4506		73.8	5	935	640
		5496	Fine Jewelry	C6	389	543		140	389	543		140	9459	12155		128.5	9459	12155		128.5	5	1691	1417
	5566	5576	Petites Collection	C6	106	0			106	0			2760	130		4.7	2760	130		4.7	5	461	25
	5624	5620	Missy Updated/Tren	C6	113	152		135	113	152		135	2631	3766		143.1	2631	3766		143.1	5	493	0
		5625	Missy Active	C6	458	204		45	458	204		45	10818	7707		71.2	10818	7707		71.2	5	1992	839
		5626	Missy Classic Casu	C6	1699	2840		167	1699	2840		167	37237	45090		121.1	37237	45090		121.1	5	7388	7047
		5635	Missy Classic Care	C6	1640	1449		88	1640	1449		88	42648	33140		77.7	42648	33140		77.7	5	7134	5792
		5638	Missy Traditional	C6	2020	2236		111	2020	2236		111	48098	40729		84.7	48098	40729		84.7	5	8786	5370
		5662	Missy Collections	C6	1943	1557		80	1943	1557		80	46520	35125		75.5	46520	35125		75.5	5	8451	4308
		SUB		C6	11007	10072		92	11007	10072		92	262081	224288		85.6	262081	224288		85.6		47874	32637
C	GIBBS				13453	13136		98	13453	13136		98	320078	283145		88.5	320078	283145		88.5		58515	41220

The analysis of all this information, although not used in maintaining the **retail method of inventory**, per se, allows for evaluation of sales as well as stock position and should result in optimizing sales performance and profit margin.

Employee Discounts

As described in Unit II, an employee discount is a common practice in retail stores, allowing store employees a percentage off the retail price when making purchases for themselves. It is essential to record the difference between the retail price and the price paid by the employee. The procedure and form of record used for this transaction vary widely from store to store. Typically, employee discounts are listed under "Retail Reduction" but are classified separately from markdowns, even though they are reductions in retail price.

Figure 23. District Flash Sales by Store Records

District Flash Sales by Store
Week 25 ending 07/22/2013

Store			Sun $	Mon $	Tue $	Wed $	Thu $	Fri $	Sat $	WTD $	WTD %	MTD $	MTD %	HTD $	HTD %	YTD $	YTD %	STD%	%CHG STD
5044	Brattleboro	TY	2838	3533	4572	3639	0	0	0	14583	-8	75	-10	764	17	764	17	38.31	0
		LY	3547	3154	4961	4122	5130	6548	5412	15784		84		654		654			1993
5070	Geneva	TY	5239	5402	8105	11797	0	0	0	30543	3	155	11	1317	-4	1317	-4	42.01	0
		LY	3124	7069	7229	12341	13951	14910	10804	29763		139		1376		1376			3135
5072	Rochester	TY	0	2155	2280	6085	0	0	0	10519	13	41	-8	451	-13	451	-13	39.61	0
		LY	0	2381	2206	4685	4056	3986	2299	9272		44		520		520			1139
5095	Johnstown	TY	8725	11018	13333	18347	0	0	0	51424	-3	249	-2	2170	-9	2170	-9	40.95	0
		LY	8951	10068	11425	22578	18798	23726	21461	53022		255		2387		2387			5299
5121	St Albans	TY	3360	3831	5176	4295	0	0	0	16661	-4	81	-7	673	-6	673	-6	36.83	0
		LY	3405	4801	4681	4437	6538	6197	7053	17324		87		718		718			1826
5129	Hornell	TY	2680	2473	3870	5861	0	0	0	14885	9	66	3	656	-1	656	-1	42.03	0
		LY	1694	2663	1799	7551	6964	6577	6149	13706		64		660		660			1561
5165	Hudson	TY	4148	5959	7125	10427	0	0	0	27660	12	155	28	1284	3	1284	3	45.66	0
		LY	4794	5280	6214	8329	8152	8101	10705	24618		121		1245		1245			2812
5170	Belmont	TY	2962	3680	4744	4410	0	0	0	15796	-8	89	-12	728	-7	728	-7	39.10	0
		LY	3115	4133	4568	5439	6454	6800	6721	17255		102		781		781			1863
5174	Barkhamsted	TY	4398	2691	2423	5008	0	0	0	14520	0	78	0	695	0	695	0	46.58	0
		LY	0	0	0	0	0	0	0	0		0		0		0			1492
5175	Carbondale	TY	3324	3192	3914	5516	0	0	0	15946	22	75	2	654	62	654	62	39.04	0
		LY	2940	3665	3147	3341	3914	4073	4582	13094		73		402		402			1674
5182	Springfield	TY	2663	3508	4481	5156	0	0	0	15809	0	68	0	588	0	588	0	35.39	0
		LY	0	0	0	0	0	0	0	0		0		0		0			1661

Store			Sun $	Mon $	Tue $	Wed $	Thu $	Fri $	Sat $	WTD $	WTD %	MTD $	MTD %	HTD $	HTD %	YTD $	YTD %	STD%	%CHG STD
Dist. Total	Comp	TY	29953	38053	49204	64861	0	0	0	182071	1	910	2	7355	-5	7355	-5		
		LY	28630	39549	43083	69481	70043	76844	70604	180743		895		7771		7771			
Dist. Total	ALL	TY	40337	47444	60023	80541	0	0	0	228345	18	1131	17	9979	14	9979	14		
		LY	31569	43214	46231	72823	73956	80917	75186	193836		969		8744		8744			
Comp Store %	Dist.	TY	5	-4	14	-7	-100	-100	-100										
	Chain	TY	-6	1	-3	-13	-100	-100	-100		-7		-2		-5		-5		
		LY	-3	-2	3	76	47	39	34		22		6		7		7		
All Store %	Dist.	TY	28	10	30	11	-100	-100	-100										
	Chain	TY	2	7	4	-7	-100	-100	-100		0		5		3		3		
		LY	7	7	12	87	58	49	44		31		15		16		16		

Figure 24. District Flash Sales by Group: Week 25 Ending 07/22/2013

Group		Sun $	Mon $	Tue $	Wed $	Thu $	Fri $	Sat $	WTD $	WTD DI%	WTD Ch%	MTD $	MTD DI%	MTD Ch%	HTD $	HTD DI%	HTD Ch%	YTD $	YTD DI%	YTD Ch%
MENS	TY	4876	4715	6535	8832	0	0	0	24958	20	2	118	12	5	1119	11	4	1119	11	4
	LY	3705	4892	4541	7662	7582	8175	9379	20799			106			1009			1009		
YOUNG MENS	TY	2459	2731	2614	3920	0	0	0	11725	3	3	62	19	7	526	8	5	526	8	5
	LY	2313	2660	2647	3740	3969	5549	5000	11360			52			489			489		
SHOES	TY	3748	3668	5740	9961	0	0	0	23117	13	5	116	25	12	1041	13	1	1041	13	1
	LY	3442	4122	4695	8247	8566	9837	8187	20506			93			918			918		
CHILDRENS	TY	2908	4157	4644	7024	0	0	0	18733	-5	-10	98	8	-2	1015	17	3	1015	17	3
	LY	3588	4396	4134	7663	7369	8753	7972	19782			91			865			865		
COSMETICS/FRAGRANCES	TY	1886	2465	3289	3022	0	0	0	10663	0	7	64	0	1	524	17	5	524	17	5
	LY	2009	2506	3201	2916	4513	5269	4577	10631			64			448			448		
INTIMATE	TY	1131	1392	2508	2569	0	0	0	7599	2	-12	38	4	-9	340	15	-1	340	15	-1
	LY	743	2189	2064	2471	3219	3120	1885	7466			36			297			297		
HOME/GIFTS	TY	1295	1646	1818	2691	0	0	0	7450	33	-6	35	31	17	288	16	-2	288	16	-2
	LY	980	1168	1318	2120	2324	2038	2520	5586			27			249			249		
ACCESSORIES	TY	2279	2891	3215	4394	0	0	0	12779	8	-11	64	3	-3	676	17	7	676	17	7
	LY	2176	2689	2480	4450	4409	4951	4407	11796			62			579			579		
OUTERWEAR	TY	54	18	58	12	0	0	0	142	-45	-59	1	15	-39	86	10	-15	86	10	-15
	LY	0	61	22	177	87	69	127	260			1			78			78		
SWIMWEAR	TY	1813	1889	1920	2043	0	0	0	7665	83	20	28	22	8	82	-20	-12	82	-20	-12
	LY	697	1114	1492	884	1028	574	1336	4187			23			103			103		
SP SIZE SPORTSWEAR	TY	2953	3664	4728	6589	0	0	0	17933	28	-4	89	17	4	804	16	1	804	16	1
	LY	2142	3012	2715	6120	5989	6190	5345	13988			75			696			696		
MISSY SPORTSWEAR	TY	10697	12473	15891	21220	0	0	0	60281	41	9	292	33	13	2382	21	6	2382	21	6
	LY	6006	9137	10498	17104	16635	16144	14567	42745			219			1971			1971		
JR SPORTSWEAR	TY	3304	4675	5393	5808	0	0	0	19180	8	-4	98	9	2	843	3	-5	843	3	-5
	LY	3127	3741	4176	6638	6527	7822	7732	17682			90			821			821		
DRESSES	TY	827	1058	1469	2197	0	0	0	5551	-20	-21	25	-11	-9	211	-3	-9	211	-3	-9
	LY	620	1513	2224	2588	1703	2393	2100	6946			29			218			218		
MISCELLANEOUS	TY	106	1	200	261	0	0	0	568	446	979	3	420	660	42	568	456	42	568	456
	LY	23	13	24	45	35	34	52	104			1			6			6		
Dist. Total Comp	TY	29953	38053	49204	64861	0	0	0	182071	1	-7	910	2	-2	7355	-5	-5	7355	-5	-5
	LY	28630	39549	43083	69481	70043	76844	70604	180743			859			7771			7771		
Dist. Total All	TY	40337	47444	60023	80541	0	0	0	228345	18	0	1131	17	5	9979	14	3	9979	14	3
	LY	31569	43214	46231	72823	73956	80917	75186	193836			969			8744			8744		
Comp St. % Dist.	TY	5	-4	14	-7	-100	-100	-100												
Chain	TY	-6	1	-3	-13	-100	-100	-100												
All St. % Dist.	TY	28	10	30	11	-100	-100	-100												
Chain	TY	2	7	4	-7	-100	-100	-100												

Maintaining a Perpetual Book Inventory Figure Practice Problems

1. On July 15, a statistical inventory indicates an on-hand retail stock of $64,250. A physical count on that date reveals a stock of $62,875. What is the opening retail book inventory figure for the period commencing July 16?

2. Opening inventory at retail for an outerwear department is $175,000. Purchases retail for the following six-month period are $490,000, net sales are $400,000, markdowns are $30,000, returns to vendors are $10,000, transfers (transfers out) to the third floor boutique are $15,000, and employee discounts are $6,000. Find the retail book inventory at the end of this six-month period.

3. Using the following figures from an accessories department, find the closing book stock at retail.

Physical inventory January 15	$85,000
Purchases retail January 16 through July 15	$165,000
Gross sales	$170,000
Returns from customers	$30,000
Returns to vendors	$5,000
Markdowns	$10,000

4. The following figures are from a juniors' sportswear department:

Markdowns	$12,000
Purchases (retail)	$315,000
Returns to vendors	$20,000
Transfers in (retail)	$8,000
Transfers out (retail)	$4,000
Net sales	$265,000
Opening book inventory (retail)	$180,000

    a. Determine the closing book inventory for the period at retail.

    b. How would the opening retail inventory for the coming six-month period be determined?

5. The following figures are from a small boutique, which has a 49% markup:

Opening book inventory at retail	$16,000
Net sales	$31,000
Markdowns	$2,000
Purchases (retail)	$40,000

    a. Determine the retail book inventory for the period.

    b. Convert the closing retail book inventory figure to the cost value.

6. Distinguish between physical inventory and book inventory. Which one is more likely to be affected by human error? Why? Which one has become more accurate since the advent of electronic capability?

7. A lingerie department buyer was given the following data:

	Cost	Retail
Opening inventory	$320,000	$530,000
Purchases	$1,118,000	$2,271,000
Net sales	$1,400,000	
Markdowns	$90,000	

(Includes employee discounts)

Calculate

a. The closing book inventory at retail.

b. The closing book inventory at cost.

8. The athletic footwear department had a closing book inventory at retail of $400,000 and had achieved a 53.5% markup on total merchandise handled. Determine the closing inventory at cost.

9. Find the closing inventory at cost of a furniture department if:

	Cost	Retail
Net sales		$330,000
Opening inventory	$150,000	$325,000
Markdowns		$25,000
Returns to vendors	$13,000	$18,000
Employee discounts		$6,500
Gross purchases	$200,000	$390,000

10. Utilize the following figures to calculate:

   a. The closing book inventory at retail.

   b. The cost value of this closing book inventory.

	Cost	Retail
Opening inventory	$390,500	$774,000
Gross purchases	$690,000	$1,360,000
Returns to vendors	$6,400	$12,000
Freight	$3,260	
Gross sales		$1,117,000
Customer returns		$25,000
Markdowns		$93,000

UNIT IV.III
SHORTAGES AND OVERAGES

Physical inventories at current retail prices are taken at the end of the accounting period. At this same time, the "book stock" at retail is adjusted to agree with the dollar value of the physical count. Any discrepancy between the dollar value of the "book stock" and the dollar value of stock determined by the physical count of merchandise on hand is classified as a **shortage** (or shrinkage) or an **overage**. As described, shortages exist if physical inventory is lower than book inventory; overages exist if the physical count exceeds the statistical tally.

It is almost impossible to run a merchandising operation with 100% accuracy. Shortages or overages nearly always result and are actually expected to occur. The shortage or overage is commonly expressed as a percentage of the net sales. Regardless of the cause, the inventory shortage is fundamentally the buyer's or department manager's problem and responsibility. To keep discrepancies to a minimum is one of the many challenges a merchant must face. For internal control purposes, it is sometimes desirable to estimate shortages. This estimate is also expressed as a percentage of net sales. Furthermore, even though merchandise planning is devised with estimated planned shortages in mind, generally the actual shortage exceeds the expected shortage.

Figure 25, a typical shortage report, which is usually calculated at the end of the accounting period, shows typical shortage information. From the data in this report, a multistore operation can pinpoint prevention, causes, and shortage remedies and can attempt to improve the shortage results. Figure 26 indicates the current average annual shrink percentage in the retail industry.

Figure 25. Shortage Report

DVI 10						DATE
	----------SHORTAGES IN DOLLARS----------			----------SHORTAGES IN PERCENTS----------		
STORE	CURRENT SEASON	CURRENT –1	CURRENT –2	CURRENT SEASON	CURRENT –1	CURRENT –2
00						
01	8,731	2,395	3,920	2.8	0.8	1.3
06	891-	717	1,112	0.5-	0.5	1.1
09	999-	867-	1,583	0.9-	0.9-	1.5
12	293-	668	1,518	0.3-	0.8	1.6
14	5,107	501	524	5.0	0.6	0.6
15	1,056	1,361	1,928	0.8	1.2	1.6
DIV 10	12,711	4,781	11,185	1.4	0.6	1.3

Figure 26. Average Annual Shrink Percentage

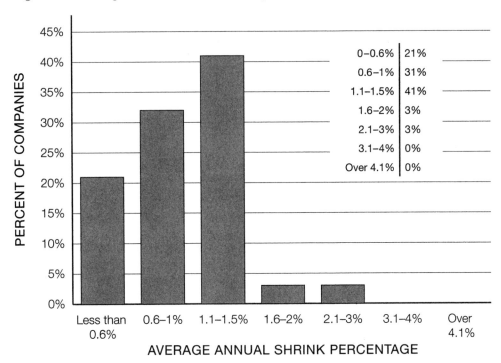

0–0.6%	21%
0.6–1%	31%
1.1–1.5%	41%
1.6–2%	3%
2.1–3%	3%
3.1–4%	0%
Over 4.1%	0%

Source: Tenth Annual Retail Horizons: Benchmarks for 2011, Forecasts for 2012 (KPMG/NRF Foundation)

CAUSES OF SHORTAGES AND OVERAGES

Shortages may stem from inaccurate record-keeping and/or faulty physical counts. Another principal cause of shortages is pilferage, which, realistically, can never be prevented completely. Overages, however, can only be caused by faulty record-keeping.

The common causes of shortages and overages are:

- Clerical errors in the calculation of the book and/or physical inventory, which include:

  - Failure to record markdowns properly.

  - Incorrect "retailing" of invoices.

  - Errors in charging invoices to departments.

  - Errors in recording transfers.

  - Errors in recording returns to vendor.

  - Errors in recording physical inventory.

    (Note: The computer processing of these forms has minimized these clerical errors.)

- Physical merchandise losses, which include:
  - Theft by customers and/or employees.
  - Unrecorded breakage and spoilage.
  - Sales clerks' errors in recording sales.
  - Overweighting.
  - Borrowed merchandise.
  - Lost or incorrect price tickets.
  - Sampling.

CALCULATING SHORTAGES AND OVERAGES

The Physical Inventory Count as a Determining Factor in the Calculation of Shortages or Overages

CONCEPT

$$\text{Shortage (or overage)} = \text{Closing book inventory at retail} - \text{Physical inventory count}$$

PROBLEM

Find the shortage or overage in dollars from the following figures:

Opening inventory at retail	$22,000
Purchases at retail	$17,500
Net sales	$18,000
Markdowns	$300
Employee discounts	$600
Physical inventory, end of period	$19,200

SOLUTION

Opening book inventory retail	=	$22,000		
+ Purchases retail	=	+ 17,500		
Total merchandise handled (retail)	=	$39,500	→	$39,500
Net sales	=	$18,000		
+ Markdowns	=	+ 300		
+ Employee discounts	=	+ 600		
Total retail deductions	=	$18,900	→	− 18,900
Book inventory retail	=			$20,600
− Physical inventory	=			− 19,200
Dollar shortage	=			$1,400

Expressing the Amount of Shortages or Overages for a Period as a Percentage of the Net Sales for the Same Period

$$\text{Shortage \%} = \frac{\$ \text{ Shortage}}{\$ \text{ Net sales}} \times 100$$

CONCEPT

For the period under consideration, the net sales of Department 23 are $100,000. The physical count revealed a $5,000 shortage. What was the shortage percentage for this period?

PROBLEM

$$\frac{\$ \text{ Shortage}}{\$ \text{ Net sales}} = \frac{\$5,000}{\$100,000} \times 100$$

Shortage % = 5%

SOLUTION

Estimating Dollar Shortages that Are Expressed as a Percentage of the Planned Net Sales Figure for Internal Control Purposes

$$\text{Estimated dollar shortage} = \text{Estimated shortage percentage} \times \text{Planned net sales}$$

CONCEPT

The seasonal plan for a department showed planned sales of $350,000, with a planned shortage of 2.5%. What was the planned dollar shortage?

PROBLEM

Planned dollar shortage	=	$350,000	Net sales
	×	2.5%	Planned shortage
Planned dollar shortage	=	$8,750	

SOLUTION

11. A costume jewelry department showed the following figures for a six-month period:

Net sales	$125,000
Purchases (at retail)	$105,000
Opening retail inventory (Feb. 1)	$64,000
Markdowns	$9,000
Employee discounts	$2,600
Physical count (July 31)	$31,000

   a. What was the shortage in dollars?

   b. What was the shortage in percentage?

   If the planned shortage was estimated at 2%, was the actual shortage more or less? By how much in dollars? In percentage?

12. Find the shortage or overage percentage if:

Net sales	$137,000
Opening inventory (retail)	$140,000
Markdowns	$7,000
Employee discounts	$1,000
Retail purchases	$96,000
Closing physical inventory	$89,150

13. Last year, the net sales in a home fashions department were $365,000. The book inventory at year-end was $67,500, and the physical inventory was $66,000. What was the shortage percentage?

14. Find the shortage or overage percentage using the following data:

Opening inventory (retail)	$204,000
Net sales	$342,000
Vendor returns	$4,000
Transfers to branches	$8,000
Employee discounts	$1,000
Purchases (at retail)	$495,000
Markdowns	$46,000
Closing physical inventory	$287,000

15. If the retail book inventory at the close of the year is $1,500,000 and the physical inventory totals only $1,275,000, what will be the shortage percentage if net sales were $15,000,000?

16. The merchandise plan for Fall shows planned sales of $35,000, with an estimated shortage of 0.7%. What are the planned dollar shortages for Fall?

17. A new shop owner was reviewing figures with the store's accountant. Net sales for the first three months of business were $87,000 and the book inventory was $72,000. It was noted that the physical inventory was 2.5% lower than the book inventory. Find the shortage percentage for this three-month period.

18. For the six-month period ending in January, your department showed the following figures:

Opening inventory (retail)	$262,000
Customer returns	$10,000
Returns to vendor	$6,200
Employee discounts	$3,800
Gross sales	$910,000
Retail purchases	$870,000
Markdowns	$30,000
Transfers in	$5,100
Transfers out	$4,000
Physical inventory	$170,000

a. What is the percentage of employee discounts?

b. Determine the overage or shortage in both dollars and percentage.

c. Using a 49% markup, convert the retail opening and closing inventories to cost values.

UNIT IV.IV
AN EVALUATION OF THE
RETAIL METHOD OF INVENTORY

THE ADVANTAGES OF THE
RETAIL METHOD OF INVENTORY

The benefits of the retail method of inventory are that:

- It permits control over profit because the figures for markup obtained (i.e., the difference between the cost and the retail of the total merchandise handled) and markdowns taken (upon which the realized gross margin depends) frequently are available, and immediate action can be taken to protect the desired profit margin.

- It simplifies the physical inventory process because the physical inventory is taken at retail prices, which is less difficult and less expensive. Additionally, because all entries are made rapidly and no decoding is necessary, the personnel do not require special training or experience.

- It provides a book inventory and, therefore, discrepancies (i.e., shortages and/or overages) in stock can be determined, shortage causes may be discovered, and preventive/corrective measures can be taken.

- It provides an equitable basis for insurance and adjustment claims.

THE LIMITATIONS OF THE
RETAIL METHOD OF INVENTORY

The disadvantages of the retail method of inventory are that:

- It is a system of averages and therefore does not provide a precise cost evaluation of the inventory at its present cost price. This figure (i.e., cost evaluation of inventory) is calculated by applying the markup complement percentage to the retail value of the inventory. This may result in a figure that is either greater or smaller than the invoice cost of the merchandise currently received. This is the most significant weakness of this method.

- It depends upon extensive record-keeping for system accuracy.

- It is essential that all price changes be recorded.

FINDING THE COST OF GOODS SOLD AND THE GROSS MARGIN WITH THE RETAIL METHOD OF INVENTORY VALUATION

The retail method of inventory was introduced in department stores because it allowed a more simplified method to constantly monitor the all-important gross margin figure. The retail method of inventory eliminated a whole system of records formerly necessary to determine the valuation of an inventory at cost. Because the calculation of profit depends on cost data, the subsequent steps shown are taken in the calculation of a book inventory and in the determination of a continual gross margin figure. The following problem illustrates the calculation of gross margin on stock plus purchases (i.e., total merchandise handled) (see Figure 27):

Figure 27. Calculating Gross Margin on Stock Plus Purchases

	Cost	Retail	% of Sales	Cum. MU%
Opening Inventory	$49,000	$100,000		51.0%
	$\left(\begin{array}{c} \$100{,}000 \times (100\% - MU\%) \\ \$100{,}000 \times 49\% \end{array}\right)$			
(Plus) New Purchases & Freight	+ $240,000	+ $500,000		
Total Mdse. Handled	$289,000	$600,000		51.8%
(Minus) Total Deductions		− $475,000		
		$\left(\begin{array}{l} \text{Sales} \quad \$425{,}000 \\ + \text{Markdown} \quad \$45{,}000 \\ + \text{Shortages} \quad \$5{,}000 \end{array}\right)$		
(Minus) Closing Inventory	− $60,250	$125,000		
	$\left(\begin{array}{c} \$125{,}000 \times (100\% - MU\%) \\ \$125{,}000 \times 48.2\% \end{array}\right)$			
Gross Cost of Mdse. Sold	$228,750			
		$\begin{array}{l} \text{Net Sales} \quad \$425{,}000 \\ - \text{Gross Cost of Msde.} \\ \quad \text{Sold} \quad \$228{,}750 \end{array}$		
Merchandise Margin		$196,250	46.2%	
(Plus) Cash Discounts		+ $13,000		
		$209,250		
(Minus) Workroom Costs		− $1,000		
Gross Margin		$208,250	49%	

	Cost	Retail	MU %
PROBLEM	A juniors' sportswear buyer wants to calculate the gross margin figure to ascertain whether the department is "on target" and will achieve the planned gross margin goals for the season. The available season-to-date information is:		

PROBLEM

A juniors' sportswear buyer wants to calculate the gross margin figure to ascertain whether the department is "on target" and will achieve the planned gross margin goals for the season. The available season-to-date information is:

	Cost	Retail	MU %
Opening inventory		$100,000	51%
New purchases and freight	$240,000	$500,000	

SOLUTION

Step 1: Begin with a retail opening inventory figure: $100,000. The opening inventory at retail ($100,000) was determined when the stock-on-hand was physically counted at the end of the previous accounting period. The cumulative markup of 51% was achieved.

Step 2: Determine a cost opening book inventory figure:

$100,000 × (100% − 51%)

= $100,000 × 49%

= $ 49,000

Step 3: All new purchases ($240,000 cost, $500,000 retail) are added to the opening book inventory figures ($49,000 cost, $100,000 retail) to find total merchandise handled (TMH) figures ($289,000 at cost and $600,000 at retail), resulting in a 51.8% cumulative markup.

Step 4: The sum of $475,000 ($425,000 Total of net sales + $45,000 Markdowns + $5,000 Shortages) is subtracted from the retail figure of TMH ($600,000) to find the retail closing book inventory figure ($125,000).

Step 5: Determine a cost closing book inventory figure:

$125,000 × (100% − 51.8%)

= $125,000 × 48.2%

= $60,250

Step 6: The closing book inventory at cost ($60,250) is subtracted from TMH at cost ($289,000) to find the cost of goods sold ($228,750).

Step 7: The cost of goods sold ($228,750) is then subtracted from the net sales ($425,000) to find the merchandise margin ($196,250).

Step 8: The cash discounts ($13,000) are added to the merchandise margin ($196,250), which equals $209,250.

Step 9: The workroom costs ($1,000) are subtracted from $209,250 to find the gross margin ($208,250).

From an accounting viewpoint, in the calculation of gross margin, the cash discounts and workroom costs are adjusted after the margin on the merchandise itself (i.e., maintained markup) is determined. Nonetheless, because merchants frequently negotiate cash discounts or influence the workroom factor, their impact on the gross margin must be considered.

THE RELATIONSHIP OF PROFIT TO INVENTORY VALUATION IN THE RETAIL METHOD OF INVENTORY

The value placed on an inventory has a decided effect on profits. In this unit there is a detailed examination of the mathematical calculations and records adopted by departmentalized retailers who use the retail method of inventory to establish a continuing gross margin figure, as well as to verify if a profit has been achieved. By illustrating the relationship between sales volume, cost of merchandise sold, given expenses, and the operating profit, the example that follows shows the application of the data collected through this method of inventory valuation. (For ease of comprehension of this system, the same figures are used as in the preceding calculation of gross margin to the operating profit.)

Net Sales		Cost	Retail	% of Sales
			$425,000	100%
Opening book inventory		$49,000		
+ Purchases	+	240,000		
Total mdse. handled	=	$289,000		
− Closing book inventory	−	60,250		
Gross cost of mdse. sold	=	$228,750		
− Cash discounts	−	13,000		
		$215,750		
+ Workroom costs	+	1,000		
Net cost of mdse. sold	=	$216,750	− 216,750	− 51%
Gross margin			$208,250	49%
− Operating expenses			− 191,250	− 45%
Net profit			= $17,000	4%

19. The shortage in the legwear department is $3,500. This is 5% of that department's net sales. What is the sales volume of the department?

20. The coat department's net sales were $225,000, markdowns taken amounted to $15,000, and employee discounts were $3,000. The retail opening inventory for this period was $75,000, the purchases made at retail were $210,000, and the buyer estimated the shortages at 2%. Determine the estimated physical count.

21. A store with net sales of $3,500,000 has estimated its shortages to be 2%. The actual dollar shortage amounted to $72,000.

    a. Was this shortage a higher or lower percentage than anticipated? By how much?

    b. What was the dollar difference between the estimated and the actual shortage?

22. The net sales of a lingerie department were $295,000; inventory on February 1 was $150,000; markdowns were 8% of net sales; purchases for this period were $362,000; the physical inventory taken July 31 was $188,400.

    a. Was there a dollar shortage for this period?

    b. What was the shortage or overage percentage for this period?

23. Describe in detail the various methods that a merchant might use to reduce excessive departmental shortage.

24. Research and Discussion: One of the major duties of any merchant is to control inventory discrepancies (e.g., excessive shortages or overages). Prepare a brief fact sheet for new assistant buyers that outlines the actions a merchant at the departmental level can take to effectively accomplish this responsibility. Briefly explain each action mentioned.

25. A men's outerwear department had an opening inventory of $340,000. The net purchases were $78,000, gross sales were $140,250, customer returns were $11,150, and markdowns—including employee discounts—were $4,800. Shortages of 1.2% were estimated. Calculate:

 a. The closing retail book inventory.

 b. The estimated physical inventory.

26. For the Spring season, the underwear department had net sales of $700,000. On July 31, the physical inventory was $174,220 and the retail book inventory was $185,220.

 a. What was the shortage percentage for the season?

 b. If a 2% shortage was estimated, was the actual shortage percentage higher or lower than anticipated? By how much?

27. The men's furnishings buyer received the following data:

	Cost	Retail
Total merchandise handled	$451,608	$940,850
Net sales		$650,000
Markdowns		$40,000
Employee discounts		$10,000
Operating expenses		$292,500

Calculate:

   a. The closing inventory at cost and retail.

   b. The gross margin in dollars and percentage.

   c. Net profit in dollars and percentage.

CASE STUDY 1
RETAIL METHOD OF INVENTORY

Two years ago, Ms. Carol, the misses' sportswear buyer, agreed with management that a separate petite sportswear department should be created. Because of increasing sales, she felt that petite sportswear had outgrown its status as a classification and deserved, in its own right, to become a separate department. Ms. Carol continued as the buyer for the newly created department, and with her enthusiastic and skillful attention, the impressive sales increases continued for the first year. The second year, however, the sales increases were minute. Ms. Carol now questioned if the category should remain a separate department or be reincorporated into the misses' sportswear department. To make an appropriate judgment, she requested the following data for analysis. The department had an opening inventory of $750,000 at retail that carried a 53% markup. During this period, the gross purchases of $570,000 at retail were priced with a 56.1% markup. The freight charges were $9,600. The merchandise returned to vendors amounted to $14,000 at cost, and $30,000 at retail. Transfers from the misses' sportswear department were $3,500 at cost, and $7,600 at retail. Transfers to the misses' sportswear department were $8,000 at retail, with an agreed cost of $3,700. The gross sales were $720,000; customer returns and allowances were $30,000. The markdowns taken were 12%, and employee discounts were 1%.

As Ms. Carol determined the gross margin achieved by the petite sportswear department, she weighed this against the 46.1% gross margin of the misses' department. Should this "new" department continue as a separate entity? Why? Justify your decision with a mathematical comparison of the performance of the petites versus misses' sportswear departments.

CASE STUDY 2
CONTROLLING SHORTAGES

At the end of the Fall season, Gary Abbott, the buyer, received the shortage report for the Gift Shop. This report revealed that the overall department shortage for this six-month period was 1.3%, or 0.2% less than the previous season. Gary was delighted to notice this decline in shortage, small as it was. As he analyzed the results of the individual stores, he found that Store 01 had a shortage of 1.2% while Store 09 had a 5.0% shortage.

Because the store uses a bar code scanning system to take inventory, the accuracy of the amount of inventory taken is ensured. However, Gary reviews the figures for each store before trying to determine the causes of the vast shortage differences. He refers to the following data:

	Store 01			Store 09		
	Cost	*Retail*	*MU %*	*Cost*	*Retail*	*MU %*
Opening inventory		$450,000	52%		$300,000	52%
Purchases (including freight)	$142,500	$300,000		$71,250	$150,000	
Reductions		$7,000			$4,000	
Sales		$375,000			$150,000	
Shortage		1.2%			5%	

Store 01 had a physical inventory figure of $363,500, and Store 09's physical count was $288,500. Other differences between these two stores are:

1. Store 01 is one of the oldest existing branches of the chain, while Store 09 is the newest branch, having been opened one year ago.

2. Store 01 is located in a high-income area, while Store 09 is in a medium-income-bracket location.

3. Store 01 is one of the most profitable units of the chain, and because of its high productivity enjoys a commensurate sales force.

4. Since 09 is so young, it has been staffed with a minimum permanent sales organization supplemented by part-time employees.

Gary takes three steps:

1. He decides (though can the computers ever be wrong?) to first determine the closing book inventory from the above figures.

2. Having done that, he adjusts the physical count to the book inventory to determine the shortage percentage.

3. Having satisfied himself as to the accuracy of the shortage percentage, he attempts to determine the possible causes. If you were the buyer, what causes would you investigate more thoroughly in order to decrease shortages, and why? What effect, if any, would the large shortage percentage of Store 09 have on the overall department net profit?

DOLLAR PLANNING AND CONTROL

"The best way to predict the future is to create it."

PETER DRUCKER

OBJECTIVES

- Understanding and recognition of the elements of a six-month merchandise plan.

- Knowledge and ability to plan sales.

- Calculation of changes in sales as percentages.

- Facility to plan stock levels, using:

    - Stock-sales ratio method.

    - Week's supply method.

    - Basic stock method.

- Calculation of GMROI.

- Proficiency to plan markdowns.

- Skill to plan purchases at retail and at cost.

- Calculation of open-to-buy figures.

KEY TERMS

average retail stock

basic stock method

BOM stock

dollar merchandise plan

EOM stock

GMROI

on order

open-to-buy (OTB)

planned purchases/ receipts

six-month seasonal dollar merchandise plan

stock-sales ratio method

turnover

week's supply method

KEY CONCEPT FORMULAS

Average retail stock

$$\text{Average retail stock} = \frac{\text{Planned sales for period}}{\text{Turnover rate}}$$

$$\text{Average retail stock} = \frac{\left(\begin{array}{c}\text{Sum of beginning} \\ \text{inventories}\end{array} + \begin{array}{c}\text{Ending inventory} \\ \text{for given period}\end{array}\right)}{\text{Number of inventories}}$$

$$\textbf{GMROI} = \frac{\text{Gross margin \% } \times \text{ Turnover}}{100\% - \text{Markup \%}}$$

$$\textbf{Number of weeks supply} = \frac{\text{Weeks}}{\text{Desired turnover}}$$

Open-to-buy

$$\text{OTB} = \text{Planned purchases for the month} - \begin{array}{c}\text{Outstanding orders to} \\ \text{be delivered that month}\end{array}$$

$$\begin{array}{c}\text{OTB for balance} \\ \text{of month}\end{array} = \begin{array}{c}\text{Planned purchases} \\ \text{for month}\end{array} - \begin{array}{c}\text{Merchandise} \\ \text{received to date}\end{array} - \begin{array}{c}\text{Merchandise} \\ \text{on order}\end{array}$$

$$\begin{array}{c}\text{OTB for} \\ \text{balance} \\ \text{of month}\end{array} = \begin{array}{c}\text{Planned} \\ \text{EOM} \\ \text{stock}\end{array} + \begin{array}{c}\text{Planned} \\ \text{sales for} \\ \text{balance} \\ \text{of month}\end{array} + \begin{array}{c}\text{Planned} \\ \text{markdowns} \\ \text{for balance} \\ \text{of month}\end{array} - \begin{array}{c}\text{Actual} \\ \text{stock-} \\ \text{on-hand}\end{array} - \begin{array}{c}\text{On} \\ \text{order}\end{array}$$

Planned purchases

$$\begin{array}{c}\text{Planned monthly} \\ \text{purchases at} \\ \text{retail}\end{array} = \begin{array}{c}\text{Planned} \\ \text{EOM} \\ \text{stock}\end{array} + \begin{array}{c}\text{Planned sales} \\ \text{for month}\end{array} + \begin{array}{c}\text{Planned} \\ \text{markdowns} \\ \text{for month}\end{array} - \begin{array}{c}\text{Planned} \\ \text{BOM} \\ \text{stock}\end{array}$$

$$\begin{array}{c}\text{Planned monthly} \\ \text{purchase at cost}\end{array} = \text{Planned retail purchases} \times (100\% - \text{Planned markup \%})$$

Seasonal markdowns

$$\text{Planned total seasonal dollar markdowns} = \begin{array}{c}\text{Planned total} \\ \text{seasonal sales}\end{array} \times \begin{array}{c}\text{Total seasonal} \\ \text{markdown \%}\end{array}$$

$$\text{Total seasonal markdown \%} = \frac{\text{Last year (LY) total dollar markdowns}}{\text{LY total sales}} \times 100$$

Stock ratios

$$\text{Stock-sales ratio} = \frac{\text{Retail stock at given time in the period}}{\text{Sales for the period}}$$

$$\text{BOM stock} = \text{Planned monthly sales} \times \text{Stock-sales ratio}$$

$$\text{BOM stock} = \text{Basic stock} + \text{Planned sales for the month}$$

$$\text{Planned stock} = \text{Average weekly sales} \times \text{Number of weeks supply}$$

$$\text{Sales increase \%} = \frac{\text{This year (TY) planned sales} - \text{LY actual sales}}{\text{LY actual sales}} \times 100$$

$$\text{Seasonal planned sales} = \text{LY sales} + \text{Dollar increase}$$

$$\text{Dollar increase} = \text{LY sales} \times \text{Planned increase \%}$$

$$\text{Turnover} = \frac{\text{Net sales for period}}{\text{Average retail stock for the same period}}$$

Profit in retailing is determined largely by maintaining a proper proportion between sales, inventories, and prices. The merchandiser is responsible for providing an inventory that reflects customer demand and also remains within the financial limits set by management. For each department, a sales goal in dollar amounts is forecast, and the size of the inventory necessary to meet these goals is planned. A budget that coordinates these sales and stocks is called a **dollar merchandise plan**. It schedules planned sales month by month, the amount of stock planned for each of these months, and the amount of projected reductions. The budget is prepared in advance of the selling period to which it applies. It typically covers a six-month period, e.g., Spring season (February 1 to July 31), or Fall season (August 1 to January 31).

The information in this budget permits the merchandiser to determine the amount of purchases required. In no way does the dollar merchandise plan address the issue of what merchandise should be purchased. The development of an assortment that reflects customer demands is another important aspect of the total planning process. Because of the quantitative nature of this book, this unit focuses on the mathematics used in this process; concepts and principles are briefly defined and discussed for better comprehension.

Although the dollar merchandise plans used by different stores vary considerably in scope and detail, when properly planned and administered, the sales, stocks, markdowns, and projected cumulative markup percentage (i.e., the original retail price of the total merchandise handled minus the cost) are the indispensable figures that should result in a satisfactory net profit.

The main reason for planning purchases is to assist the buyer in making purchases at the proper time and in the correct amounts so that the stock level is in ratio to sales. Consequently, the dollar merchandise plan also provides a control figure called **open-to-buy (OTB)**. This figure represents the dollar amount of merchandise the buyer may receive during the balance of a given period, without exceeding the planned stock figure at the end of the period under consideration. Because of the benefits that result from this process, most large and many small retailers are committed to comprehensive planning activities. The dollar merchandise system of planning and control discussed in this unit is designed to protect a store's major investment, that is, its inventory. As the art of this merchandising technique is broad in scope and requires an in-depth examination, this subject must be included in any study related to buying for retail.

UNIT V.I
SIX-MONTH SEASONAL DOLLAR MERCHANDISE PLAN

As a device for unifying merchandising operations, the objectives of the dollar plan are:

- To procure a net profit by providing an instrument that plans, forecasts, and controls the purchase and sales of merchandise.

- To research previous results in order to repeat and improve prior successes and to avoid failures.

- To integrate the various merchandising activities involved in determining the purchases necessary to achieve the estimated planned sales.

THE PROCEDURE OF DOLLAR PLANNING BY ELEMENT

Planning Sales

The planning of this figure is most significant because it is the basis for establishing the stock, markdown, and purchase figures. Thus, it should be calculated first. However, its calculation requires the greatest skill and judgment because its accuracy depends on detailed investigation and analysis.

Step 1: Carefully forecast future total dollar sales volume for the entire period by:

a. Reviewing and analyzing past sales performance for the same time period.

b. Considering factors that may cause a change in sales. These factors include:

- Current sales trends.

- Previous rate-of-growth patterns.

- Economic conditions.

- Local business conditions.

- Fashion factors.

- Influencing conditions within and outside of the store or department (e.g., changes in store concepts, market direction, competition, etc.).

c. Establishing, for the season, a percentage of estimated sales change after analyzing the sales performance and current conditions that cause sales changes. Then, calculate the total dollar sales volume for the period. The following calculations are used in this procedure.

Calculating the Percentage of Sales Increase or Decrease When
Last Year's Actual Sales and This Year's Planned Sales Are Known

CONCEPT

Percentage of sales increase   =   This year (TY) planned sales

                                –   Last year (LY) actual sales
                               ―――――――――――――――――――――

                               =   Sales increase

                               = $\dfrac{\text{Sales increase}}{\text{LY actual sales}} \times 100$

                               =   % Sales increase

PROBLEM

If last year's actual sales were $1,834,900 and this year's planned sales are $2,000,000, what is the percentage of sales increase?

SOLUTION

Percentage of sales increase   = $2,000,000   Planned sales

                                –   1,834,900   LY actual sales
                               ――――――――――――――――――――

                               = $165,100   Sales increase

                                  $\dfrac{\$165{,}100 \text{ Sales increase}}{\$1{,}834{,}900 \text{ LY sales}} \times 100$

                               =   0.090 or 9%

Percentage of sales increase =   9%

There are circumstances under which the sales volume of a department or classification is reduced because of a decreased demand. The concept for a decrease in sales is the same as for an increase in sales.

PROBLEM

The sales of the boot classification declined significantly because of the current fashion emphasis. Consequently, the shoe buyer planned sales for this category at $500,000 this season, although last year's actual sales amounted to $650,000. What was the planned percentage of sales decrease for this classification?

Percentage of sales decrease $=$ $\dfrac{\text{(LY actual sales} - \text{TY planned sales)}}{\text{LY actual sales}}$

	$=$	$650,000	LY actual sales
	$-$	500,000	TY planned sales
	$=$	$150,000	Sales decrease
	$=$	$\dfrac{\$150,000 \text{ Sales decrease}}{\$650,000 \text{ LY actual sales}}$ $\times$ 100	

Percentage of sales decrease $=$ 23.1%

Calculating a Total Planned Seasonal Sales Figure When Last Year's Sales and the Planned Percentage of Increase Are Known

CONCEPT

Seasonal planned sales	$=$	Last year (LY) sales $\times$ Planned increase %
	$=$	Dollar increase
	$=$	LY sales $+$ Dollar increase

PROBLEM

If last year's seasonal sales are $1,834,900 and there was a planned 9% sales increase, what are the seasonal planned sales for this year?

SOLUTION

Seasonal planned sales	$=$	$1,834,900	LY sales
	$\times$	9%	Sales increase
	$=$	$165,141	Sales increase
		$1,834,900	LY sales
		$+$ 165,141	Sales increase
TY seasonal planned sales	$=$	$2,000,041	

Step 2: To set the individual monthly sales goals, use as a guideline the seasonal distribution of the previous year's sales for the same period. When adjusting the planned monthly sales increase or decrease, the three essential processes that influence a buyer's judgment are:

- Considering the department's past experience with respect to the normal percentage distribution of sales for the planning period.

- Comparing the monthly percentage distribution with industry performance (see Figure 28).

- Adjusting monthly sales figures due to shifting dates of certain holidays, planned special promotions, and other merchandising strategies (Figure 29).

Figure 28. Typical Conventional Department Stores Monthly Sales Distribution

Month	Feb	Mar	Apr	May	June	July	Aug	Sept	Oct	Nov	Dec	Jan
Percentage	7.0	7.6	7.8	7.9	7.8	7.1	7.8	7.2	7.9	9.9	16.1	6.0

Source: U.S. Department of Commerce, Bureau of the Census: Combined Annual and Revised Monthly Report

Figure 29. Daily Flash Sheets

Daily Flash Sales

Daily Flash Sales for Wednesday 2/20/2013   Date: per 09 wk 2 day 4

*****PLAN NUMBERS REPRESENT AN END-OF-WEEK CUMULATIVE TOTAL*****

	(3) TODAY		(4) PTD ($1000)				(5) STD	
LOC	TY	LY	TY	LY	PLAN	PCT	TY	PLAN
(1) DEPT 220 BELTS								
(2) 01 NY	3680	2147	40	37	55	7.5+	277	284
02 BR	301	403	4	3	5	7.8+	32	22
03^ FM	0	0	0	0	0	0.0+	0	0
04^ ST	0	0	0	0	0	0.0+	0	0
05 BC	61	506	5	5	8	6.1-	38	36
06 SH	216	207	5	4	5	27.5+	31	28
07 CP	0	0	0	0	0	0.0+	0	0
08 NM	719	243	7	5	8	36.3+	57	46
09 GC	471	276	5	4	5	38.4+	32	27
10 PG	402	77	2	2	2	25.6+	13	8
11 CH	695	343	5	3	5	38.4+	34	31
12 WP	322	320	6	5	7	1.4+	41	42
13 WF	293	859	3	5	6	46.2-	21	27
14 TC	185	237	3	4	5	9.6-	22	23
16 KP	265	306	4	3	4	16.0+	22	21
17 WG	177	170	2	2	2	12.4+	17	14
20^ VV	0	0	0	0	0	0.0+	0	0
21* FA	0	580	0	6	7	102.9-	12	35
22* FR	0	0	0	0	0	0.0+	0	0
24 FN	0	0	0	0	0	0.0+	0	0
25* MI	50	0	3	0	6	100.0+	25	29
TOT-CMP	7787	6094	90	83	117	8.4+	638	609
TOT-ALL	7837	6674	94	90	130	4.5+	675	673
PCT	17.4+		4.5+					

*****PLAN NUMBERS REPRESENT AN END-OF-WEEK CUMULATIVE TOTAL*****

	TODAY		PTD ($1000)				STD	
LOC	TY	LY	TY	LY	PLAN	PCT	TY	PLAN
DEPT 231 SCARVES								
01 NY	4822	4191	59	64	81	8.6-	316	301
02 BR	122	59-	2	2	0	35.8+	13	3
03^ FM	0	0	0	0	0	0.0+	0	0
04^ ST	0	0	0	0	0	0.0+	0	0
05 BC	661	488	8	6	10	24.8+	43	33
06 SH	478	740	6	7	9	14.8-	35	32
07 CP	0	0	0	0	0	0.0+	0	0
08 NM	368	848	7	6	11	27.0+	55	40
09 GC	407	155-	4	3	5	29.8+	24	18
10 PG	56	44	1	0	0	131.2+	4	1
11 CH	571	82	5	6	7	11.6-	35	22
12 WP	73	602	10	6	10	72.4+	53	38
13 WF	170	315	3	4	5	33.1-	19	21
14 TC	85	483	3	3	5	17.3-	18	20
16 KP	485	311	4	4	5	10.4+	22	23
17 WG	26	465	3	3	4	5.3-	19	15
20^ VV	0	0	0	0	0	0.0+	0	0
21* FA	0	57	0	1	2	100.0-	4	7
22* FR	0	0	0	0	0	0.0+	0	0
24 FN	0	0	0	0	0	0.0+	0	0
25* MI	349	0	4	0	0	100.0+	23	0
TOT-CMP	8324	8356	113	113	152	0.2+	658	567
TOT-ALL	8673	8413	117	115	154	2.5+	685	574
PCT	3.0+		2.5+					

*****PLAN NUMBERS REPRESENT AN END-OF-WEEK CUMULATIVE TOTAL*****

	TODAY		PTD ($1000)				STD	
LOC	TY	LY	TY	LY	PLAN	PCT	TY	PLAN
MGM 105 DRESS ACCESSORIES								
01 NY	13709	12232	162	163	223	0.6-	1038	1008
02 BR	1001	1376	16	15	20	3.9+	122	97
03^ FM	0	0	0	0	0	0.0+	0	0
04^ ST	0	0	0	0	0	0.0+	0	0
05 BC	1324	2362	20	20	30	2.3+	151	129
06 SH	1284	1786	23	21	27	12.9+	152	136
07 CP	0	0	0	0	0	0.0+	0	0
08 NM	2636	2871	29	29	44	0.7-	231	215
09 GC	1163	687	14	13	17	13.8+	96	80
10 PG	874	519	7	5	8	24.1+	44	38
11 CH	2751	821	19	17	22	8.0+	139	110
12 WP	968	1248	27	21	30	32.0+	176	151
13 WF	1043	2045	11	17	21	33.4-	83	100
14 TC	921	1389	12	13	17	10.3-	88	80
16 KP	1504	1352	13	11	15	22.1+	86	80
17 WG	616	1008	9	11	12	11.5+	63	58
20^ VV	0	0	0	0	0	0.0+	0	0
21* FA	0	1847	0	17	23	101.1-	41	114
22* FR	0	0	0	0	0	0.0+	0	0
24 FN	0	0	0	0	0	0.0+	0	0
25* MI	634	0	13	0	16	100.0+	102	85
TOT-CMP	29794	29696	363	355	486	2.2+	2470	2282
TOT-ALL	30428	31543	376	372	525	0.9+	2613	2481
PCT	3.5-		0.9+					

*****PLAN NUMBERS REPRESENT AN END-OF-WEEK CUMULATIVE TOTAL*****

	TODAY		PTD ($1000)				STD	
LOC	TY	LY	TY	LY	PLAN	PCT	TY	PLAN
DEPT 252 SOCKS								
01 NY	6382	6578	76	82	81	7.6-	334	386
02 BR	368	313	3	3	0	0.3-	22	7
03^ FM	0	0	0	0	0	0.0+	0	0
04^ ST	0	0	0	0	0	0.0+	0	0
05 BC	1017	1673	12	13	10	2.0-	52	54
06 SH	754	1002	13	11	9	18.5+	56	52
07 CP	0	0	0	0	0	0.0+	0	0
08 NM	1348	1133	16	15	11	6.2+	77	85
09 GC	839	1000	12	11	5	7.1+	51	44
10 PG	38	27	1	1	0	16.0-	6	7
11 CH	802	516	8	7	7	21.8+	35	33
12 WP	1129	775	13	13	10	0.4-	59	62
13 WF	399	958	6	9	5	35.7-	25	42
14 TC	469	429	6	6	5	4.2+	22	24
16 KP	335	772	4	6	5	26.2-	19	31
17 WG	307	515	4	5	4	15.3-	17	21
20^ VV	0	0	0	0	0	0.0+	0	0
21* FA	0	296	0	3	2	100.0-	5	21
22* FR	0	0	0	0	0	0.0+	0	0
24 FN	0	0	0	0	0	0.0+	0	0
25* MI	534	0	4	0	0	100.0+	23	45
TOT-CMP	14187	15691	175	181	152	3.7-	776	848
TOT-ALL	14721	15987	179	184	154	3.2-	805	914
PCT	7.9-		3.1-					

Planning Stocks

Because the merchandising policies of retail stores differ, there is no absolute formula for developing the variety of a stock assortment. However, the planning phase of stock investment is accomplished through the dollar plan. In the planning and control of dollar stocks, every merchandiser's objective is to:

- Maintain adequate assortments (i.e., reasonably complete from a customer's viewpoint).

- Regulate the dollar investment of stocks in relation to sales in order to obtain a satisfactory balance between these two factors.

Daily computerized sales reports provide the buyer with information on the actual performance and any variance from the planned performance. This information requires analysis for appropriate action and decisions. These computerized reports provide the basis for dollar control of inventories. This report helps alert the merchandiser to the most current sales position to make any revisions deemed necessary.

After planned monthly sales are established, the amount of dollar stock that is required to be on hand at the beginning of each month (**BOM stock**) and/or the end of each month (**EOM stock**) must be determined. The EOM stock for a particular month is the same as the BOM stock for the following month; for example, if $230,000 is the EOM stock for February, this same figure is the BOM stock for March.

There are variations in the methods of calculating individual monthly stock figures. Before discussing these possible techniques, it is essential to examine turnover because it represents the degree of balance between sales and stocks. The rate of stock turnover measures the velocity with which merchandise moves into and out of a department or store. **Turnover**, or rate of stock turnover, is a merchandising figure. It indicates the number of times that an **average retail stock** has been sold and replaced during a given period, the number of times goods have been turned into money, and, subsequently, money turned back into goods. Although turnover is a resultant figure, it can be planned and controlled, and for convenience of comparison, it is usually expressed as an annual or semiannual figure.

Determining the Turnover Figure

Every retailer should understand the importance of turnover to make better use of capital investment, control inventories, and, ultimately, realize optimum profits. It acts as an index to efficient merchandising. Successful stock planning does not begin with turnover but results in achieving the desired rate of stock turnover. This term indicates the number of times that an average stock is sold for a given period of time, which, unless otherwise stated, refers to a period of one year. However, turnover may be computed on a weekly, monthly, or seasonal basis (Figure 30). The actual number of stock turns varies with the type of merchandise and price. Generally speaking, merchandise in lower price ranges turns more rapidly than in higher ranges; apparel and accessories turn more rapidly than home furnishings. Typical average turnover figures for a particular type of goods are most important as a method of comparison. The following average rates of turnover show the range that may occur:

Misses' dresses:	2.8
Men's furnishings:	2.1
Loungewear and robes:	2.1
Children's footwear:	1.9
Linen and domestics:	1.9
Handbags:	2.8

Turnover is important to a merchandising operation because it:

- Stimulates sales by presenting fresh merchandise to the customer.

- Reduces markdowns by keeping the flow of new goods constant, thereby curbing the accumulation of large amounts of older stock.

- Lowers cost of goods sold because the "open-to-buy" position permits the buyer to take advantage of special prices and offerings.

- Decreases interest, merchandise taxes, and other operating expenses as a percentage of net sales.

The stock turnover rate can be calculated on either a unit or dollar basis, but for the purposes of this text, the dollar basis will be examined.

Calculating Turnover When Average Retail Stock and Sales for the Period Are Known

The dollar figures of stock turn can be determined on either a cost or retail basis. Generally, in stores that use the retail method of inventory, the rate of stock turn is determined on a retail basis. Essential for accuracy, however, is that both sales and inventory be calculated on the same foundation.

CONCEPT

$$\text{Turnover} = \frac{\text{Net sales for period}}{\text{Average retail stock for the same period}}$$

PROBLEM

For the year, the infants' department had net sales of $2,000,000. The average retail stock during this period was $500,000. What was the rate of stock turn?

SOLUTION

$$\text{Turnover rate for the period} = \frac{\$2,000,000 \text{ Net sales}}{\$500,000 \text{ Average retail stock}}$$

$$\textbf{Turnover} = 4.0$$

Figure 30. Inventory Turnover

Ended Inventory Turnover	Percent of Companies
Fewer than 1.5 times	4%
1.6–2	14%
2.1–2.5	14%
2.6–3	14%
3.1–3.5	7%
3.6–4	14%
4.1–4.5	14%
4.6–5	4%
5.1–7.5	4%
More than 7.5	11%

Source: Tenth Annual Retail Horizons: Benchmarks for 2011, Forecasts for 2012 (KPMG/NRF Foundation)

Calculating Average Retail Stock When Planned Sales and Turnover Are Known

CONCEPT

$$\text{Average retail stock} = \frac{\text{Planned sales for period}}{\text{Turnover rate}}$$

PROBLEM

The women's slipper department planned sales of $2,000,000 with a stock turn of 4.0 as the goal. What should be the average stock carried for the period under consideration?

SOLUTION

$$\text{Average retail stock for period} = \frac{\$2,000,000 \text{ Planned sales}}{4.0 \text{ Turnover rate}}$$

Average retail stock for period = $500,000

By understanding the relationship of the average stock, planned sales, and turnover, and by substituting the known factors of the basic formula, the unknown can be calculated (e.g., Net sales = Stock turnover × Average stock at retail).

Calculating Average Retail Stock When Monthly Inventories Are Known

Because the determination of the average inventory directly affects the rate of stock turn, there is a need for a common method among stores and retail establishments to determine the average stock amounts so that the comparison of stock turns can be meaningful. Under the retail method of inventory, an average retail stock is the sum of the retail inventories at the beginning of each year, season, month, or week. This is added to the ending inventory and then divided by the number of inventories used. This is the most accurate and commonly used method because a monthly book inventory figure is available through the retail method of inventory. For example, to obtain an average retail stock figure for a year, the 12 stock inventories at the beginning of each month are added to the ending inventory and the total sum is divided by 13. If the stock turnover rate is computed for a shorter period than one year, the same principle is applied (e.g., for determining a six-month turnover rate, add the 7 stock-on-hand figures and divide by 7). This turnover rate, which has been computed for a period of less than a year, can then be converted to an equivalent annual rate.

In addition, an average stock figure can be calculated in cost as well as retail dollars. The method of finding an average monthly inventory at cost is exactly the same as determining the average stock at retail. For reasons that should be apparent, it is incorrect to mix cost figures with those at retail in the same turnover calculation, so when this type of figure is desired, only the cost inventory figures are used.

$$\text{Average retail stock} \ = \ \frac{\left(\begin{array}{c}\text{Sum of beginning} \\ \text{inventories}\end{array} + \begin{array}{c}\text{Ending inventory} \\ \text{for given period}\end{array}\right)}{\text{Number of inventories}}$$

Find the average retail stock and the turnover for this period:

	Sales		BOM stock		Ending Inventory
January	$10,000	Jan. 1			$13,000
February	8,000	Feb. 1			12,000
March	14,000	Mar. 1			17,000
April	16,000	Apr. 1			19,000
May	12,000	May 1			15,000
June	14,000	June 1			18,000
July	10,000	July 1			14,000
August	6,000	Aug. 1			10,000
September	12,000	Sept. 1			16,000
October	11,000	Oct. 1			15,000
November	12,000	Nov. 1			15,000
December	15,000	Dec. 1			18,000
Total	$140,000				$182,000
		Dec. 31			$13,000

Sum of 12 BOM stocks = $182,000

\+ Ending inventory = + 13,000

= $195,000

Average retail stock = $\dfrac{\$195,000 \text{ (Sum of 13 figures)}}{13 \text{ (Number of inventories)}}$

Average retail stock for one year = $15,000

After calculating an average stock figure, the formula of net sales for the period under consideration divided by the average stock is applied to determine the turnover rate. For example:

Turnover rate = $\dfrac{\$140,000 \text{ (Sum of 12 monthly sales figures)}}{\$15,000 \text{ (Average retail stock for the period)}}$

Turnover rate = 9.3

This same method is used to calculate an average retail stock for a shorter period. The next problem applies the formulas for average inventory and turnover. It illustrates how to determine the average retail stock for a period shorter than one year and how to convert the turnover to an annual rate.

PROBLEM

	Stock-on-hand	Sales (book inventory)	
Feb. 1	$20,000	$50,000	
Mar. 1	27,500	60,000	
Apr. 1	35,000	75,000	
May 1	32,500	70,000	
May 31		60,000	
Total sales	$115,000	$315,000	Sum of inventories

SOLUTION

Average stock = $\dfrac{\$315,000}{5}$ $\dfrac{\text{Sum of inventories}}{\text{Number of inventories}}$

= $63,000

Stock turn rate = $\dfrac{\$115,000}{\$63,000}$ $\dfrac{\text{Net sales for period}}{\text{Average stock for same period}}$

= 1.83 for 4 months or 1/3 year

Annual rate = 1.83 × 3

Annual turnover rate = 5.49

In planning stocks for a season, from the standpoint of stock turnover, merchandise is apportioned so that the average stock is related to the sales for the entire period. This approach does not offer a basis for planning a specific amount of stock to be on hand in order to achieve a planned sales figure.

Determining Gross Margin Return by Dollar Inventory

While retailers have stock turn goals to judge the efficiency of the balance between sales and stocks, when money is tight greater emphasis is placed on the relationship between the inventory investment, or working capital, and its ability to produce gross margin dollars. The objective is to produce a maximum gross margin from a minimum dollar amount investment.

The ratio of productivity of each dollar invested in inventory is similar to a share of stock, and the productivity of this dollar is equivalent, to some degree, to earnings per share. Stock turnover influences and affects the utilization of money invested in inventory. The more times money is converted into sales and gross margin, the greater the return per dollar of inventory. Today, the frequency of this "reinvestment" is an increasingly significant factor. The measurement of the efficiency of investment in inventory is referred to as **gross margin return on investment**, which is commonly known as **GMROI** (pronounced *jimroy*). This element is used by financial analysts to measure capital turnover.

Merchandisers in retailing are responsible for a successful stock turnover and, consequently, give it much focus. Both stock turn and GMROI are involved with inventory productivity, and the relationship between these two elements is that the calculation of stock turn utilizes an average inventory at retail, while GMROI uses an average inventory at cost.

The following example illustrates this concept:

Net sales	=	$1,200,000
Gross margin	=	$480,000
Average inventory (retail)	=	$480,000
Average inventory (cost)	=	$240,000

a. Stock turn $= \dfrac{\$1,200,000}{\$480,000}$ Net sales / Average inventory at retail

$= 2.5$

b. GMROI $= \dfrac{\$480,000}{\$240,000}$ Gross margin / Average inventory at cost

$= 2.0$

This is the simplest level of calculating GMROI. It is apparent that as more sales and gross margin dollars are generated, without increasing inventory, GMROI will increase.

It is more practical to think of GMROI in terms commonly used in merchandising. These factors, which can be managed and influenced, are:

- Markup percentage.

- Gross margin percentage.

- Turnover.

Another way to think of the calculation is:

$$\frac{\text{How much is made on a sale} \times \text{How long it takes to sell it}}{\text{How much was paid for it}}$$

This results in the following calculation:

CONCEPT

$$\textbf{GMROI} = \frac{\text{Gross margin \%} \times \text{Turnover}}{100\% - \text{Markup \%}}$$

PROBLEM

The year-to-date results of the intimate apparel department are:

Gross margin: 40%

Turnover: 2.5

Markup: 50%

What is the GMROI achieved by this department?

SOLUTION

$$\text{GMROI} = \frac{\text{Gross margin \%} \times \text{Turnover}}{100\% - \text{Markup \%}}$$

$$= \frac{40\% \text{ GM} \times 2.5 \text{ Turnover}}{100\% - 50\% \text{ MU}}$$

$$= \frac{0.40 \times 2.5}{1.0 - 0.50}$$

$$= \frac{1}{0.50}$$

$$\textbf{GMROI} = 2.0$$

The GMROI result is identical for either calculation, but the second example shows the relationship of the components and demonstrates how future results can be improved.

The key to successful retailing is achieving more dollar sales without a corresponding increase in inventory. Through the determination of turnover, the stock level that produces an optional sales level can be measured. The calculation of GMROI shows the profitability or cash flow that these sales produce.

Figure 31 compares department and specialty stores' inventory productivity or stock turn and the profitability or GMROI for a five-year period. These measurements, once established as acceptable industry performance, do not vary significantly from year to year.

Figure 31. Inventory Productivity and Profitability

Note: Department and Specialty store figures are weighted by the aggregate net sales of the companies reporting.

METHODS OF STOCK PLANNING

It is common to plan monthly stock figures for the beginning of the period by a **stock-sales ratio method**. This technique, illustrated in the following examples, indicates the relationship between stock-on-hand at the beginning of the month and the retail sales for the same month.

Setting Individual First-of-Month
Stock Figures by the Stock-Sales Ratio Method

After planned monthly sales figures are established, the amount of dollar stock that is required on hand at the beginning of each month (BOM stocks) and the end of each month (EOM stocks) must be determined. This relationship is referred to as a stock-sales ratio. Generally, the BOM stock-sales ratio is used to balance planned monthly stocks with the planned monthly sales. Standard stock-sales ratios in departments can be established by evaluating the actual past stock-sales ratio performance of a department. This has proven to provide the proper relationship. Additionally, researched guidelines of data showing typical monthly stock-sales ratios are available and can be used as a source of information in planning monthly stock proportions. Because monthly stock-sales ratio proportions vary according to location, customer type, etc., the best source of information in establishing a proper ratio for each individual month is a store's own records. Figure 32 illustrates typical monthly stock-sales ratios.

Figure 32. Typical Stock-Sales Ratio

Feb	Mar	Apr	May	June	July	Aug	Sept	Oct	Nov	Dec	Jan
5.43	4.17	5.19	4.95	4.03	4.83	4.75	4.34	5.13	4.18	2.10	6.17

Calculating Stock-Sales Ratio When Retail Stock and Sales for a Given Period Are Known

CONCEPT

$$\text{Stock-sales ratio} = \frac{\text{Retail stock at given time in the period}}{\text{Sales for the period}}$$

PROBLEM

On February 1, the boys' wear department had a retail stock of $120,000. The planned sales for this month were $20,000. Find the stock-sales ratio for the month of February.

SOLUTION

$$\text{Stock-sales ratio} = \frac{\$120,000 \text{ BOM stock}}{\$20,000 \text{ February sales}}$$

$$\textbf{Stock-sales ratio} = 6.0$$

Calculating BOM Stock When Planned Sales and Stock-Sales Ratio Are Known

BOM stock = Planned monthly sales × Stock-sales ratio

CONCEPT

The fabric department planned sales of $40,000 for the month of July. Experience in the department showed that an 8.2 stock-sales ratio was successful. What should be the planned BOM stock for July?

PROBLEM

BOM July stock	=	$40,000	Planned July sales
	×	8.2	Stock-sales ratio
BOM stock	=	$328,000	

SOLUTION

Setting Stock Figures by the Week's Supply Method

The **week's supply method** plans inventory size on a weekly basis. The set amount of stock equals a calculated number of weeks supply. The number of weeks supply that is to be "on hand" depends on the planned turnover figure to be achieved and is used as a guide to set the inventory. This technique of stock planning is best used in a department that primarily carries staple merchandise and/or has a relatively stable sales volume. Note that because the stock size is in direct relation to the planned weekly sales, it can result in an excessive stock condition at the peak selling periods or in dangerously low stocks during the slower months.

Calculating the Number of Weeks Supply

$$\text{Number of weeks supply} = \frac{\text{Weeks}}{\text{Desired turnover}}$$

CONCEPT

Department #32 has a planned stock turnover of 4.0 for the six-month period. Determine the number of weeks supply needed to achieve the desired turnover.

PROBLEM

$$\text{Number of weeks supply} = \frac{26 \text{ Weeks (6 months)}}{4.0 \text{ Turnover}}$$

Number of weeks supply = 6.5

SOLUTION

Finding Planned Stock, Given Turnover, and Weekly Rate of Sales

CONCEPT	Planned stock = Average weekly sales × Number of weeks supply
PROBLEM	A department has an average weekly sales rate of $9,800 and a planned turnover rate of 4.0 for the six-month period. Calculate the amount of stock to be carried.
SOLUTION	**Step 1:** Find the number of weeks supply given the turnover and the supply period.

$$\text{Number of weeks supply} = \frac{26 \text{ Weeks (6 months)}}{4.0 \text{ Turnover}}$$

Number of weeks supply   =   6.5

Step 2: Find planned stock given the average weekly sales and the number of weeks supply.

Planned stock   = $9,800 Average weekly sales × 6.5 Number of weeks supply

Planned stock   = $63,700

Setting Beginning of the Month (BOM) Stock Figures by Basic Stock Method

Another approach to balancing stocks and sales is the **basic stock method**, which is the average inventory for the period. This average inventory is derived simply from the planned sales and turnover. For example, if the anticipated six-month sales total $960,000, and a turnover of 2.0 is desired for the season, average inventory can be calculated by applying the following formula:

$$\text{Average inventory} = \frac{\$960,000 \quad \text{Sales}}{2.0 \quad \text{Turnover}}$$

Average inventory   = $480,000

This technique presumes that the retailer will begin each month with a minimum amount of basic stock that remains constant regardless of the monthly sales to be achieved. Generally it is best to apply this basic stock (i.e., fixed quantity of stock maintained throughout the season) when the annual turnover rate is 6.0 or less, because using it with higher-stock-turn merchandise would result in unrealistic basic stocks.

Calculating the Average Monthly Sales
Planned sales

February	$110,000
March	150,000
April	160,000
May	180,000
June	210,000
July	150,000
Total sales	$960,000

$$\text{Average monthly sales} = \frac{\$960,000 \text{ Total sales}}{6 \text{ Months}}$$

$$\textbf{Average monthly sales} = \$160,000$$

Finding a Basic Stock Given the Average Monthly Sales and the Average Inventory

The average inventory minus the average monthly sales produces a basic stock at retail. For example:

Average inventory	=	$480,000
− Average monthly sales	=	− 160,000
Basic stock	=	$320,000

Finding a BOM Stock When a Basic Stock and Planned Sales for the Month Are Known

The calculated basic stock figure is added to each month's planned sales to determine the BOM amount for the month.

BOM stock = Basic stock + Planned sales for the month

CONCEPT

In an accessories department that has planned a turnover of 4.0 for the Fall season, the estimated sales are as follows:

PROBLEM

August	$28,000		November	$36,000
September	$30,000		December	$40,000
October	$32,000		January	$26,000

Calculate the BOM stocks using the basic stock method.

SOLUTION

Step 1: Determine average monthly sales.

August		$28,000
September		30,000
October		32,000
November		36,000
December		40,000
January	+	26,000
Total for the season		$192,000

$$\text{Average inventory} = \frac{\$192,000}{6\ \text{Months}}$$

Average monthly sales = $32,000

Step 2: Calculate average inventory.

$$\text{Average inventory} = \frac{\$192,000\ \text{Sales}}{4.0\ \text{Turnover}}$$

Average inventory = $48,000

Step 3: Find basic stock.

Basic stock at retail	=	Average inventory	$48,000
	–	Average monthly sales	– 32,000
		Basic stock =	$16,000

Step 4: Calculate BOM stock by adding basic stock to monthly planned sales.

BOM stock =	Monthly sales		Basic stock		BOM stock
August	$28,000	+	$16,000	=	$44,000
September	$30,000	+	$16,000	=	$46,000
October	$32,000	+	$16,000	=	$48,000
November	$36,000	+	$16,000	=	$52,000
December	$40,000	+	$16,000	=	$56,000
January	$26,000	+	$16,000	=	$42,000

Planning Markdowns

In dollar planning, markdowns are important because they reduce the total value of the stock available for sale. Careful planning of markdowns helps reduce the amount of markdowns taken, which in turn helps increase net profit figures. The amount of planned markdowns to be taken is expressed both in dollars and as a percentage of planned sales. Because the dollar markdowns vary greatly, the percentage data is more significant for comparison between past and present performance. The percentage of markdowns also varies with different lines of merchandise, different months, and different seasons. The planned markdown figure is usually based on a normal amount determined from experience. Typical markdown percentages by department are available for industry comparison, as illustrated in Figure 33.

Figure 33. Typical Markdown Percentages (Including Employee Discounts)

Women's Footwear —	19.4%	Boys' Clothing —	21.8%
Fine Jewelry & Watches —	5.6%	Small Appliances —	15.7%
Infants & Toddlers —	22.9%	Cosmetics & Toiletries —	1.9%

Figure 34. Monthly Markdowns (% of Monthly Total Company Net Owned Sales)

Feb	Mar	Apr	May	June	July	Aug	Sept	Oct	Nov	Dec	Jan
13.88	10.74	10.93	7.87	12.57	17.88	15.73	8.60	10.43	10.16	15.95	17.54

It is common when planning markdowns for a season to:

Step 1: Set the total markdown amount (stated as a percentage of the total season's sales) for the entire period by:

a. Reviewing and analyzing past markdown performance for the same period and for the entire period under consideration.

b. Considering factors that may effect a change in markdowns.

$$\text{Total seasonal markdown \%} = \frac{\text{Last year (LY) total dollar markdowns}}{\text{LY total sales}} \times 100 \qquad \text{CONCEPT}$$

Step 2: Convert the planned markdown percentage of sales to a total dollar figure for the season.

$$\text{Planned total seasonal dollar markdowns} = \text{Planned total seasonal sales} \times \text{Total seasonal markdown \%} \qquad \text{CONCEPT}$$

Step 3: Apportion total dollar planned markdowns by month. (Note that the distribution of monthly markdown goals does not necessarily mean that markdowns and sales will be in the same proportion during each of the months of the season.) Figure 34 illustrates storewide monthly markdown percentages.

EXAMPLE

Last year, net sales for the season in the swimwear department were $100,000. The total amount of markdowns taken during the entire period totaled $5,000. The buyer, upon reviewing the performance of the department and in preparation for planning markdowns for the same period this year, decided that the $5,000 markdown figure taken previously was normal and compared favorably with standard markdown percentages established for this type of merchandise. Consequently, last year's dollar markdown amount was converted to a percentage:

$$\text{Markdown \%} = \frac{\$5,000 \text{ LY markdown}}{\$100,000 \text{ LY net sales}} \times 100$$

$$\text{Markdown \%} = 5\%$$

The total planned sales figure established by the buyer for the season under consideration was set at $110,000. Because a repetition of the percentage of markdowns was desired for the forthcoming season, the dollar amount of markdowns to be taken was determined by:

$$\begin{array}{c}\$110,000 \\ \text{Planned sales}\end{array} \times \begin{array}{c}5\% \text{ Planned} \\ \text{markdowns}\end{array} = \begin{array}{c}\$5,500 \text{ Planned total markdown} \\ \text{for the season}\end{array}$$

The amount of $5,500 would then be apportioned by dollars to the individual months of the period.

Planning Markups

Although markup planning and calculations are discussed in Unit III, it is necessary to understand that after the initial markup has been carefully planned, the buyer will have to constantly manipulate the actual markup to date in relation to the markup on additional purchases for the season in order to obtain the planned seasonal markup percentage. To "protect" profitability, the gross profit figure, including an estimated shortage amount, can be calculated easily as in the following example, which shows the facts that should be considered:

1. For the Spring season, a department has planned:

   • Sales @ $2,000,000

   • Markdowns @ $200,000 (10%)

   • Shortages @ $40,000 (2%)

2. The department came into the period under consideration with an opening inventory at retail of $500,000 and a cumulative markup for the period of 52%.

3. A closing inventory of $500,000 at retail is projected for the end of the Spring period.

4. Management projects a desired gross margin of 48.5% for the Spring period.

5. Based on a 48.5% gross margin, the cumulative markup (Stock + Purchases) is calculated:

a. $$\text{Cumulative MU \%} = \frac{48.5\% \text{ Gross margin} + (10\% \text{ Markdowns} + 2\% \text{ Shortages})}{100\% \text{ Sales} + 12\% \text{ Reductions}}$$

$$= \frac{60.5\%}{112\%}$$

$$= 54\%$$

b. The markup percentage required on new purchases to meet desired goals is determined by the following method:

$$\text{Total retail MDSE requirements} = \text{Net sales} + \text{Markdowns} + \text{Shortages} + \text{Closing retail inventory}$$

	$2,000,000	Net sales
+	200,000	Markdowns
+	40,000	Shortages
+	500,000	Closing retail inventory

Total retail MDSE requirements = $2,740,000

Cost = Total retail MDSE requirements × (100% − MU %)

= $2,740,000 × (100% − 54%)

= $2,740,000 × 46%

= $1,260,400

New purchases at retail = Total retail MDSE requirements − Opening inventory

= $2,740,000 − $500,000

New purchases at retail = $2,240,000

New purchases at cost = New purchases at retail × (100% − Cumulative MU %)

= $2,240,000 × (100% − 52%)

= $2,240,000 × 48%

= $1,075,200

$$\text{Markup \% on new purchases} = \frac{\$2,240,000 \text{ Retail (new purchases)} - \$1,075,200 \text{ Cost (new purchases)}}{\$2,240,000 \text{ Retail}} \times 100$$

$$= \frac{\$1,164,800 \text{ Markup (new purchases)}}{\$2,240,000} \times 100$$

$$= 52\%$$

Planned gross profit percentage is determined by the following method:

Given:

Dollar sales (from plan)	=	$2,000,000
Dollar markdown (from plan) (10%)	=	$200,000
Anticipated shortage percentage	=	2%

Anticipated dollar shortage = Planned shortage % × Total planned dollar sales

$$= (2\% \times 2,000,000)$$

Anticipated dollar shortage	=	$40,000
Planned markup % on Planned stock + Purchases	=	54.0%
Cost or complement % on Planned stock + Purchases	=	46.0%

Cost of planned sales:

Planned markdown	=	$200,000 × 0.46	=	$92,000
Planned shortage	=	$40,000 × 0.46	= +	18,400
Planned sales	=	$2,000,000 × 0.46	= +	920,000
Total cost of planned sales			=	$1,030,400
Planned dollar sales			=	$2,000,000
Cost of planned sales			= −	1,030,400
Planned dollar gross profit			=	$969,600

$$\text{Planned gross profit percentage} = \frac{\$969,600}{\$2,000,000} \times 100$$

Planned gross profit percentage = 48.5%

Planned Purchases—Planned Receipts

One objective of planning is to assist the buyer in proper timing and in purchasing the correct amounts of goods. Therefore, when the planned sales, stocks, and markdowns have been determined, the amount of monthly purchases is automatically calculated by a formula. **Planned purchases**, which is more accurately termed **planned receipts**, refers to the dollar amount of merchandise that can be brought into stock during a given period. Store reports frequently identify these figures as receipts. Generally, purchases are preplanned at retail value for each month and then converted, by formula, to a cost figure by applying the planned markup.

Calculating Planned Monthly Purchases at Retail

CONCEPT

Planned monthly purchases at retail	=	Planned EOM stock
	+	Planned sales for month
	+	Planned markdowns for month
	=	Total merchandise requirements
	−	Planned BOM stock
	=	Planned purchase amount

PROBLEM

From the following planned figures for the lingerie department, calculate the planned purchase amount for June:

Planned stock June 1	$38,000
Planned sales for June	$100,000
Planned markdowns for June	$5,000
Planned stock for July 1	$40,000

SOLUTION

	Planned June sales		$100,000
+	Planned EOM stock (July 1)		40,000
+	Planned June markdowns	+	5,000
	Total merchandise requirements	=	$145,000
−	Planned BOM stock (June 1)	−	38,000
	Planned monthly retail purchases		$107,000

Converting Retail Planned Purchases to Cost

The planned purchase figure at retail must be established first before the planned purchase figure at cost is determined by conversion.

CONCEPT	$\dfrac{\text{Planned monthly}}{\text{purchase at cost}}$ = Planned retail purchases × (100% − Planned markup %)

PROBLEM The planned retail purchases for June were $107,000 and the planned markup percentage was 41.5%. Calculate the planned purchase amount at cost.

SOLUTION

Planned purchases = $\dfrac{\$107{,}000 \text{ Planned}}{\text{retail purchases}}$ × (100% − 41.5% Planned MU)

= $107,000 × 58.5%

= $62,595

Planned purchases at cost = $62,595

Based on the above examination of the procedures, elements, and computations that relate to the creation of a dollar plan, analyze Figures 35–39, which are examples of typical **six-month seasonal dollar merchandise plans**. The formats differ, yet there are certain common features. These forms are included for familiarization with their differences and similarities. In large stores, the statistical departments furnish this kind of historical data to assist the buyers and the divisional merchandise managers in making decisions on which the required purchases—also known as **planned receipts**—are calculated. It is common for a general merchandise manager and/or controller to contribute to the planning function.

Figure 35. Worksheet for Annual Merchandise Plan

$(000)

SALES ($)	FEB.	MARCH	APRIL	MAY	JUNE	JULY	SPRING	AUG.	SEPT.	OCT.	NOV.	DEC.	JAN.	FALL	ANNUAL
00 PLAN							2007								
13 ACT.	1817	3396	3476	3066	3041	2070	16865	2303						2303	19168
13 PLAN	1643	3265	3207	3238	3034	1608	15996	2231	4095	3071	3161	4233	1681	18471	34467
12 ACT.	1427	2619	2550	2701	2742	1438	13478	1766	3157	2322	2112	3077	1457	13891	27368
11 ACT.	1224	2250	2065	2366	2447	1379	11730	1725	2536	1842	1847	2620	959	11530	23260
10 ACT.	1115	2018	1947	1977	1951	1170	10177	1451	2159	1412	1377	1988	833	9221	19399

SALES % CHG.	FEB.	MARCH	APRIL	MAY	JUNE	JULY	SPRING	AUG.	SEPT.	OCT.	NOV.	DEC.	JAN.	FALL	ANNUAL
04P/05A															
03P/04A	27.3	29.6	36.3	13.5	10.9	43.9	25.1	30.4	−100.0	−100.0	−100.0	−100.0	−100.0	−83.4	−30.0
02P/03A	15.1	24.7	25.8	19.9	10.6	11.9	18.7	26.3	29.7	32.3	49.7	37.6	15.3	33.0	25.9
01P/02A	16.6	16.4	23.5	14.2	12.1	4.3	14.9	2.4	24.5	26.0	14.3	17.4	52.0	20.5	17.7
00P/01A	9.8	11.5	6.1	19.7	25.4	17.9	15.3	18.9	17.5	30.4	34.1	31.8	15.1	25.0	19.9

EOM STOCK	FEB.	MARCH	APRIL	MAY	JUNE	JULY	AVG. SPRING	AUG.	SEPT.	OCT.	NOV.	DEC.	JAN.	AVG. FALL	AVG. ANNUAL
00 PLAN							10513								
13 ACT.	7449	9578	9714	8979	8518	7581	8337	10555							
13 PLAN	8971	9703	9586	8712	7410	6950	8241	11613	12270	11810	11256	9000	8431	10190	9390
12 ACT.	7204	8802	9009	8225	6474	6105	7339	7577	8098	8536	8138	5959	6538	7279	7401
11 ACT.	5389	5986	6182	6056	5261	5140	5477	6122	6120	6460	6692	5368	5551	5922	5742
10 ACT.	5349	6188	5614	4691	4069	4481	4916	4578	5285	5031	4998	4057	4323	4679	4822

EOM – WKS OF SUPPLY	FEB.	MARCH	APRIL	MAY	JUNE	JULY	TURNOVER SPRING	AUG.	SEPT.	OCT.	NOV.	DEC.	JAN.	T.O. FALL	T.O. ANNUAL
00 PLAN							1.95								
13 ACT.	9.8	13.0	15.7	14.9	13.1	10.5	2.02	13.3							
13 PLAN	12.1	13.6	16.1	15.2	12.4	9.8	1.94	14.5	17.3	18.1	17.7	14.9	12.1	1.81	3.67
12 ACT.	12.0	15.2	17.6	16.6	13.2	11.0	1.84	13.0	15.0	18.1	16.6	13.0	10.5	1.91	3.70
11 ACT.	10.8	11.2	13.0	14.0	12.3	10.9	2.14	12.8	12.6	15.9	16.2	13.6	11.4	1.95	4.05
10 ACT.	11.8	14.1	14.4	13.3	11.4	11.5	2.07	11.9	15.4	15.7	15.1	12.4	10.6	1.97	4.02

NET RECEIPTS	FEB.	MARCH	APRIL	MAY	JUNE	JULY	SPRING	AUG.	SEPT.	OCT.	NOV.	DEC.	JAN.	FALL	ANNUAL
00 PLAN															
13 ACT.	2728	5525	3611	2331	2580	1133	17909	5276						5276	23185
13 PLAN															
12 ACT.	3080	4217	2756	1918	992	1069	14032	3238	3677	2760	1714	898	2036	14323	28355
11 ACT.	2290	2846	2261	2240	1652	1258	12547	2707	2534	2183	2079	1296	1142	11942	24489
10 ACT.	2442	2857	1373	1054	1330	1581	10637	1549	2866	1158	1345	1047	1099	9064	19700

MARKDOWN ($)	FEB.	MARCH	APRIL	MAY	JUNE	JULY	SPRING	AUG.	SEPT.	OCT.	NOV.	DEC.	JAN.	FALL	ANNUAL
00 PLAN															
13 ACT.	395	380	456	773	797	448	3249	452						452	3700
13 PLAN															
12 ACT.	165	533	342	628	743	122	2533	314	488	479	578	996	31	2885	5418
11 ACT.	250	233	294	228	649	162	1816	253	365	489	362	1002	90	2560	4376
10 ACT.	216	216	350	252	504	292	1830	168	223	315	366	450	204	1725	3555

MARKDOWN %	FEB.	MARCH	APRIL	MAY	JUNE	JULY	SPRING	AUG.	SEPT.	OCT.	NOV.	DEC.	JAN.	FALL	ANNUAL
00 PLAN															
13 ACT.	21.7	11.2	13.1	25.2	26.2	21.6	19.3	19.6						19.6	19.3
13 PLAN															
12 ACT.	11.6	20.3	13.4	23.2	27.1	8.5	18.8	17.8	15.5	20.6	27.4	32.4	2.1	20.8	19.8
11 ACT.	20.4	10.3	14.3	9.6	26.5	11.7	15.5	14.7	14.4	26.6	19.6	38.2	9.4	22.2	19.8
10 ACT.	19.4	10.7	18.0	12.8	25.8	25.0	18.0	11.5	10.3	22.3	26.6	22.6	24.5	18.7	18.3

A13 – RTW C DRESSES
A13 – RTW C DRESSES

Figure 36. Six-Month Merchandise Plan (By Store)

	SALES														
	FEBRUARY		MARCH		APRIL		MAY		JUNE		JULY		TOTAL SEASON		
STORE	PLAN	L Y	PLAN	L Y	PLAN	L Y	PLAN	L Y	PLAN	L Y	PLAN	L Y	PLAN	L Y	STORE
01	27.8	26.5	43.9	40.4	57.6	55.0	79.0	75.5	46.1	43.5	26.8	25.4	281.2	266.3	01
02	43.8	42.3	59.5	55.8	84.1	81.3	120.1	116.0	61.2	58.4	39.2	37.9	407.9	391.7	02
03	44.3	42.8	56.7	53.6	84.7	81.8	123.2	118.9	69.3	65.7	43.8	42.4	422.0	405.3	03
05	14.9	14.1	23.8	22.2	33.2	31.7	48.8	46.6	27.5	26.3	15.6	15.0	163.8	155.9	05
07	10.8	10.5	15.0	14.3	18.6	18.1	29.3	28.3	17.7	17.1	9.8	9.4	101.2	97.7	07
08	18.8	18.1	32.1	30.3	39.1	37.7	59.4	57.2	33.9	32.6	20.3	19.4	203.6	195.3	08
09	10.8	10.3	13.9	12.9	19.0	18.2	31.9	30.5	20.3	19.3	11.0	10.5	106.9	101.7	09
12	23.3	22.2	27.3	25.5	47.4	43.8	77.5	72.0	44.5	41.3	31.1	28.9	251.1	233.7	12
13	28.0	26.2	34.1	31.6	60.1	56.1	96.3	89.7	52.8	49.4	31.2	29.1	302.5	282.1	13
14	7.3	6.6	8.4	7.5	10.5	9.5	21.8	19.5	13.3	12.0	6.5	5.9	67.8	61.0	14
15	10.1	8.7	12.5	10.4	20.2	16.9	35.6	30.7	24.9	22.2	16.1	14.6	119.4	103.5	15
16	17.2	15.8	21.5	19.5	32.1	29.5	52.8	48.2	30.2	27.9	17.3	15.9	171.1	156.8	16
17	1.4	1.4	2.2	2.2	3.7	3.6	5.8	5.7	4.3	4.2	4.1	4.0	21.5	21.1	17
18	12.0	11.2	15.1	13.7	24.9	23.3	43.9	40.1	18.4	17.0	15.2	14.0	129.5	119.3	18
19	14.3	13.6	16.9	15.6	23.0	21.7	40.3	38.0	25.5	24.0	14.7	13.8	134.1	126.7	19
20	10.8	9.7	14.6	12.9	14.4	13.4	34.5	31.4	23.7	21.6	10.9	10.0	108.9	99.0	20
21	6.1	5.5	11.6	10.2	8.9	8.3	17.9	16.3	17.0	15.5	9.9	9.0	71.4	64.8	21
TOT	301.7	285.5	409.1	378.6	581.5	549.9	918.1	864.6	530.6	498.0	323.5	305.2	3064.5	2881.8	TOT

	STOCK														
01	58.0	42.8	72.0	50.1	88.0	73.4	116.0	99.2	80.0	77.7	72.0	59.8	69.0	51.6	01
02	94.0	95.5	99.0	70.6	121.0	94.8	159.0	152.3	110.0	106.6	99.0	87.3	95.0	63.1	02
03	79.0	73.3	108.0	63.5	132.0	110.0	174.0	169.6	120.0	146.9	108.0	105.9	102.2	73.1	03
05	36.0	24.3	54.0	37.6	66.0	49.6	87.0	41.8	60.0	46.0	54.0	30.3	51.0	25.0	05
07	29.0	19.5	36.0	29.4	44.0	42.0	58.0	39.4	40.0	38.5	36.0	31.4	27.0	20.9	07
08	44.0	31.3	63.0	33.8	77.0	49.7	102.0	56.7	70.0	47.7	63.0	48.9	58.0	35.5	08
09	29.0	23.0	45.0	30.5	55.0	48.6	73.0	44.5	50.0	53.8	45.0	36.2	43.0	20.3	09
12	65.0	49.3	76.0	42.6	94.0	70.5	123.0	115.0	85.0	87.5	77.0	47.9	74.0	40.0	12
13	72.0	53.0	81.0	50.0	99.0	67.1	130.0	107.7	90.0	72.7	81.0	60.0	77.0	54.7	13
14	15.0	12.2	27.0	21.6	33.0	21.2	44.0	24.3	30.0	25.5	27.0	26.2	26.0	16.9	14
15	33.0	18.1	41.0	25.8	49.0	38.1	65.0	40.9	45.0	49.7	40.0	37.1	38.0	29.2	15
16	44.0	34.3	54.0	35.5	66.0	53.1	87.0	73.9	60.0	63.7	54.0	49.0	52.0	43.2	16
17	7.0	8.6	9.0	11.0	11.0	13.8	15.0	21.5	10.0	16.8	9.0	13.7	9.0	5.7	17
18	33.0	25.3	41.0	39.7	50.0	50.4	65.0	63.9	45.0	59.8	41.0	42.5	39.0	31.7	18
19	40.0	26.0	40.0	33.5	49.0	46.1	65.0	69.7	45.0	71.9	40.0	38.4	39.0	33.8	19
20	29.0	24.0	32.0	31.4	39.0	43.6	51.0	51.5	35.0	50.3	32.0	35.9	30.0	31.8	20
21	18.0	12.8	22.0	37.1	27.0	35.8	36.0	28.2	25.0	38.6	22.0	26.8	21.0	15.8	21
TOT	725.0	573.3	900.0	643.7	1100.0	907.8	1450.0	1200.1	1000.0	1053.7	900.0	777.3	850.0	592.3	TOT
PL. RCPTS.	476.7		609.1		931.5		468.1		430.6		273.5		3189.5		PL. RCPTS.
*MD	125.0	126.3	70.0	52.0	113.0	117.2	285.0	264.6	172.0	195.6	45.0	32.3	810.0	788.0	*MD

TOTAL SEASON		PLAN	L Y			PLAN	L Y	DEPT. NUMBER: _____
	MARKUP %	58.0	57.4	GM & DISC %		50.6	49.9	DEPT. NAME: MS. BUDGET COORDINATES
	MD & ED %	26.9	27.8	TURNOVER		3.1	3.5	BUYER: _____

* (EXCLUDING ED)

234 | MATHEMATICS FOR RETAIL BUYING

Figure 37. Six-Month Merchandise Plan

		AUGUST SALES	AUGUST BOM STOCK	SEPTEMBER SALES	SEPTEMBER BOM STOCK	OCTOBER SALES	OCTOBER BOM STOCK	NOVEMBER SALES	NOVEMBER BOM STOCK	DECEMBER SALES	DECEMBER BOM STOCK	JANUARY SALES	JANUARY BOM STOCK	SEASON SALES	SEASON AVER STOCK	FEBRUARY SEASON T.O.	FEBRUARY BOM STOCK
CHAIN	LY PLAN	365.8	576	348.8	790	306.4	704	376.5	612	310.0	607	130.9	278	1836.4	595	3.09	321
T.O.	LY PLAN	0.63		1.04		1.48		2.08		2.59		3.09		3.09			
O.T.B.	LY PLAN																
M.D.$	LY PLAN	64.8		46.3		37.8		70.8		59.2		75.1		354.0			
M.D.%	LY PLAN	17.72		13.36		12.33		18.80		19.10		57.40		19.28			
MU: PUR	LY PLAN	50.40		49.73		48.80		50.07		44.64		48.61		49.64			
MU% S&P	LY PLAN	50.12		49.69		49.20		49.49		49.26		49.07		49.07			
SHORT%	LY PLAN	2.07		2.04		2.08		2.18		2.15		2.18		2.11			
G.P.$	LY PLAN	147.2		143.6		124.3		149.9		115.5		20.6		701.0			
G.P.%	LY PLAN	40.24		41.40		40.55		39.80		37.25		15.76		38.17			
BEG SEAS STK MU%	LY PLAN	49.80															

Figure 38. Total Corporate Six-Month Plan

SPRING 2013 — Total Corporate Six-Month Plan

CLASS		FEB BOM	FEB SALE	FEB MD	FEB REC	MAR BOM	MAR SALE	MAR MD	MAR REC	APR BOM	APR SALE	APR MD	APR REC	MAY BOM	MAY SALE	MAY MD	MAY REC	JUN BOM	JUN SALE	JUN MD	JUN REC	JUL BOM	JUL SALE	JUL MD	JUL REC	AUG BOM	AUG SALE	AUG MD	AUG REC	TOTAL SALE	AVE. STOCK	TURN	RECEIPTS RETAIL	RECEIPTS LCC
EARS	R.PLAN ACT.	533	58	42	115	548	100	25	120	543	105	25	126	539	135	35	135	504	125	35	212	559	180	50	130	459								
	P.PLAN	533	58	42	115	548	100	25	120	543	105	25	126	539	135	35	135	504	125	35	215	559	180	50	130	459				703	526	1.34	841	210
	LY	371	60	4	66	365	90	4	140	398	85	8	140	406	113	5	207	564	99	5	232	534	145	9	116	323				592	423	1.40	867	217
STRAN	R.PLAN ACT.	268	31	2	61	296	50	10	40	276	55	10	57	268	70	15	85	268	60	10	98	296	90	20	64	275								
	P.PLAN	268	31	2	61	296	50	10	40	276	55	10	57	268	70	15	85	268	60	10	98	296	90	20	64	250				356	275	1.30	405	101
	LY	301	34	0	0	256	48	2	47	245	50	4	83	259	69	0	114	282	61	2	106	308	89	0	68	241				351	270	1.30	418	105
FASHI BASIC	R.PLAN ACT.	170	21	3	93	239	45	10	24	208	45	10	40	193	55	10	54	182	50	10	85	202	75	15	66	183								
	P.PLAN	170	21	3	93	239	45	10	24	208	45	10	40	193	55	10	54	182	50	10	85	207	75	15	66	183				291	197	1.47	362	91
	LY	119	18	3	9	103	36	3	59	118	31	3	91	165	46	4	130	229	38	6	32	206	50	3	34	119				219	151	1.45	355	89
COLO	R.PLAN ACT.	114	17	4	0	93	15	5	117	190	20	5	23	188	30	10	0	148	30	10	16	124	35	10	20	99								
	P.PLAN	114	17	4	0	93	15	5	117	190	20	5	23	188	30	10	0	148	30	10	16	124	35	10	20	99				147	137	1.08	176	44
	LY	114	24	10	59	143	34	3	135	240	39	4	135	248	49	16	55	230	39	16	40	266	52	6	79	266				237	215	1.10	415	104
GOLD	R.PLAN ACT.	170	8	2	0	160	25	10	79	204	25	5	44	218	20	10	0	188	25	10	15	168	40	15	30	143								
	P.PLAN	170	8	2	0	160	25	10	79	204	25	5	44	218	20	10	0	188	25	10	15	168	40	15	30	143				143	179	0.80	168	42
	LY	26	5	0	42	58	16	1	41	81	20	1	107	160	11	14	112	145	19	11	22	223	43	2	43	116				114	116	0.99	361	90
FASHI	R.PLAN ACT.	172	26	3	118	261	60	15	98	284	50	20	214	424	60	20	68	412	55	20	60	397	75	30	30	322								
	P.PLAN	172	26	3	118	261	60	15	98	284	50	20	210	424	60	20	68	412	55	20	60	397	75	30	30	322				326	325	1.00	594	149
	LY	301	33	6	38	291	59	8	122	301	52	10	86	304	61	11	112	315	42	12	44	283	42	11	16	224				289	288	1.00	418	105

Figure 39. Purchase Planning

```
                                        Planned
Planned purchases for October        $20,000   Planned Sales
   based on planned figures        +  42,000   Planned EOM Stock

                                   +     500   Planned Markdowns
                                     $62,500   Total Merchandise Requirements
                                   -  40,000   Planned BOM Stock
PLANNED PURCHASES—                    22,500


                                        Revised
Planned purchases for October        $22,000   Rivised Sales
   based on revised figures        +  42,000   Planned EOM Stock

                                   +     500   Revised Markdowns
                                     $64,500   Total Merchandise Requirements
                                   -  40,000   Revised BOM Stock
ADJUSTED PLANNED PURCHASES—          $24,500
```

As a guide to merchandising, the real value of dollar planning is that the figures projected for each element reflect goals that are reasonably attainable. Because the buyer is responsible for interpreting and achieving the projected figures, it is essential that the buyer be involved in the preparation of the figures. Also, a buyer who has helped to set these guidelines will be more inclined to use them. Once completed, a dollar plan must be adjusted to actual conditions and results during the season under consideration.

Adjusting the Planned Purchases

During the season, as the merchandising activities are performed, the actual results are checked against the planned figures. Sometimes this reveals the need to adjust the original planned figures either for a specific month or for the balance of the season, because of a deviation from the planned sales thus far or because of a change in circumstances. For example, if sales and/or markdowns are actually larger than planned, purchases must be greater than planned to achieve the level of stock planned. Conversely, if these factors are actually less than planned, a downward revision of purchases is required. Figure 39 illustrates the variation between planned figures and actual results.

Explanation of Merchandise Statistics Report

The elements that affect profit are included in a merchandise statistics report, as well as the status of the size of the stock and sales trends. It is a guide to the six-month projections, shows the current performance, and enables the buyer to make necessary adjustments. The annotated information in Figure 40 is numbered (1) to (8), and the following information corresponds to those numbers:

Figure 40. Merchandise Statistics Report

MERCHANDISE STATISTICS REPORT

SPRING 20___

CURRENT WEEK
SALES, MARKDOWNS, STOCK,
GROSS MARGIN DATA ESTIMATED

DEPT ____

1. WEEK ENDING and WEEK NO.: Example: FEB 05 is WEEK NO. 01.

2. NET SALES (in 100s): This category is divided into the following two sections:

   a. WEEKLY: Figures that show the sales of TY, PLAN, and LY. Example:

      WEEK ENDING FEBRUARY 05

TY	$62.5
PLAN	$68.8
LY	$62.7

   b. CUMULATIVE: Cumulative sales for the period for TY, PLAN, LY, and % CHG (percent change) for existing stores, but also excluding any new store(s). Example:

      WEEK ENDING FEBRUARY 12

TY	$122.7
PLAN	$123.8
LY	$123.5
% CHG	– 0.7%
EXCLUDE NEW STORE:	– 4.6%

3. MARKUP % CUMULATIVE SALES: Markup on of all merchandise handled, season-to-date, before the adjustments of cash discounts for TY and LY. Example:

   WEEK ENDING FEBRUARY 05

Opening: TY	38.2%
LY	37.8%

4. MARKDOWNS—CUMULATIVE INCLUDING EMPLOYEE ALLOWANCE: Markdowns both in DOLLARS and the % (of change), TY, and LY. Example:

   WEEK ENDING FEBRUARY 05

	DOLLARS	*%*
TY	$3.6	5.7%
LY	$6.6	10.5%

5. STOCK ON HAND: Merchandise in stock for TY, PLAN, and LY. Example:

   WEEK ENDING FEBRUARY 05

TY	$1,954.20
PLAN	$1,450
LY	$1,498

6. PLATFORM RECEIPTS: Merchandise received TY and LY for the reported end of week. Example:

   WEEK ENDING FEBRUARY 05

TY	$74.7
LY	$118.0

7. OUTSTANDING ORDERS: Amount of open orders. Example:

WEEK ENDING FEBRUARY 05

TY	$394.5
LY	$126.9

8. STATISTICS BELOW ON FISCAL MONTH BASIS: Comparison of operational factors that affect ultimate profit, such as GROSS MARGIN, STOCK TURN, DISC. EARNED, etc., TY over LY. Example:

9 WEEKS—GROSS MARGIN MMO AFTER SHORTAGE %

TY	30.5%
PLAN	30.6%
LY	22.6%

Applying the concepts to Figure 40:

PROBLEM

Buyers use reports to plan future sales and stock levels. Use Figure 40 from "WEEK ENDING DATE FEB 05 TO APR 30," columns (2a) "NET SALES: WEEKLY: TY/PLAN/LY" and (5) "STOCK ON HAND: TY/PLAN/LY" to answer the following six questions.

1. Calculate the percentage by which current sales in March were above or below planned sales.

2. Calculate the percentage by which current sales in March were above or below last year's sales.

3. Based on this information, how would you evaluate the planned sales for April?

4. What was the opening cumulative markup percentage for this department? What percentage change was this over LY?

5. Season to date, which week ending had the largest dollar sales TY? What was the dollar amount of those sales? Which week ending had the best sales increase percentage for the season TY over LY?

6. For both the months of February and March, were the sales TY larger or smaller than PLAN? State the percentage of change for each month.

Planning Sales Practice Problems

1. In the children's department, the August sales were planned at $247,500 because of additional promotional events. The actual sales for this month last year were $225,000. What is the percentage increase in planned sales for August of this year?

2. For the Spring period, the handbag department's total seasonal sales volume for last year was $750,000. If there is an 8% increase this year, what is the dollar amount of sales planned?

3. During the month of August, sales for a sporting goods store are planned at $900,000, which is 15% of the planned season's total sales. Calculate the monthly sales for the balance of the season, if sales are planned as follows:

August:	15%	November:	18%
September:	14%	December:	25%
October:	16%	January:	12%

4. A small retailer is planning a 10% reduction in sales due to competition from a major new department store. If last year's sales were $500,000, what sales figure should be planned for this year?

5. After a detailed analysis of sales by classification, the hosiery buyer determined a decline in the panty hose category. Last year's sales for this category were $75,000. This year the sales for this classification are planned at $60,000. What is the percentage of sales decline?

6. Seasonal sales for last year were $855,000, and this year the merchandise manager planned for a sales increase of 8%. What is the estimated planned dollar sales figure for this year?

7. If actual sales for last year were $855,000, and this year's planned sales are $923,400, calculate the percentage of sales increase for this year.

Calculating Average Retail Stock Turnover and GMROI Practice Problems

8. The net sales in the neckwear department were $240,000, with a stock turnover of 3.0. Find this department's average stock at retail.

9. What amount of average stock should be carried by a costume jewelry department with net sales of $920,000 for the year and a stock turn of 4.0?

10. What is the average stock of a department with annual sales of $1,350,000 and an annual stock turn of 4.5?

11. Find the average stock from an activewear department's inventory figures:

BOM January	$62,000	BOM July	$120,000
BOM February	$64,000	BOM August	$78,000
BOM March	$70,000	BOM September	$78,000
BOM April	$74,000	BOM October	$68,000
BOM May	$88,000	BOM November	$64,000
BOM June	$100,000	BOM December	$60,000

12. Determine the seasonal stock turnover on the basis of the following information:

	Retail inventory	Sales
Aug. 1	$36,000	$20,000
Sept. 1	$68,000	$28,000
Oct. 1	$60,000	$44,000
Nov. 1	$40,000	$28,000
Dec. 1	$28,000	$24,000
Jan. 1	$28,000	$10,000
Jan. 31	$18,000	

13. A housewares department has an average inventory of $112,000 at retail, with a stock turnover of 2.0. What are the department sales for the period?

14. Calculate the yearly turnover using the following figures from an outer-wear department:

Gross sales	$497,500
Customer returns	$47,500
Inventory 8/1	$85,000
Inventory 10/1	$105,000
Inventory 12/1	$250,000
Inventory 2/1	$53,000
Inventory 4/1	$90,000
Inventory 6/1	$80,000
Inventory 8/1	$85,000

15. For the year, a shoe department has net sales of $2,500,000. The average stock carried during this period was $1,000,000. What was the annual rate of stock turn?

16. Departmental gross sales for the year were $220,000, with customer returns of 10%. During the year these inventories were taken:

Date	Inventory value (retail)
Jan. 1	$37,000
April 1	$36,500
July 1	$41,500
Oct. 1	$46,500
Jan. 1 of following year	$38,500

Find:

    a. The average stock for the year.

    b. The annual rate of turn.

17. The sales for October were $8,000; the stock on October 1 at retail value was $24,000; the stock on October 31 was $28,000. What was the stock turn for the month?

18. The sales in the children's department amounted to $416,000 for the year. The stock at the beginning of the year was $120,000 at retail, and for the end of the year, the retail stock figure was $140,000. What was the stock turn for the year?

19. The men's furnishings department had the following performance for the period under consideration:

- 26.1% Gross margin.

- 2.8 Turnover.

- 30.7% Markup.

What GMROI was achieved?

20. The same men's furnishings buyer (in problem 19) made some spectacular purchases for an annual store event that increased the markup to 33.8%, with the other factors being constant. What GMROI resulted from this strategy?

21. Last Fall, the active sportswear department achieved a 45.9% gross margin with a stock turn of 2.1. The markup was 60.3%. During this Fall season, the gross margin was increased to 50.5%. Compare the GMROI performance from last year with this year.

22. The budget sportswear department achieved a 26.1% gross margin and had the same 30.7% markup as the men's furnishings department, with a stock turn of 8.0. What was the resultant GMROI for this department?

23. What is the planned stock-sales ratio in the handbag department when beginning of the month stock is planned at $19,000 and planned sales are $9,100?

24. Planned sales in the costume jewelry department for April are $130,000, and the planned stock-sales ratio is 2.4. What should be the stock figure on April 1?

25. The outerwear department buyer decided that a stock-sales ratio of 2.5 for the month of February would be appropriate. If the sales for February were planned at $12,000, how much stock should be carried on February 1?

26. The glove department's stock at the beginning of March was $67,500, with sales for the month at $15,900. What was the stock-sales ratio for March?

Finding Weekly Rate of Sales
Practice Problems

27. The hosiery department sells control-top panty hose at the rate of 48 dozen per week at a retail price of $4.50 per pair. Calculate the amount of stock that should be carried to achieve a turnover of 6.0 for the six-month season in this category.

28. A stationery store has sales of $18,000 per week and a planned turnover of 4.0 for a six-month period. Calculate the amount of stock that should be carried in this store.

29. A handbag department plans a stock turn at 6.0 for a twelve-month period. What figure represents the number of weeks supply needed to achieve the desired turnover?

30. A knit accessories department has an average weekly sales figure of $14,500 and a planned turnover rate of 3.0 for the six-month period. Calculate the amount of stock to be carried.

31. Calculate the basic stock figure of a men's suit department that has annual sales of $1,650,000 and an annual stock turn of 4.0.

32. For May, the gift department had planned sales of $180,000. For the Spring season, the department's planned sales were $900,000, with a planned stock turnover of 3.0. Determine the BOM figure for May, using the basic stock method.

33. The small leather goods department had planned the following figures for the Fall season:

    Planned total sales for season: $102,000

    Planned turnover for season: 2.0

    Planned sales for November: $26,000

    Calculate the November BOM figure for this department, using the basic stock method.

Planning Markup Practice Problems

34. Calculate the planned gross profit, in dollars, given the following data:

Planned dollar sales (given)	$900,000
Planned dollar markdowns (given)	$135,000
Estimated planned dollar shortage	$18,000
Percentage planned markup on stock and purchases	48.5%
Reciprocal percentage planned markup	51.5%

35. Department #580, on August 1, had an opening retail inventory of $1,000,000, with a cumulative 55% markup. For the Fall season, the department planned:

Sales	$4,000,000	
Markdowns	$400,000	(10%)
Shortages	$80,000	(2%)
Closing inventory	$1,000,000	
Gross margin for the season	52%	

Based on these projected figures for the season, calculate the markup percentage needed on new purchases made during this period to achieve these goals.

Planned Purchases Practice Problems

36. Find the planned purchases for June, if:

Planned June sales	$72,000
Planned June markdowns	$3,000
Planned stock June 1	$150,000
Planned stock July 1	$155,600

37. Calculate the planned July purchases at cost using the following figures:

Planned July sales	$175,000
Planned July markdowns	$20,000
Planned stock July 1	$250,000
Planned stock July 31	$125,000
Planned markup	52%

38. Note the following figures:

Planned September sales	$18,000
Planned September markdowns	$800
Planned stock September 1	$49,200
Planned stock October 1	$50,400
Planned markup	51.5%

Determine:

    a. The planned September purchases at retail.

    b. The planned September purchases at cost.

    c. The turnover for September.

39. The hosiery department has an initial markup of 54%. The planned sales for April are $10,000 and $12,000 for May. The desired BOM stock-sales ratio for April is 2.0 and 1.5 for May. The planned markdowns are $600.

Calculate:

    a. The planned April purchases at retail.

    b. The planned April purchases at cost.

40. The following figures are from a shoe department:

Planned stock November 1	$147,000
Planned stock December 1	$110,000
Planned November markdowns	$2,000
Planned November sales	$63,000
Actual stock November 1	$140,000
Actual November sales	$61,000

Find:

a. The original planned purchases.

b. The adjusted planned purchases.

41. The petite sportswear department had the following seasonal planned figures for October:

	Dollars	Percentages
Sales	$150,000	
Markdowns		11%
BOM stock	$136,000	
EOM stock	$108,000	
Markup		51.5%

Determine:

    a. The planned purchases at retail.

    b. The planned purchases at cost.

42. The children's clothing department had projected the following figures for January:

- Sales of $46,000.
- Stock-sales ratio of 3.0.
- Reductions of $13,800.
- EOM inventory of $140,000.

What are the planned retail purchases for January?

43. A men's furnishings department had the following figures planned for December:

Planned sales	$450,000
Planned markdowns	$45,000
Planned stock (December)	$900,000
Planned stock (January)	$600,000

However, the following figures reflect the actual performance:

Actual sales	$430,000
Actual stock (January 1)	$620,000

Find:

a. The original planned purchases.

b. The adjusted planned purchases.

UNIT V.II
OPEN-TO-BUY CONTROL

Merchandise control results from effective use of data that is available through the dollar planning procedure. In purchasing merchandise, a buyer is guided by the timing and quantity goals established in the six-month seasonal dollar plan. To provide an even tighter control on the amount of merchandise received in a specific period, and to achieve as precisely as possible the sales and stock plans, the buyer refers to a merchandising figure called **open-to-buy**. This term, abbreviated OTB, denotes the amount of unspent (i.e., order limit) money that is available for purchasing merchandise that will be delivered during a given period. Usually, it is calculated on a monthly basis and indicates that the buyer has not yet spent all of the planned purchases or receipts for the period in question. It represents the difference between the planned purchases for a period and the merchandise orders already placed for that period. Unfilled orders, generally known as open orders, or "**on order**," should be charged to those months during which delivery is expected so that the buyer is able to control and time buying activities to correlate with selling activities. The purpose of this control is to identify the deviations between actual results and planned goals, and so that the buyer can take corrective measures when needed.

The planned purchase figure for a particular month indicates the sum available to purchase goods during that month, but this figure does not indicate the distribution of the money throughout the month. Experienced buyers attempt to distribute purchases over the entire month to:

- Reorder or replace fast-selling goods.

- Fill in stocks so that complete stocks are offered.

- Compete advantageously when buying special purchases and/or new and interesting items as they become available.

- Test offerings of new resources.

Information showing current developments helps ensure that all the planned factors will proceed according to plan. Consequently, it is common in large stores that the controller's office periodically issues a report. The typical report (see Figure 41) contains information that covers:

- **Sales, including:**
  - Plans for month.
  - This month to date.
  - Adjusted plan for month.

Figure 41. Open-to-Buy Monthly Report

CO P1, MD A, RD 4, DG 026 SUITS		Last Month (MAY)	Current Month (JUN)	JUN-1/5 #22	JUN-2/5 #23	JUN-3/5 #24	JUN-4/5 #25	JUN-5/5 #26	JUL-1/4 #27	CURR. MO. (MTD)	Next Month (JUL)	2 Nxt Month (AU6)	3 Nxt Month (SEP)
THIS WEEK (JUN-3/5) #24													
$ NET SALES	LAST YEAR	0	0	0	0	0	0	0	0	0	0	0	0
	PLAN	10,000	5,000	950	1,000	1,000	1,050	1,000	0	1,950	0	8,000	20,000
	ACTUAL	3,801		558						558			
	% PLAN: LY	0	0	0	0	0	0	0	0	0			0
	% ACT.: LY	0	0	0	0	0	0	0	0	0			
	% ACT.: PLAN	(62)		(41)	(100)					(71)			
$ STOCK/SALES	LAST YEAR		0.0	0.0	0.0	0.0	0.0	0.0	0.0				
	ACTUAL			9.4	0.0								
$ MARK-DOWNS	LAST YEAR	0	0	0	0	0	0	0	0	0	0	0	0
	PLAN	2,000	5,000	950	1,000	1,000	1,050	1,000	0	1,950	0	0	1,000
	HOME OFF.	0								0			
	P.O.S.	0								0			
	TOTAL	0								0			
MARK-DOWNS/ SALES	% LAST YEAR	0	0	0	0	0	0	0	0	0	0	0	0
	% PLAN	20	100	100	100	100	100	100	0	100	0	0	5
	% ACTUAL	0		0	0								
# NET SALES	LAST YEAR	0	0	0	0	0	0	0	0	0	0	0	0
	PLAN	68		10	0					10			
	ACTUAL												
# STOCK/SALES	LAST YEAR		0.0	0.0	0.0	0.0	0.0	0.0	0.0				
	ACTUAL	0.00		9.2	0.0								
# AVERAGE SALE	LAST YEAR	0.00	0.00	0.00	0.00	0.00	0.00	0.00	0.00	0.00	0.00	0.00	0.00
	PLAN	55.90		55.80						55.80			
	ACTUAL	0.00	0.00	0.00	0.00	0.00	0.00	0.00	0.00	0.00	0.00	0.00	0.00
# AVERAGE STOCK	LAST YEAR	58.55	57.05	57.05	57.07	0.00	0.00	0.00	0.00				
	PLAN												
	ACTUAL												
	LAST YEAR	0	0	0	0	0	0	0	0	0	0	0	0
	PLAN	22,000	10,000	5,249	4,680						15,000	15,000	30,000
	ACTUAL	6,558	5,249	5,249	4,680								
$ RECEIVED NOT SHIPPED		2,568				0				0			
$ SHIPMENTS				0		0				0			
MARK UP	% LAST YEAR	32	0	0	0	0	0	0	0	0	0	0	0
	% PLAN	35	32	32						32		35	35
	% ACTUAL									0			
# RECEIVED NOT SHIPPED		48		0	0	0				0			
# SHIPMENTS				0	0					0			

		Next Month (JUL)	2 Nxt Month (AU6)	3 Nxt Month (SEP)
# OPEN-TO-RECEIVE	0	0	0	0
# ON ORDER	0			
# OPEN TO BUY	0	0	0	0
$ OPEN-TO-RECEIVE	0	15,000	23,160	16,400
$ ON ORDER	0	0	0	0
% MARK UP	0	0	0	0
$ OPEN TO BUY	0	15,000	23,160	16,400
$ CUM. OPEN-TO-BUY	0	15,000	38,160	54,560

(CGMRTO) PAGE: 58 09:50 AM

- **Markdowns, including:**
  - Season-to-date at BOM in dollars.
  - Season-to-date at BOM in percent to sales.
  - Month-to-date.
- **Stocks, including:**
  - First of month.
  - Balance for current month.
  - Receipts to date (additions).
  - On hand today.
- **Open-to-buy, including:**
  - Planned EOM stock.
  - Adjusted EOM stock.
- **Outstanding orders, including:**
  - For delivery by month.
- **Purchases, including:**
  - Plans for month.
  - Adjusted plan for month.
  - Plan for next month.
- **Cumulative markup, including:**
  - Plan for month.
  - Actual to date.

Because it is critical to be able to determine at any time the dollar amount still available to purchase future merchandise, the computerized report, Figure 42, controls the merchandising facts planned and identifies deviation between the planned goals and the actual reports, so that necessary corrective measures can be taken. Generally, it is prepared on a weekly basis.

Figure 42. Open-to-Buy Report

(1) 10/10/13 (2) WEEK 01 OF 04	FALL 2014 OPEN TO BUY	(3) DEPT 736 BRIDGE SUITS

(The table in Figure 42 is a dense Open-to-Buy Report with sections labeled (5) SALES, (6) STOCKS, (7) ORDERS, (8) MARKDOWNS, and (9) OPEN TO REC. Data rows are organized by store (NY, BR, BC, SH, NM, GC, PG, CH, WP, WF, TC, KP, WG, FA, MI, RTV, EB, ES, T, etc.) with TY (this year), PL (plan), and LY (last year) subrows.)

Explanation of Open-to-Buy Report

Figure 42 illustrates the information that is contained in a typical OTB report (e.g., sales, stocks, markdowns, outstanding orders, and open-to-receive). The report format and frequency of issuance can vary with organizational size and needs. This particular report shown gives the reviewer the opportunity to analyze the department's performance by individual store or on a combined all-store basis. The annotated information in Figure 42 is numbered (1) to (9), and the following information corresponds to those numbers:

1. Date: Published date of the report. Example: 10/10/13.

2. WEEK 01 OF 04: Week of the month being viewed.

3. DEPT 736 BRIDGE SUITS: Department number and name.

4. Branch store listing: Listing of all the stores by location. Example: Store NY (left-hand column). At the bottom of the sheet is the total (T) section, which designates the total for all stores.

5. SALES: Net sales, by store, and the percent change, which indicates the variance of CURRENT sales figures from PLAN and LY's actual sales. This category is divided into the following sections:

a. CURRENT WEEK: Sales in dollars and percentages by store, for the current week. Example:

For Store NY, CURRENT WEEK:

	Dollars	*Percentages*
TY	$18.6	
PLAN	$14.4	29%
LY	$22.2	– 16%

These figures show that for the current week, Store NY had net sales of $18.6, which was 29% ahead of PLAN, but 16% behind LY.

b. LAST WEEK: Sales in dollars and percentages by store, for the prior week. Example:

For Store NY, LAST WEEK:

	Dollars	*Percentages*
TY	$9.7	
PLAN	$14.2	– 32%
LY	$24.2	– 60%

These figures show that for LAST WEEK, Store NY had net sales of $9.7, which was 32% under PLAN, and 60% behind LY.

c. 2 WKS AGO: Sales in dollars and percentages by store, for 2 weeks prior. Example:

For Store NY, 2 WKS AGO:

	Dollars	*Percentages*
TY	$23.3	
PLAN	$14.2	64%
LY	$17.0	37%

These figures show that for 2 WKS AGO, Store NY had net sales of $23.3, which was 64% ahead of PLAN, and 37% over LY.

d. PRIOR 4 WKS: Total sales in dollars and percentages by store, for prior 4 weeks. Example:

For Store NY, PRIOR 4 WKS:

	Dollars	*Percentages*
TY	$24.2	
PLAN	$28.5	– 15%
LY	$26.5	– 9%

These figures show that for PRIOR 4 WKS, Store NY had net sales of $24.2, which was 15% under PLAN, and 9% behind LY.

e. MTD (Month-to-date): Total sales in dollars and percentages by store, for fiscal month. Example:

For Store NM, MTD:

	Dollars	Percentages
TY	$3.8	
PLAN	$4.3	– 11%
LY	$8.5	– 55%

These figures show that for MTD, Store NM had net sales of $3.8, which was 11% under PLAN, and 55% behind LY.

f. STD (Season-to-date): Total net sales in dollars and percentages by store, from beginning of season to the current date. Example:

For Store BR, STD:

	Dollars	Percentages
TY	$13.1	
PLAN	$5.4	145%
LY	$15.8	– 17%

These figures show that for MTD, Store BR had net sales of $13.1, which was 145% ahead of PLAN, but 17% behind LY.

g. OCT $, NOV $, DEC $: Planned sales in dollars for the present month and the next two months, compared to the same months LY. Example:

For Store BC:

OCT	NOV	DEC
$6.0 PLAN	$6.6 PLAN	$8.0 PLAN
$1.8 LY	$1.8 LY	$3.3 LY

6. STOCKS: Retail dollar value of stock currently received, which is planned by the month. This category is divided into the following sections:

a. LAST WK: Dollar value of stock LAST WK, compared to PLAN and LY amounts for the same week. Example:

For Store NY, LAST WK:

TY	$141.5
PLAN	$177.3
LY	$272.0

b. CURRENT WK: Current week's dollar value of stock compared to PLAN and LY amounts for the same week. Example:

For Store NY, CURRENT WK:

TY	$126.7
PLAN	$166.4
LY	$289.7

c. OCT $, NOV $, DEC $: Comparison of the PLAN EOM with LY's stock dollars for the current month, and the next two months. Example:

For Store NY:

OCT	NOV	DEC
$166.4 PLAN	$142.1 PLAN	$99.3 PLAN
$270.4 LY	$283.9 LY	$305.3 LY

d. WKS OF STOCK: This subcategory is divided into two sections:

   i. WKS OF STOCK ONPLN: Number of weeks merchandise should last based on planned sales. They indicate how many future weeks of planned sales will be covered by the current week's stock. Example:

     For Store NY: 11 (weeks)

   ii. WKS OF STOCK ON TRD: Weeks of stock adjusted for actual vs planned sales performance. Example:

     For Store NY: 8 (weeks)

7. ORDERS: Commitments by retail value of merchandise ordered. This category is divided into the following sections:

a. PRIOR MOS. PAST DUE: Alerts the buyer to past-due orders, TY vs LY. Example:

For Store NY:

TY	$37.0
LY	$17.2

b. OCT $, NOV $, DEC $: Orders due for the current month, and the next two months. Example:

For Store NY:

OCT	NOV	DEC
$76.9 TY	$27.0 TY	
$117.2 LY		

c. FUTURE: Figures for orders that would be due in future months, subsequent to the current month, and the next two months. Blank spaces indicate no future commitments.

d. TOTAL: Figures that are the total of orders due for the present month, and next two months. Example:

For Store NY:

TY	$103.9
LY	$117.2

e. STOCK AND ORDERS (S & O): Figures, which are a combination of the stock with the total orders, used to compare TY figures with LY figures. Example:

For Store NY:

TY	$230.70
LY	$406.90

8. MARKDOWNS: Dollar reductions taken. This category is divided into the following sections:

a. CURRENT WEEK: Markdowns for the current week, comparing TY with LY. Example:

For Store NY:

TY	$8.0
LY	$0.3

b. MTD $: Total dollar reductions taken month-to-date, comparing TY with LY. Example:

For Store NY:

TY	$8.0
LY	$0.3

c. STD $: Total dollar reductions taken season-to-date, comparing TY with LY. Example:

For Store NY:

TY	$27.7
LY	$43.3

d. STD % SLS: Total reductions expressed as percentages of sales, comparing TY with LY. Example:

For Store NY:

TY	21.9%
LY	32.0%

9. OPEN TO REC: Comparison of the planned and actual receipts at a given point in time during the month. It lists by month the retail dollar amount of merchandise open to be bought and received and is calculated by subtracting the month's orders from the month's planned receipts (i.e., planned purchases) figure. The positive numbers indicate money still available, while the negative numbers show an overextended or overbought condition. This overbought condition occurs when the month's orders placed exceed that month's planned receipts. Example:

For Store NY:

OCT	NOV	DEC
– $23.7 TY	$13.4 TY	$28.3 TY
$65.1 LY	$40.4 LY	$28.3 LY

CALCULATING RETAIL OPEN-TO-BUY
AT THE BEGINNING OF A MONTH

OTB: Planned purchases for the month minus outstanding orders to be delivered that month

A buyer has planned January sales of $60,000, with an opening January stock planned at $50,000, a closing stock of $30,000, and markdowns planned at $500. If the orders that have already been placed for January delivery amount to $10,000 at retail, what is the buyer's January open-to-buy?

January EOM stock		$30,000
+ January sales	+	60,000
+ January markdowns	+	500
Total merchandise requirements	=	$90,500
− January BOM stock	−	50,000
January planned purchases	=	$40,500
− January on order	−	10,000
January OTB at retail	=	$30,500

When the retail open-to-buy for any period is established, it can be converted to a cost open-to-buy figure. For example, $30,500 retail open-to-buy is converted to a cost figure by multiplying the retail open-to-buy by 100% (minus the planned mark-up percentage).

CALCULATING RETAIL OPEN-TO-BUY DURING THE MONTH

If the buyer wishes to calculate the OTB figure at a certain time during the period, the calculations may be based on the predetermined planned purchases, or the open-to-buy figure may be determined for the balance of the period using the planned closing stock figure. The problems that follow illustrate these calculations.

OTB for Balance of Month Based on Predetermined Planned Purchases

CONCEPT

OTB for balance of month   =

    Planned purchases for month

  − Merchandise received to date

  − Merchandise on order

  = OTB for balance of month

PROBLEM

The merchandise plan shows that the planned purchases for September amounts to $17,000. The store's records indicate that from September 1 to September 15 the department received $8,300 worth of new goods, and there is an order of $700 for September delivery. What is the open-to-buy for the balance of the month?

SOLUTION

	September planned purchases		$17,000
&minus;	Merchandise received	&minus;	8,300
&minus;	On order	&minus;	700
	September OTB balance		$8,000

OTB for Balance of Month Based on Planned Closing Stock

OTB for balance of month =

    Planned EOM stock

 + Planned sales for balance of month

 + Planned markdowns for balance of month

 = Total merchandise requirements

 – Actual stock-on-hand

 – On order

 = OTB for balance of month

On September 15, an infants' department has a stock of $26,000 and merchandise on order amounting to $700. The planned sales for the balance of September are $8,000, with planned markdowns for the balance of the month at $500. The stock planned for September 30 is $31,800. What is the OTB for the balance of the month?

Planned sales for balance of month		$8,000
+ Planned markdowns for balance of month	+	500
+ Planned EOM stock	+	31,800
Total merchandise requirements	=	$40,300
– Actual stock-on-hand	–	26,000
– On order	–	700
September OTB balance		$13,600

44. What is the open-to-buy for a department that has planned purchases of $71,500 and outstanding orders of $74,000?

45. The actual stock on April 1 is $116,000, with "on order" in April amounting to $18,000. Sales are planned at $75,000, with markdowns estimated to be 3.5%, and the stock on April 30 is planned at $112,000. What is the OTB for this month?

46. On March 13, stock-on-hand is $16,300, with planned sales for the balance of the month at $9,000. Merchandise on order comes to $3,000, and the planned April 1 stock is $10,000. Find the balance of the OTB for March.

47. The May portion of a six-month plan for a shop is as follows:

Planned May sales	$37,500
Planned May markdowns	10%
Planned May BOM stock	$66,000
Planned June BOM stock	$59,000
Planned markup	49%

    a. What are the planned May purchases at retail?

    b. On May 1, the buyer is notified that $8,000 worth of goods (retail value) is on order. What is the open-to-buy at cost for May?

48. Find the OTB balance for December when on December 10 the stock-on-hand is $265,000 and the planned sales for the balance of the month are $171,000. Markdowns are planned at $11,000, and planned inventory for December 31 is $150,000, with outstanding orders totaling $71,500.

49. A major West Coast retail store has a housewares department that operates on a planned stock turn figure of 4.0 for the six-month period August 1 to February 1. Find the number of weeks supply.

50. The annual turnover figure for a plus-size apparel department is projected at 5.0. Express the stated relationship in terms of week's supply.

51. Average weekly sales in an automotive supply department of a major national chain is stated at $3,400,000. Turnover in this classification of merchandise is 4.0 annually. Using the week's supply method, calculate the appropriate stock figure.

52. Turnover is planned at 2.5 for the six-month period February 1 through July 31. Average weekly sales for that period are $75,000. What average stock should be carried in this situation?

53. After careful analysis of economic projections from the U.S. Department of Commerce, a major department store chain set a figure of 7.5% as a realistic increase for this year's sales volume over last year. The previous year, the corporate volume was $3,700,000,000 with an overall 11.2% markdown.

    a. What would be the projected sales volume for this year?

    b. What would be the amount of dollar markdowns to be taken if the 11.2% markdown percentage was projected for this year?

54. A Dallas-based specialty chain had sales of $196,000,000 last year. It plans $216,000,000 for the coming year. What percentage increase is being projected?

55. March figures for a shoe department are:

Planned sales	$510,000
Planned markdowns	$6,000
Planned March 1 stock	$906,000
Planned April 1 stock	$630,000
Outstanding March orders	$126,000
Planned markup	52%

Calculate:

    a. The planned March purchases at retail.

    b. The March open-to-buy at cost.

56. A juniors' sportswear buyer was shown the following data:

Planned sales	$22,000
BOM stock June	$44,000
BOM stock July	$40,000
Planned June markdown	$1,000

Find:

    a. The OTB at retail, if "on order" for June delivery is $16,000 at retail.

    b. The OTB at cost, if the planned markup is 56%.

57. Note the following figures:

Planned sales	$85,000
Planned markdowns	$1,000
Planned BOM stock	$151,000
Planned EOM stock	$105,000
Merchandise on order	$21,000
Planned markup	51%

Determine:

    a. The original planned purchases at cost.

    b. The OTB at retail.

58. What is the OTB for a coat department with planned purchases of $56,000 and an "on order" of $19,000?

59. The stock-sales ratio in the men's shirt department has been set at 3.4 for June. Sales are planned at $34,500. What is the BOM stock for June?

60. Determine the BOM stock-sales ratio when the planned sales for April are $56,000 and the retail value of stock-on-hand for April 1 is $84,000.

61. The shoe department planned the following figures for October:

Planned sales	$46,000
Planned markdowns	$6,500
Planned September EOM stock	$68,000
Planned October EOM stock	$54,000
Planned markup	48%

a. Find the planned purchases for October at retail and at cost.

b. On October 1, the buyer calculates that $16,000 worth of merchandise at retail is on order. What is the OTB at cost for October?

62. A boutique had net sales of $760,000 for a six-month period ending July 31. The monthly retail inventories were:

Dates	Stock-on-hand
Feb. 1	$78,000
March 1	130,000
April 1	217,600
May 1	306,600
June 1	197,840
July 1	132,880
July 31	118,700
	$1,181,620

a. Find the turnover for the six-month period.

b. Calculate the stock-sales ratio for May, if sales for the month were $146,000.

63. An infants' wear buyer takes a physical inventory of stock every three months. Last year, the stock counts showed the following inventory valuations:

Dates	Stock-on-hand
January 3	$16,390
April 2	18,412
July 1	14,473
October 2	19,670
December 31	15,880
	$84,825

What was the department's average stock for last year?

64. In a juniors' dress department, planned sales for the six-month period February through July were $250,000. The monthly inventories at retail for this period were:

Dates	Stock-on-hand
February 1	$90,000
March 1	87,000
April 1	92,000
May 1	90,000
June 1	84,000
July 1	79,000
July 31	62,000
	$584,000

a. What is the planned average stock for the period?

b. What is the planned annual turnover based on the performance of this six-month period?

c. If planned sales in April were $23,000, what is the stock-sales ratio for April?

65. For the Fall season, a boutique with a 3.0 turnover has planned the following sales:

August	$100,700	November	$116,900
September	$113,500	December	$118,200
October	$150,000	January	$100,000

Using the basic stock method, find the BOM stock figures for each month.

66. Consider the following figures:

	BOM stocks	Net sales
January	$50,000	$15,000
February	46,000	18,000
March	46,000	20,000
April	46,000	14,000
May	40,000	12,000
June	40,000	16,000
July	45,000	14,000
August	45,000	14,000
September	50,000	18,000
October	60,000	18,000
November	80,000	38,000
December	44,000	16,000
January (following year)	46,000	
	$638,000	$213,000

Find:

    a. The yearly average stock figure.

    b. The turnover for the year.

    c. The turnover for September.

    d. The stock-sales ratio for June.

67. The statistical division provides an accessories buyer with the following computerized information:

Planned sales for balance of month	$162,000
Planned markdowns for balance of month	$4,000
Planned EOM stock	$200,000
Merchandise on order this month	$64,000
Stock figure this date	$214,000

Determine the OTB for the balance of the month.

68. Research and Discussion: Describe how a buyer may use turnover and stock-sales ratio figures in planning a future departmental operation.

69. Research and Discussion: Are turnover and stock-sales ratio related? Explain.

70. Research and Discussion: Does an increased turnover rate always mean that the department is functioning more effectively and profitably? Explain.

71. When the buyer for the juniors' dress department started to develop the merchandise plan for the Spring season, the following data was received. It represents the department's performance last year. Preparing to plan the goals of the department for this year, the buyer refers to the factors of the plan located on the six-month merchandising plan in Figure 43.

  a. What judgmental decision must be made first? Why?

  b. What figures can be calculated from the incomplete information in the plan to either improve or repeat last year's results?

Figure 43. Six-Month Merchandising Plan

Department Name _____   Department No. _____

<table>
<tr><td rowspan="7" colspan="2">

SIX-MONTH MERCHANDISING PLAN</td><td></td><td colspan="2">**PLAN** (This Year)</td><td colspan="2">**ACTUAL** (Last Year)</td></tr>
<tr><td>Workroom Cost</td><td colspan="2"></td><td colspan="2"></td></tr>
<tr><td>Cash Discount %</td><td colspan="2"></td><td colspan="2"></td></tr>
<tr><td>Season Stock Turnover</td><td colspan="2"></td><td colspan="2"></td></tr>
<tr><td>Shortage %</td><td colspan="2"></td><td colspan="2"></td></tr>
<tr><td>Average Stock</td><td colspan="2"></td><td colspan="2"></td></tr>
<tr><td>Markdown %</td><td colspan="2"></td><td colspan="2"></td></tr>
</table>

<table>
<tr><td colspan="2">**SPRING 2013**</td><td>**FEB.**</td><td>**MAR.**</td><td>**APR.**</td><td>**MAY**</td><td>**JUNE**</td><td>**JULY**</td><td>**SEASON TOTAL**</td></tr>
<tr><td rowspan="5">**SALES $**</td><td>Last Year</td><td>140,000</td><td>160,000</td><td>200,000</td><td>175,000</td><td>165,000</td><td>160,000</td><td>$1,000,000</td></tr>
<tr><td>Plan</td><td></td><td></td><td></td><td></td><td></td><td></td><td></td></tr>
<tr><td>Percent of Increase</td><td></td><td></td><td></td><td></td><td></td><td></td><td></td></tr>
<tr><td>Revised</td><td></td><td></td><td></td><td></td><td></td><td></td><td></td></tr>
<tr><td>Actual</td><td></td><td></td><td></td><td></td><td></td><td></td><td></td></tr>
<tr><td rowspan="4">**RETAIL STOCK (BOM) $**</td><td>Last Year</td><td>325,000</td><td>475,000</td><td>550,000</td><td>500,000</td><td>375,000</td><td>275,000</td><td></td></tr>
<tr><td>Plan</td><td></td><td></td><td></td><td></td><td></td><td></td><td></td></tr>
<tr><td>Revised</td><td></td><td></td><td></td><td></td><td></td><td></td><td></td></tr>
<tr><td>Actual</td><td></td><td></td><td></td><td></td><td></td><td></td><td></td></tr>
<tr><td rowspan="5">**MARKDOWNS $**</td><td>Last Year</td><td>20,000</td><td>20,000</td><td>30,000</td><td>35,000</td><td>45,000</td><td>50,000</td><td>200,000</td></tr>
<tr><td>Plan (dollars)</td><td></td><td></td><td></td><td></td><td></td><td></td><td></td></tr>
<tr><td>Plan (percent)</td><td></td><td></td><td></td><td></td><td></td><td></td><td></td></tr>
<tr><td>Revised</td><td></td><td></td><td></td><td></td><td></td><td></td><td></td></tr>
<tr><td>Actual</td><td></td><td></td><td></td><td></td><td></td><td></td><td></td></tr>
<tr><td rowspan="4">**RETAIL PURCHASES**</td><td>Last Year</td><td>310,000</td><td>255,000</td><td>180,000</td><td>85,000</td><td>110,000</td><td>235,000</td><td></td></tr>
<tr><td>Plan</td><td></td><td></td><td></td><td></td><td></td><td></td><td></td></tr>
<tr><td>Revised</td><td></td><td></td><td></td><td></td><td></td><td></td><td></td></tr>
<tr><td>Actual</td><td></td><td></td><td></td><td></td><td></td><td></td><td></td></tr>
<tr><td rowspan="4">**PERCENT OF INITIAL MARKON**</td><td>Last Year</td><td>50.4</td><td>49.8</td><td>50.8</td><td>51.3</td><td>48.0</td><td>50.8</td><td></td></tr>
<tr><td>Plan</td><td></td><td></td><td></td><td></td><td></td><td></td><td></td></tr>
<tr><td>Revised</td><td></td><td></td><td></td><td></td><td></td><td></td><td></td></tr>
<tr><td>Actual</td><td></td><td></td><td></td><td></td><td></td><td></td><td></td></tr>
<tr><td rowspan="4">**ENDING STOCK JULY 31**</td><td>Last Year</td><td>300,000</td><td></td><td></td><td></td><td></td><td></td><td></td></tr>
<tr><td>Plan</td><td></td><td></td><td></td><td></td><td></td><td></td><td></td></tr>
<tr><td>Revised</td><td></td><td></td><td></td><td></td><td></td><td></td><td></td></tr>
<tr><td>Actual</td><td></td><td></td><td></td><td></td><td></td><td></td><td></td></tr>
</table>

Comments

Merchandise Manager _____   Buyer _____

Controller _____

72. Under the present conditions, the buyer plans a 7% sales increase because it is realistic. On the basis of this planned sales increase, project, for the forthcoming Spring season only, the monthly sales, stocks, markdowns, and retail purchases on the six-month merchandising plan provided in Figure 44. Attach a separate sheet showing all calculations.

    a. Justify why a particular month was changed in the monthly sales distribution.

    b. State the method of stock planning used in calculating the BOM stocks. The ending stock is $300,000, which is the same as last year.

    c. Justify a change, if any, in monthly planned dollar markdowns and/ or seasonal total percentage.

    d. Calculate the monthly planned retail purchases.

Figure 44. Six-Month Merchandising Plan

Department Name _____ Department No. _____

SIX-MONTH MERCHANDISING PLAN		PLAN (This Year)	ACTUAL (Last Year)
	Workroom Cost		
	Cash Discount %		
	Season Stock Turnover	2.0	
	Shortage %		
	Average Stock	$530,000	
	Markdown %	5.0%	

SPRING 2013		FEB.	MAR.	APR.	MAY	JUNE	JULY	SEASON TOTAL
SALES $	Last Year							
	Plan	80,000	120,000	145,000	300,000	315,000	100,000	$1,060,000
	Percent of Increase							
	Revised							
	Actual	78,194	119,873					
RETAIL STOCK (BOM) $	Last Year							
	Plan	350,000	550,000	650,000	700,000	650,000	450,000	
	Revised							
	Actual	325,312	552,100	651,325				
MARKDOWNS $	Last Year							
	Plan (dollars)	3,000	5,000	5,000	8,000	16,000	16,000	53,000
	Plan (percent)							
	Revised							
	Actual	3,000	5,000					
RETAIL PURCHASES	Last Year							
	Plan							
	Revised							
	Actual							
	Outstanding Orders				$160,000	50,000		
ENDING STOCK JULY 31	Last Year							
	Plan	360,000						
	Revised							
	Actual							

Comments

Merchandise Manager _____ Buyer _____

Controller _____

CASE STUDY 1
OPEN-TO-BUY

It is the beginning of the third week in April. Mr. Johnston, the handbag buyer for a women's specialty store in California, studies the position of this department as he approaches the second quarter of the Spring season.

Before Mr. Johnston analyzes the actual results of the season-to-date performances, he examines the classification reports for the department to ascertain if the composition of his stock is in balance with the sales records. He finds that the leather handbag category—in which the price lines are highest—has fewer unit sales, which result in a high dollar inventory. The "fashion" fabrication of the season—sisal and straw, combined with new styling—has caused an out-of-proportion increase in the unit sales of this group when compared to the sales of previous years. This trend has surpassed even Mr. Johnston's originally high expectations of this fashion. Additionally, the weather, which has turned unusually warm for this time of year, has been a catalyst to this vigorous selling in the Spring-Summer look. On the six-month merchandise plan, the season-to-date figures for the department are shown in Figure 44.

As Mr. Johnston examines these figures, he considers the following facts:

- The February and March sales are almost on target for the plan, but the post-Easter sales sagged. (Mr. Johnston estimates that there will be a 10% decrease in sales from the plan during the first quarter because the sales before Easter were slightly off and have been decreasing since that time.) A 5% increase is required over planned sales for the second quarter to achieve, if not surpass, the total seasonal planning goals in relation to sales, markdowns, and turnover.

- Unless immediate action is taken, the lowered actual sales to date will result in a higher than planned May 1 inventory figure.

- Both the dollar amount in the inventory and the outstanding orders in the straw category are entirely too low to generate possible sales increases because the demand for this merchandise has exploded. (This requires instant correction.)

- The sales at the beginning of the third week for the month are $60,000, and the inventory figure is $795,000.

To accomplish the second-quarter objectives (i.e., to attain the originally planned figures regarding sales, markdowns, and turnover), what actions must Mr. Johnston take? What are the alternatives, if any? What adjustments do you recommend? Justify your suggestions mathematically.

CASE STUDY 2
PLANNING FOR EFFECTIVE BUYING

You were recently promoted to the position of buyer for the hosiery department in a large specialty store. Your market is about to open, and in anticipation of this you must be prepared with certain dollar goals for the coming season.

It is the policy of your store that the buyer be responsible for the formulation of the departmental dollar six-month plan. You know that if this plan is to be of value, the figures established must be ones that you can actually achieve. You also know that despite your inexperience you will have to be prepared to explain and justify the plans and strategies you will use as guidelines when merchandising for the period under consideration.

Where shall you begin? You know a sound basis for future planning is to analyze the past results of your "new" department. So before you develop your plan for Fall, you decide to review the figures below, which show the performance achieved by the hosiery department for Fall of last year.

Month	BOM stock	Sales	Markdowns
August	$455,500	$75,000	$2,000
September	$850,000	$205,000	$2,000
October	$550,000	$135,000	$7,500
November	$600,500	$135,000	$7,500
December	$850,000	$230,000	$8,300
January	$440,000	$120,000	$24,000
February	$454,000		
Total	$900,000		$51,300
Turnover for period	1.5		
Markdown %	5.7%		

Your Divisional Merchandise Manager (DMM) informed you that though the sales increases for the Fall season of last year had been greater than planned, there were other areas in the overall operation that needed improvement.

You are aware of the following facts: the nationwide economy is moving briskly; top management has planned on an overall storewide sales increase of 7%; legwear has had a strong surge of sales for the first six-month period (sales were planned with a 15% increase but actually were ahead 23% over the year before); fashion influences of long, leggy looks with slits in dresses and skirts continue as important apparel looks; the rising trend for legwear in the Spring season, after four dismal years, also saw the revival of body suits, which has stabilized to a fair contribution of total sales. The textured hosiery introduced in the spring retailing at 20% higher retail prices is expected to create big business. . . .

Your DMM (divisional merchandise manager) requested a meeting with you to discuss your projected goals for the six months before they are finalized. You feel the following issues should be addressed:

- How should the LY figures be used by you in preparation for your plan for the Fall season of this year?

- It would seem as if the sales trend in your department lends itself to a further increase of sales. Why must you estimate as accurately as possible (neither too high nor too low) the amount of sales you can generate during this season?

- As the buyer, what three strategies can you plan in order to achieve the sales gain you propose?

- Having set your projected sales figures, you now want to adjust your stocks to the proper size in order to achieve the planned monthly sales figures. Your DMM gave you August 1 stock figures of $460,000 and February 1 stock figures of $450,000. He told you to work out the BOM stock figures for each of the other months in your six-month plan. There are three approaches to planning the amount of stock necessary for projected sales figures. Which will you choose? Why?

- After you have determined all BOM stock figures for the entire period, what measurement will tell you how well you balanced your stock and sales for the entire period?

- In addition to planning sales and stocks, the markdown amounts are to be included. The typical markdown percentage in the industry for a hosiery department is 8%. The amount taken by your predecessor was 5.7%. In planning the amount of reductions for the entire period, how will you plan the markdowns on your current plan? In dollars? In percentages? Higher? Lower?

- Because your predecessor only achieved a turnover of 1.5, and the typical turnover in the industry for your department is 3.7, you realize that this was one of the "areas that needs improvement." How can you show an increased turnover on the dollar plan you are going to submit at present?

It is September 15. The following table shows the figures of your six-month plan. Should you make any revisions in your plan in light of the fact that your department for August had a 10% decrease in planned sales? If so, why and what revision(s) would you make? If not, why not?

	Aug	Sept	Oct	Nov	Dec	Jan	Seasonal total
Sales	$100.00	$235.00	$165.00	$165.00	$265.00	$150.00	$1,080.00
LY	$175.00	$205.00	$135.00	$135.00	$130.00	$120.00	$900.00
Plan	$100.00	$235.00	$165.00	$165.00	$265.00	$150.00	$1,080.00
Actual	$90.00						
Revised							
BOM stock	$460.00	$840.00	$525.00	$655.00	$860.00	$410.00	
LY	$455.50	$850.00	$550.00	$600.50	$850.00	$440.00	
Plan	$460.00	$840.00	$525.00	$655.00	$860.00	$410.00	
Actual							
Revised							
Outstanding orders					$200.00	$250.00	$450.00

From this information, calculate the OTB figure for the month of November. What could cause the OTB figure for September to change after it is established? Can you convert an overbought condition to an OTB position? If so, how? If not, why?

During the course of the six-month period, as you review your actual sales performance, should the actual results be compared to last year's sales or the planned sales figures, or both, in order to have a meaningful comparison? Which? Why?

CASE STUDY 3
DOLLAR PLANNING AND CONTROL

The sales performance of the Luggage Department in a sporting goods store last Fall was:

August $80,000   November $140,000

September $90,000   December $160,000

October $100,000   January $120,000

Total seasonal sales = $690,000

As the six-month merchandising plan for this department was being formulated for this Fall season, the following decisions were made:

1. An 8% sales increase could be attained this year with the introduction and addition of a new classification of carry-on travel luggage that is well priced and of exceptional value.

2. The planned BOM stock-sales ratio for each month this year would be the same as last year—i.e., August 3.3, September 3.1, October 2.9, November 2.5, December 2.2, January 2.6—with an ending retail inventory for the period of $288,000.

3. The planned total reductions for last year were 11.6% and were distributed with 7% in August, 9% in September, 18% in October, 12% in November, 26% in December, and 28% in January.

Compute:

- The planned monthly retail receipts (purchases) for each month.

- The planned average stock and the planned stock turnover.

MERCHANDISING FOR A PROFIT

UNIT 6

"The purpose of a business is to create a customer."

PETER DRUCKER

OBJECTIVES

- Recognition of the importance of profit calculations in merchandising decisions.

- Identification of components of a profit and loss statement.

- Completion of a profit and loss statement.

- Identification of types of business expenses and their impact on profit.

- Utilization of profit calculations to:

    - Make comparisons between departments and/or stores.

    - Detect trends.

    - Make changes in merchandising strategy to achieve an increase in profits.

KEY TERMS

alteration and
workroom costs

billed cost

cash discounts

closing inventory

contribution

controllable expenses

cost

cost of goods sold

customer returns
and allowances

direct expenses

final profit and
loss statement

gross margin

gross sales

indirect expenses

inward freight

net loss

net profit

net sales

opening inventory

operating expenses

operating income

profit and loss
statement

retail

sales volume

skeletal profit and
loss statement

total merchandise
handled

KEY CONCEPT FORMULAS

Cost of goods sold

$$\text{Total cost of goods sold} = \text{Billed cost} + \text{Inward freight} + \text{Workroom costs} - \text{Cash discount}$$

$$\$ \text{ Cost of goods sold} = \text{Cost of goods sold \%} \times \text{Net sales}$$

$$\text{Cost of goods sold \%} = \frac{\$ \text{ Cost of goods sold}}{\text{Net sales}} \times 100$$

Gross margin

$$\text{Gross margin} = \text{Net sales} - \text{Total cost of goods sold}$$

$$\$ \text{ Gross margin} = \text{Gross margin \%} \times \text{Net sales}$$

$$\text{Gross margin \%} = \frac{\$ \text{ Gross margin}}{\text{Net sales}} \times 100$$

Net profit

$$\text{Net profit} = \text{Net sales} - \text{Cost of goods sold} - \text{Operating expenses}$$

$$\text{Net operating profit or net profit} = \text{Gross margin} - \text{All operating expenses}$$

$$\$ \text{ Net profit} = \text{Net profit \%} \times \text{Net sales}$$

$$\text{Net profit \%} = \frac{\text{Net profit in dollars}}{\text{Net sales}} \times 100$$

Net sales

$$\text{Net sales} = \text{Gross sales} - \text{Customer returns and allowances}$$

Operating expenses

$$\text{Operating expenses} = \text{Direct expenses} + \text{Indirect expenses}$$

$$\$ \text{ Operating expenses} = \text{Operating expenses \%} \times \text{Net sales}$$

$$\text{Operating expenses \%} = \frac{\text{Direct and indirect expenses in dollars}}{\text{Net sales}} \times 100$$

UNIT VI.I
PROFIT COMPONENTS

Why is the study of the calculation of profit necessary? An individual involved in retailing will inevitably have many opportunities to become involved with the concept of profit. An employee of a private organization should be aware of corporate profits. For example, many companies offer a profit-sharing plan, which is now a frequent form of incentive in many industries. An individual may be a possible investor of personal funds in publicly owned corporations. To an employee of a publicly owned corporation, profit is a significant goal in the sale of shares. Since the beginning of the twentieth century, the U.S. government has requested that all entrepreneurs declare the profits or losses of all business ventures. The profits are taxed. Competent accounting methods require a statement of net profit before and after taxes.

Because one of the major responsibilities of a merchandiser in retailing is to attain a profit for the department,[1] store, or retail business being supervised, it is logical to recognize that this can only be achieved by knowing the elements of profit, their calculation, and their importance.

USE OF PROFIT CALCULATIONS

The merchandising executive uses the calculation of profits to:

1. Exchange data and compare stores to determine relative strengths and weaknesses.

2. Indicate the direction of the business and whether it is prosperous, struggling for survival, or bankrupt.

3. Provide a statement for analysis so that knowledgeable changes in management or policy can be made.

4. Improve the profit margin by using this analysis.

This unit examines the basic profit elements, defines them, shows their relationships to one another in profit and loss statements, and describes methods practiced to manipulate these elements to improve profits.

---

1. Department (Merchandise Department): A grouping of related merchandise for which separate expense and merchandising records are kept for the purpose of determining the profit of this grouping. It is not merely a physical segregation.

THE MAJOR COMPONENTS OF
A PROFIT AND LOSS STATEMENT

Net Sales

Net sales (**operating income** or **sales volume**) are calculated from a gross sales figure adjusted by customer returns and allowances to determine how much merchandise has stayed sold

Net sales = Gross sales − Customer returns and allowances

Cost of Goods Sold

Cost of goods sold is the total amount paid for the merchandise sold, taking into consideration the necessary adjustments.

$$\text{Total cost of goods sold} = \text{Billed cost} + \text{Inward freight} + \text{Workroom costs} - \text{Cash discount}$$

Gross Margin

Gross margin (frequently called gross profit) is the amount that results when the total cost of goods sold is subtracted from the net sales. This figure measures the performance of the buyer. It must be large enough to cover expenses and allow a profit.

Gross margin = Net sales − Total cost of goods sold

Operating Expenses

Because the expenses of operating a business determine whether or not a net profit is achieved, the control and management of **operating expenses** are of major concern. For the purpose of analysis, the expenses incurred by the retailer (e.g., maintenance of store space, salaries, etc.) are classified to measure the performance of the designated function or activity. There are various approaches to classifying these items and, although there are many different kinds of expenses, each can be easily identified as just that. However, there is variation in the format used to record them. Traditionally, operating expenses fall into two major categories and are charged to a merchandise department to determine its net profit. These major categories are direct and indirect expenses.

Direct Expenses

Direct expenses exist only within a given department and cease if that department is discontinued. These might include salespeople's and buyers' salaries, buyers' traveling expenses, advertising, selling supplies, delivery to customers, and selling space. For the purpose of expense analysis in retailing, the amount of floor space occupied that generates a given department's sales volume is allotted by the square foot and charged directly to that department, even though there is no cash outlay. Each expense and/or the total direct expenses are expressed as a percentage of net sales. For example, if the net sales of a department are $100,000 and $3,500 is spent on advertising, the percentage of advertising expenses would be $3,500 ÷ $100,000, or 3.5%.

Indirect Expenses

Indirect expenses are store expenses that will continue to exist even if the particular department is discontinued. These might include store maintenance, insurance, security, depreciation of equipment, and salaries of senior executives. Many indirect expenses are distributed among individual departments on the basis of their sales volume (e.g., if a department contributes 1.5% to the store's total sales, the indirect expenses charged to this department are 1.5%).

Operating expenses = Direct expenses + Indirect expenses

PROBLEM

A children's department has net sales of $300,000, and indirect expenses are 10% of net sales. Direct expenses are:

- Selling salaries   = $24,000
- Advertising expenses   = $6,000
- Buying salaries   = $12,000
- Other direct expenses = $18,000

Find the total operating expenses of the department in dollars and as a percentage.

SOLUTION

Indirect expenses (10% × $300,000) = $30,000

Direct expenses:

Selling salaries	=	24,000
Advertising	=	6,000
Buying salaries	=	12,000
Other	=	18,000

Total dollar operating expenses   = $90,000

Operating expense %   = $\dfrac{\$90,000 \text{ Operating expenses}}{\$300,000 \text{ Net sales}} \times 100$

Operating expense %   =   30%

Controllable and Noncontrollable Expenses

There are additional expenses that further complicate expense assignments. Many, but not all, direct expenses are **controllable expenses**. For example, the rent for Branch Store Y is directly related to this store, but it is not under the control of the present store manager because this expense was previously negotiated. Utilities are another example of a direct expense to a store, but an indirect expense to a particular department. The rates are not controllable, but the utilization is.

Because retailers do not always agree on the handling of expenses, some firms use the contribution technique to evaluate the performance of a buyer or store manager. **Contribution**, also known as **controllable margin**, includes those expenses that are direct, controllable, or a combination of direct and controllable (e.g., selling salaries). Contribution is the amount the department contributes to indirect expenses and profit, as seen in Figure 45.

In learning situations, it is more important to identify expense items and to understand the control, management, and relevancy to profit of those expenses than to make the accounting decision as to which expense is direct, indirect, controllable, or noncontrollable. To eliminate the confusion of how to classify and charge a particular expense item, in this text, expenses are listed individually or are referred to simply as operating expenses.

Figure 45. Contribution Operating Statement

		Dollars	Percentages	
Net Sales		$500,000	100.0%	
(minus) **Cost of Merchandise Sold**		− $266,000	− 53.2%	
		$234,000	46.8%	
(minus) **Direct Expenses**				
Payroll	$73,000			
Advertising	$13,000			
Supplies	$7,000			
Travel	$5,000			
Other	$12,000			
		− $110,000	− 22.0%	$\left(\dfrac{\$110,000}{\$500,000}\right)$
Contribution		$124,000	24.8%	$\left(\dfrac{\$124,000}{\$500,000}\right)$
(minus) **Indirect Expenses**		− $106,500	− 21.3%	$\left(\dfrac{\$106,500}{\$500,000}\right)$
Operating Profit		$17,500	3.5%	

Net Operating Profit (or Net Profit or Loss)

The difference between the gross margin and operating expenses is **net profit** or **loss**, which is calculated by subtracting operating expenses from gross margin. To properly compare profits among retailers, it is necessary to know how the expenses are treated. In accounting there are acceptable variations in how expenses are recorded.

Net operating profit, or net profit, is the profit from the merchandising operation. This is a goal figure for the merchandising executive. "Net operating income" when added to or subtracted from net operating profit results in net profit before taxes.

The following example shows the relationships among the fundamental factors on which the amount of profit depends. For comparison, these factors are expressed in percentages as well as in dollars. The net sales figure is the basis for determining profit computations and so it is considered 100%. The other factors involved are shown and stated as a percentage of net sales.

EXAMPLE

		Dollars		Percentages	
Net sales (operating income)	=	$10,000		100%	
− Cost of merchandise sold	=	− 5,500	=	− 55%	($5,500 ÷ $10,000)
= Gross margin	=	$4,500	=	45%	($4,500 ÷ $10,000)
− Operating expenses	=	− 4,300	=	− 43%	($4,300 ÷ $10,000)
= **Net profit**	=	$200	=	2%	($200 ÷ $10,000)

Goals are set for a desired gross margin or net profit figure, but it must be understood that those figures are the result of how well merchandise is priced, how well it is bought, and how controlled the expenses are in the process.

CONCEPT

Net operating profit or net profit = Gross margin − All operating expenses

PROBLEM

The activewear department in a specialty store has a gross margin of $750,000, and the operating expenses amount to $472,500. Calculate the net operating profit.

SOLUTION

Gross margin	=	$750,000
− Operating expenses		− 472,500
Net operating profit	=	$277,500

After these topics have been analyzed, the meanings of each understood, the calculations completed, the existing interrelationships discerned, and the methods to manipulate these elements to improve profits practiced, it is possible to determine analytically whether an organization is operating at a profit or loss.

Profit Components Practice Problems

1. Analyze the expense section of the following statement:

JOHNSTON CANDY COMPANY

Operating expenses	Last year	This year	Plan
Advertising	$28,500	$24,300	$27,700
Sales salaries	$74,000	$75,100	$75,300
Misc. selling costs	$8,300	$8,300	$8,500
Total	$110,800	$107,700	$111,500
Net sales	$900,000	$1,140,000	$980,000

   a. What is the percentage of advertising expenses for each year?

   b. What is the percentage of sales salary expenses for each year?

   c. What is the percentage of miscellaneous selling costs for each year?

   d. What is the yearly percentage of total operating expenses shown?

   e. What is the trend of operating expenses?

   f. What is the trend of net sales?

2. Determine the net profit or loss in dollars and as a percentage for a small leather goods department if:

    Net sales   = $278,000
    Cost of merchandise   = $191,600
    Operating expenses   = $78,300

3. Calculate the net profit or loss in dollars and as a percentage if:

    Net sales   = $30,000
    Cost of merchandise   =   52%
    Operating expenses   =   48%

4. A drugstore has net sales of $490,000, with the cost of merchandise sold at $240,000. If the buyer must achieve a 5% net profit, calculate the allowable expenses in dollars and as a percentage.

5. The swimwear department of the ABC Department Store had the following records:

    Net sales   = $132,000
    Cost of merchandise   = $118,000
    Operating expenses   = $11,500

    What is the net profit or loss?

6. The Rappapart Ribbon Company had the following records:

Gross sales	=	$110,000
Customer returns and allowances	=	$10,000
Cost of merchandise	=	$80,000
Operating expenses	=	$35,000

What is the net profit or loss?

UNIT VI.II
PROFIT AND LOSS STATEMENTS

Businesses must keep accurate records of sales income, merchandise costs, and operating expenses to calculate profit. In retailing, one of the most important financial records is the **profit and loss statement**. Income and expenses are summarized in the form known in retailing as a profit and loss statement (for other types of organizations, this statement is frequently called an **income statement**). This statement prepared periodically by the department, store, or organization summarizes the basic merchandising factors that affect profit results, showing the difference between income and expenses. Generally, the accounting department keeps a continuous record of sales income and expenses. At set intervals, this statement is analyzed to determine whether these transactions have resulted in a profit or loss. (The interval might be a year, three months, or one month.) If income exceeds expenses, the result is profit. If expenses exceed income, the result is a loss. It is a summary of the business transactions during a given period of time expressed in terms of making or losing money. It is used to measure profitability as it evaluates the results of current performance and allows for comparison of present and possible future trends. In the calculation of a profit and loss statement, there is emphasis on an exact and rigid order of the factors included. Although adding and subtracting the appropriate figures can determine a correct profit result, the standard arrangement provides an analytical picture that allows a determination of the store's strengths and weaknesses and facilities comparisons with other counterparts. The buyer must critically examine these figures and then make a determination of causes from these results. A profit and loss statement should not be confused with a **balance sheet**, which shows the assets, liabilities, and net worth of a business.

Because this is a retailing text, the profit and loss statement will not be analyzed as a bookkeeping procedure, but in terms of how a merchant can use the data it contains to improve a merchandising operation. It is a fundamental merchandising concept that one of a buyer's chief responsibilities is to ensure that a store or department earns a profit on the merchandise sold specifically during the accounting period under consideration.

Profit and loss statements can show the performance of a department, division, branch, or the entire organization. The basic format of a profit and loss statement is as follows:

Net sales

– Cost of goods sold

= Gross margin

– Operating expenses

= Net profit or loss

SKELETAL PROFIT AND LOSS STATEMENTS

A **skeletal profit and loss statement** does not spell out all transactions in detail, but it is a quick method to determine, at any particular time, a given department's profit or loss. It contains the five major components of a profit and loss statement and is expressed in both dollars and as a percentage.

EXAMPLE

	Net sales	=		$300,000	100%
−	Cost of goods sold	=	−	180,000	60%
=	Gross margin	=		$120,000	40%
−	Operating expenses	=	−	105,000	35%
=	**Net profit**	=		15,000	5%

The value of a profit and loss statement is that it can be used to compare previous statements or to compare a company's figures with industry-wide figures to help improve profit or adjust any of the other factors mentioned in the example. Therefore, it is vital to think in terms of percentages as well as dollar amounts. For example, a buyer's statement that a net profit of $2,869 was earned during a given business period has no real meaning unless the dollar amount for each of the other contributing factors is also stated. The profit figure could be phenomenally high or dismally low by industry standards, depending on the dollar net sales volume of the department. Unless the figures for all other factors are available, it is impossible to determine which departmental operations excelled or faltered. The only meaningful way to compare departmental performances is to compare the respective results expressed as a percentage of the **net sales volume**. From this information, the deduction can be made that profit will vary upward or downward as one or more of the three major factors (i.e., net sales, cost of goods sold, or operating expenses) change.

CONCEPT

$$\text{Cost of goods sold \%} = \frac{\$ \text{ Cost of goods sold}}{\text{Net sales}} \times 100$$

$$\text{Gross margin \%} = \frac{\$ \text{ Gross margin}}{\text{Net sales}} \times 100$$

$$\text{Operating expenses \%} = \frac{\text{Direct and indirect expenses in dollars}}{\text{Net sales}} \times 100$$

$$\text{Net profit \%} = \frac{\text{Net profit in dollars}}{\text{Net sales}} \times 100$$

The juniors' sportswear department in Store A had net sales of $160,000; the cost of goods sold was $88,000, and operating expenses were $64,000. The juniors' sportswear department in Store B, for the same business period, had net sales of $260,000; the cost of goods sold was $135,200, and operating expenses were $109,200. Which store earned a higher net profit percentage?

SOLUTION

	Store A		Store B	
Net sales	$160,000	100%	$260,000	100%
− Cost of goods sold	− 88,000	− 55%	−135,200	− 52%
Gross margin	$72,000	45%	$124,800	48%
− Operating expenses	− 64,000	− 40%	−109,200	− 42%
Net profit	$8,000	5%	$15,600	6%

As a basis for comparison, the percentage figures give the clearest picture. Upon examination of this skeletal profit and loss statement, the reader can see that the junior sportswear department in Store A spent 55 cents of every dollar of sales on the cost of merchandise sold, while Store B spent 52 cents. Respectively, Store A spent 40 cents and Store B spent 42 cents of every dollar of sales on operating expenses. Gross margin, net profit, and individual transactions can be more accurately compared when these figures are recorded in a complete profit and loss statement. Also, all other figures in the skeletal profit and loss statement are then expressed as a part or a percentage of net sales. Conversely, when the respective results for cost of goods sold, gross margin, operating expenses, or net profit are expressed as a percentage of net sales, the dollar amounts of each factor can be determined.

CONCEPT

$ Cost of goods sold = Cost of goods sold % × Net sales

$ Gross margin = Gross margin % × Net sales

$ Operating expenses = Operating expenses % × Net sales

$ Net profit = Net profit % × Net sales

PROBLEM

The junior sportswear department in Store A had net sales of $160,000. The cost of goods sold was 55%; gross margin was 45%; operating expenses were 40%; and net profit was 5%. What were the dollar amounts of each?

Net sales	=	$160,000		
− Cost of goods sold	=	− 88,000	($160,000 × 55%)	
Gross margin	=	$72,000	($160,000 × 45%)	
− Operating expenses	=	− 64,000	($160,000 × 40%)	
Net profit	=	$8,000	($160,000 × 5%)	

FINAL PROFIT AND LOSS STATEMENTS

A **final profit and loss statement** shows the basic profit factors developed in detail, so that every transaction is clearly seen. The skeleton format discussed earlier shows the basic factors—that is, sales and cost of goods and expenses—and provides a quick method of monitoring profit or loss, but it is also necessary to have more detailed information on these basic factors to detect weaknesses that need strengthening or to illuminate strengths that bear repetition.

Thus, a final profit and loss statement includes additional information pertaining to stock levels. Bearing in mind that profit occurs only when the merchandise sold remains sold, the retailer must be able, from an accounting viewpoint, to determine the value of inventory or merchandise sold. Generally, retailers use an accounting method known as the retail method of inventory (see Unit IV), in which the retail stock figure at the end of the accounting period provides the basis for determining the cost value of stock. An **opening inventory** figure refers to the retail value of the merchandise in stock at the beginning of the accounting period. It is established by a physical count of the merchandise in stock at current retail prices; this figure is then converted to a cost amount. The **closing inventory** figure is the amount of merchandise in stock at the end of the period under consideration. The opening inventory, at cost, is added to the cost of new net purchases and transportation charges (**inward freight**) to determine an amount known as **total merchandise handled**. Total merchandise handled is the sum of merchandise at cost available for sale. To determine the cost of only the merchandise that was sold, the final profit calculation requires a total merchandise handled amount. It can be determined at **cost** or at **retail**. The gross cost of goods sold can be calculated when the closing inventory at cost is subtracted from the total merchandise handled amount.

Opening inventory at cost		$100,000	
+ Billed costs on new purchases		+ 500,000	
+ Inward freight		+ 1,000	
Total merchandise handled at cost	=	$601,000	
− Closing inventory at cost		− 159,000	
Gross cost of goods sold	=	$442,000	

With this information, it is now possible to determine the net cost of goods sold by the other adjustments (e.g., cash discounts). For a better understanding of the detailed final profit and loss statement shown on page 305, refer to the definitions that accompany Figure 46.

Figure 46 illustrates a final profit and loss statement, which is an amplification of the skeletal profit and loss statement. The basic profit factors (that is, sales, cost of goods sold, and expenses) are developed in detail so that each transaction is clearly seen. To analyze the results, each factor must be presented in a standard accounting arrangement. The final profit and loss statement is the only way to make a valid comparison among departments or stores because the detailed information supplied by this statement is necessary to compute the cost of goods actually sold.

- **INCOME FROM SALES** is divided into such categories as:

  - **Gross sales** ($450,000): The retail value of total initial sales.

  - **Customer returns and allowances** ($25,000): The total value of cancellation of sales by customer credit, refund, or partial rebate.

  - **Net sales figure** ($425,000): The figure derived by subtracting customer returns and allowances from the gross sales of a period. It is the dollar value of sales that "stay sold."

- **COST OF MERCHANDISE SOLD** is divided into such categories as:

  - **Opening inventory at retail** ($100,000): The amount of merchandise at the beginning of a period, counted and recorded at the current selling price.

  - **Opening inventory at cost** ($52,000): The figure derived from the retail figure by applying a markup percentage to the total merchandise handled.

  - **New net purchases** ($258,000): The **billed cost** of merchandise purchased. It is the gross purchases minus returns and allowances to vendors.

  - **Inward transportation** ($2,000): The cost of transporting goods to the premises.

  - **Total cost of goods** ($260,000): The combination of the cost of merchandise purchased and inward transportation.

  - **Total merchandise handled at cost** ($312,000): The sum of the opening inventory ($52,000) plus the total cost of the purchases ($260,000).

  - **Closing inventory at cost** ($65,000): The figure derived from the retail inventory figure that represents the merchandise in stock at the end of an operating period.

Figure 46. Profit and Loss Statement

Profit Factors	Cost			Retail		%
Income from Sales						
Gross Sales					$450,000	
− Customer Returns & Allowances					− $25,000	
Net Sales					$425,000	100%
Cost of Merchandise Sold						
Opening Inventory		$52,000	$100,000*			
New Net Purchases	$258,000					
+ Inward Transportation	+ $2,000					
	$260,000					
+ Total Cost of Goods		$260,000				
Total Merchandise Handled at Cost		$312,000				
− Closing Inventory at Cost		− $65,000				
Gross Cost of Goods Sold		$247,000				
− Cash Discount		− $13,000				
Net Cost of Goods Sold		$234,000				
+ Alteration & Workroom Costs		+ $1,000				
Total Cost of Goods Sold		$235,000			− $235,000	55.3%
GROSS MARGIN					$190,000	44.7%
Operating Expenses						
Total Direct Expenses		$101,250				
Total Indirect Expenses		$67,500				
Total Operating Expenses					$168,750	39.7%
Net Profit					$21,250	5.0%

* $100,000 represents the opening inventory figure (determined by physical count), from which $52,000, the opening cost inventory figure, is derived by applying a markup percentage.

- **Gross cost of merchandise sold** ($247,000): The total merchandise handled at cost ($312,000) less the cost of the closing inventory ($65,000 cost).

- **Cash discounts** ($13,000): Adjustments made to the cost of goods sold from paying bills in a specified time.

- **Net cost of goods sold** ($234,000): The gross cost of merchandise sold ($247,000) minus cash discounts ($13,000).

- **Alteration and workroom costs** ($1,000): The cost of preparing goods for resale. It is another adjustment to the cost of goods sold.

- **Total cost of goods sold** ($235,000 or 55.3%): The figure that results when the gross cost of merchandise sold ($247,000) is adjusted by subtracting cash discounts ($13,000) and adding alteration and workroom costs ($1,000).

- **Gross margin** ($190,000 or 44.7%): The difference between net sales ($425,000) and total merchandise cost ($235,000). This is often called gross profit.

- **OPERATING EXPENSES** are divided into such categories as:

  - **Direct expenses** ($101,250): Expenses that come into being with a department and cease if it is discontinued.

  - **Indirect expenses** ($67,500): Expenses that continue even if a department is discontinued.

  - **Total operating expenses** ($168,750): Direct ($101,250) and indirect ($67,500) expenses combined.

- **NET (OPERATING) PROFIT** ($21,250 or 5%): The result of the relationship among sales, cost of goods, and expenses. When the gross margin is larger than the operating expenses, a net profit is achieved.

7. Note the following figures:

Net profit   2.5%

Gross margin . $7,000

Operating expenses $6,600

Find:

 a. The cost of goods in dollars.

 b. The percentage of operating expenses.

8. The net profit in an appliance department for the Spring/Summer period was $20,000, which represented 2% of net sales. Operating expenses totaled $480,000. Find:

 a. The dollar amount of gross margin.

 b. The net sales figure.

9. The linen department had net sales of $80,000. There was a 2% loss, and the gross margin was 46%. Determine the operating expenses of the department and express the result in dollars and as a percentage.

10. Calculate the percentage of operating expenses for a home furnishings department that has the following figures:

Gross sales	$476,000
Customer returns	$4,000
Advertising costs	$10,000
Salaries	$101,000
Miscellaneous expenses	$6,160
Utilities	$9,000
Insurance	$11,000
Rent	$70,000

11. Set up a skeletal statement that shows the following figures as dollars and as a percentage.

Net profit	$5,500
Gross margin	2.5%
Operating expenses	47.5%

12. Suppose that the estimated net sales for the coming year are $100,000; estimated cost of merchandise purchases is $52,000; and the total estimated operating expenses are $43,000. The buyer's goal is a net profit of 5%. Determine the percentage of gross margin on sales needed to achieve this desired profit.

13. Using the following figures, set up a skeletal profit and loss statement that shows each factor in dollars and as a percentage.

Net sales	$85,000
Net profit	$1,700
Cost of goods sold	$45,000

14. What is the profit or loss in dollars if gross sales are $218,000, customer returns and allowances are $3,000, cost of goods sold are 55%, and the operating expenses are 41%?

15. Research and Discussion: In measuring gross margin performance, which is more significant: the dollar amount or the percentage figure? Why?

16. Find the net profit or loss as a percentage and the gross margin as a dollar amount.

Gross sales	$200,000
Customer returns and allowances	$15,000
Opening inventory at cost	$38,000
Billed cost of goods	$99,000
Inward transportation	$5,000
Cash discount	$6,000
Closing inventory at cost	$36,000
Payroll	$48,000
Occupancy	$28,000
Wrapping and packing	$1,200
Utilities	$2,000
Delivery	$2,800

17. Construct a profit and loss statement using the following departmental figures and show the dollar amounts for net sales, total cost of goods sold, gross margin, expenses, and profit.

Gross sales	$82,000
Customer returns and allowances	$4,000
Inward freight	$2,000
Workroom costs	$1,000
Opening inventory at cost	$17,000
Closing inventory at cost	$14,000
Purchases at cost	$36,000
Cash discounts	8%
Advertising	$5,000
Rent	$12,000
Salaries	$17,000
Miscellaneous expenses	$2,500

18. Construct a final profit and loss statement from the figures listed below and calculate the major factors as percentages and dollar amounts.

Opening inventory	$74,200
Gross sales	$248,000
Advertising	$15,000
Miscellaneous expenses	$18,000
Purchases at cost	$120,000
Closing inventory	$78,000
Customer returns	$25,800
Salaries	$26,000
Transportation charges	$8,000
Rent	$39,000
Cash discounts	3%

UNIT VI.III
How to Increase Profits

Realistically, it is impossible to list everything a retailer needs to know to merchandise at a profit, because the factors that govern are variable and net profits do not represent any fixed sum. As a frame of reference, Figure 47 lists operating profit percentage margins generated by the percentage of companies. These results illustrate that the amount of profit can be different for different organizations, and is rarely, if ever, constant. In every organization, the actual figures will change annually, but the information required for analysis will remain constant.

Figure 47. Operating Profit Margin by Percentage of Companies

Operating Profit Margin	Percent of Companies
Less than −10%	7%
−7.6 to −10%	7%
−5.1 to −7.5%	0%
−4.1 to −5%	0%
−3.1 to −4%	0%
−2.1 to −3%	10%
−1.1 to −2%	0%
0 to −1%	3%
0 to 1%	10%
1.1 to 2%	13%
2.1 to 3%	16%
3.1 to 4%	13%
4.1 to 5%	7%
5.1 to 7.5%	7%
7.6 to 10%	3%
More than 10%	7%

Source: Tenth Annual Retail Horizons: Benchmarks for 2011, Forecasts for 2012 (KPMG/NRF Foundation)

After reviewing a profit and loss statement, however, to determine how each of these factors affects profit, certain measures can be taken to improve profits. However, because these three factors (sales, cost of goods sold, and operating expenses) are interrelated, the adjustments made must keep all three factors balanced in relationship to one another. Fundamentally, profits can be improved through the following three approaches:

1. Increase sales with only a proportionate increase in the cost of the merchandise and little or no increase in expenses.

2. Decrease the cost of merchandise sold without a decrease in sales.

3. Reduce expenses.

The following example shows the application and effect of each approach. For the accounting period under consideration, a merchant estimated sales at $100,000, merchandise purchases at $70,000, and total operating expenses at $25,000. If the merchant wants to increase the previous 5% net profit, which approach should he take?

EXAMPLE

Actual Estimated Performance:

		Dollars		Percentages
Sales		$100,000		100%
− Cost of goods sold		− 70,000		− 70%
Gross margin	=	$30,000	=	30%
− Operating expenses		− 25,000		− 25%
Net profit	=	$5,000	=	5%

Approach #1:

Increase sales with only a proportionate increase in cost of goods sold and little or no increase in expenses.

		Dollars		Percentages	
Sales		$110,000		100%	(Increased sales)
− Cost of goods sold		− 75,900		− 69%	(Decreased % of cost of goods sold)
Gross margin	=	$34,100	=	31%	(Increased $ and % gross margin)
− Operating expenses		− 28,050		− 25.5%	(Increased $ and % operating expenses)
Net profit	=	$6,050	=	5.5%	(Increased net profit)

Approach #2:

Decrease the cost of goods sold without decreasing sales, which is equivalent to a larger gross margin.

		Dollars		Percentages	
Sales		$100,000		100%	(Constant)
− Cost of goods sold		− 69,500		− 69.5%	(Decreased cost of goods sold)
Gross margin	=	$30,500	=	30.5%	(Larger gross margin)
− Operating expenses		− 25,000		− 25%	(Same expenses)
Net profit	=	$5,500	=	5.5%	(Increased net profit)

Approach #3:

Lower or reduce expenses.

		Dollars		Percentages	
Sales		$100,000		100%	(Constant)
– Cost of goods sold		– 70,000		– 70%	(Constant)
Gross margin	=	$30,000	=	30%	(Constant)
– Operating expenses		– 24,500		– 24.5%	(Reduced expenses)
Net profit	=	$5,500	=	5.5%	(Increased net profit)

Mathematically, the above example demonstrates the three possible approaches to increasing profits. It shows that the manipulation of any one of the three basic profit elements studied (sales, cost of goods, and expenses) will produce different profit results.

In the real retailing arena, each approach can only be accomplished by applying specific merchandising strategies that focus on the particular initiative under scrutiny. Unless there are major management policy changes, it would be counterproductive to attempt changing all three elements at the same time. The three approaches remain the same, but the order of importance may change for any particular period under consideration.

There are many merchandising and retailing texts that examine, in depth, the principles and techniques concerning optimizing sales, decreasing cost of goods, and lowering expenses. Some of the common effective strategies used (not necessarily in order of importance) are:

1. Increasing sales:

   - Price merchandise competitively.

   - Analyze regional customer preferences to achieve proper assortment.

   - Respond quickly to product performance.

   - Minimize out-of-stock items.

   - Control amount and timing of markdowns.

2. Decreasing cost of goods:

   - Sell a larger proportion of higher-markup goods.

   - Develop and maintain vendor relationships that result in advantageous actions concerning new market developments, shipping preferences, and competitive pricing.

   - Qualify for greater quantity discounts, cash discounts, lower shipping terms, etc.

- Develop private brands that offer one-of-a-kind merchandise and exceptional value at negotiable costs.

3. Lowering or reducing expenses:

   - Practice "lean retailing," today's motto. The emphasis is not on which expenses can be further reduced, but on optimizing all the functions that pertain to the buying/selling process, from receiving room to sales floor.

   - Maximize selling-floor space with improved presentations to facilitate "easy" selling.

   - Forecast and plan all sales promotion activities to produce maximum results and effectiveness.

   - Look for innovative ideas to improve customers' in-store experiences.

Practice Problems for Review

19. The following figures are for your department:

Net sales	$490,000
Billed cost of goods	$265,000
Freight charges	$11,160
Rent	$56,640
Salaries	$111,600
Miscellaneous expenses	$25,260
Cash discounts	$37,000
Insurance	$27,800
Advertising	$16,740
Opening inventory at cost	$117,000
Closing inventory at cost	$120,000

    a. Calculate the total cost of goods sold.

    b. Determine the operating expenses in dollars.

    c. Determine the profit or loss in dollars and as a percentage.

20. If profit is $8,000 and profit percentage is 4%, what is the net sales figure?

21. If expenses are $85,340 and gross margin is $90,960, express operating profit or loss in dollars.

22. Find the net profit or loss in dollars and as a percentage if:

Opening inventory at cost	$70,000
Operating expenses	$180,000
Closing inventory	$72,000
Net sales	$400,000
Inward freight	$5,000
Purchases at cost	$210,000

23. If a department experiences a loss of 3% during a six-month period, and its gross margin is 43%, what must its expense percentage be?

24. Gross margin in the shoe department was $185,000. Operating expenses were $178,000, and the net profit was 2% of net sales. What were the net sales?

25. Determine the net sales when:

Operating expenses	$57,750
Gross margin	$56,650
Net loss	1%

26. This year for the Fall period, your entire department was estimated to produce a gross margin of $618,750 because the expenses were estimated at $562,500. The projected net profit for the period was set at 4.0%.

    a. What gross margin percentage was required to achieve the desired profit?

    b. What operating expenses percentage had to be maintained to achieve these results?

27. Set up a final profit and loss statement using the following figures:

Inward freight	$3,000
Workroom and alteration costs	$600
Opening inventory at cost	$14,400
Closing inventory at cost	$14,600
Customer returns	$8,000
Gross sales	$82,000
Purchases at cost	$35,000
Promotional expenses	$3,500
Rent and utilities	$10,000
Payroll	$15,500
Miscellaneous expenses	$2,000
Cash discounts	3%

Express results in dollar amounts and as a percentage for:

   a. Net profit or loss.

   b. Cost of goods sold.

   c. Gross margin.

   d. Operating expenses.

Then, analyze the above figures. Discuss the relationship of expenses to net profit and the size of the gross margin. Suggest strategies to improve profit.

28. Determine the dollar profit or loss in a department in which sales were $1,950,000, cost of merchandise sold was 50%, and operating expenses were $925,000.

29. Prepare a skeletal profit and loss statement showing both dollars and percentages for a department showing the following figures:

Net sales	$280,000
Cost of merchandise sold	$150,000
Loss	3%

30. Determine net sales for a handbag department with the following figures:

Gross margin	$11,500
Operating expenses	$11,000
Net profit	2%

31. Prepare a profit and loss statement for a boutique with the following figures and determine if the store operated at a profit:

Gross sales	$104,000
Customer returns	$5,000
Billed costs	$49,000
Inward freight	$10,000
Advertising	$7,500
Rent	$12,000
Alterations	$1,000
Salaries	$16,000
Miscellaneous expenses	$5,000

32. Find the gross margin percentage when:

Gross sales	$566,000
Customer returns	10%
Billed cost of goods	$258,000
Inward freight	$9,000
Workroom charges	$2,200
Cash discounts	6%

33. Set up a profit and loss statement, showing dollar amounts only, using the following figures:

Gross sales	$127,000
Closing inventory at cost	$29,000
Opening inventory at cost	$33,000
Miscellaneous expenses	$5,000
Customer returns	$6,000
Purchases at cost	$60,000
Rent and utilities	$23,000
Payroll	$30,000
Transportation charges	$1,700
Cash discounts	8%
Advertising	$6,000

34. Construct a skeletal profit and loss statement from the figures below, expressing all factors in both dollars and as a percentage.

Billed cost of goods	$90,000
Alteration and workshop costs	$2,400
Cash discounts	$1,800
Freight charges	$3,000
Direct expenses	$36,000
Customer returns	$9,000
Indirect expenses	$31,200
Gross sales	$177,000

35. Determine the percent of profit or loss if:

Gross sales	$180,000
Direct expenses	$52,000
Opening inventory at cost	$39,000
Indirect expenses	$27,000
Purchases at cost	$95,000
Customer returns	$8,000
Inward freight	$1,000
Closing inventory at cost	$44,000
Cash discounts	4%

36. Research and Discussion: Your merchandise manager has pointed out that the profit percentage in your department for the most recent period was extremely poor. In conjunction with your assistant buyers, make a list of as many ways as possible that you, as the buyer, can attempt to improve the situation directly.

37. Research and Discussion: Set up a mathematical demonstration example to show how increased profit percentage might be achieved in a department operation despite reduced volume. Explain.

CASE STUDY 1
ANALYZING PROFIT PERFORMANCE

The ABC Development Company was selected to manage a major new mall. This mall would be surrounded by a large, medium-income residential neighborhood composed of private homes and town houses ranging from $350,000 to $1,000,000.

In order to select the appropriate store type that would be successful in this area, management researched the profitability of different types of stores. The following information (Figure 48) was collected:

Figure 48. Profit Performance by Store Type

Store Type	Profits		Profits to Sales	
	Last Year	This Year	Last Year	This Year
Department stores	$1,470,655	$1,580,722	3.3%	3.5%
Mass merchandisers	$1,896,700	$2,033,300	2.8%	2.8%
Specialty stores	$555,579	$568,774	4.4%	5.0%
Discount stores	$335,336	$432,774	3.4%	3.3%
Off-price stores	$24,143	$32,073	5.4%	5.2%
Miscellaneous	$478,326	$461,537	2.3%	2.6%
Total	$4,762,739	$5,109,000	3.0%	3.2%

Using the above data:

a. Calculate the dollar profit percentage change from this year to last year.

b. Calculate the net sales for last year and this year.

c. Which store type had the most significant profit change?

d. What store type would you recommend? Why?

e. Discuss the possible causes of profit percentage change from last year to this year.

CASE STUDY 2
CONTROLLING EXPENSES

The housewares department in a specialty store had net sales of $1,500,000. The direct expenses during the period under consideration were:

Buying salaries	$125,000
Selling salaries	$275,000
Advertising	$90,000
Receiving and marking	$15,000
Wrapping and packing	$10,000

The gross margin achieved during this time was 34.0%. After reviewing this performance, management decided that expenses must be reduced. The manager was given the choice of either reducing the advertising budget to a maximum of $50,000 or eliminating a salesperson, which would reduce selling salaries by $50,000.

Which plan of action would you choose? Why? Explore the two options mathematically, and then state your choice. Justify your decision. Discuss the impact your strategy will have on net profit.

CASE STUDY 3
ANALYSIS OF PROFIT AND LOSS STATEMENTS

Ms. Kane, the china and glass buyer of Crystal Clear, Inc., was asked to present a yearly profit and loss statement in skeletal form to the divisional merchandise manager. In addition, she wanted to prepare a summary of comments that included a comparison of her performance this year with that of her major competitor, China Seas, Ltd. Ms. Kane obtained the following information from Crystal Clear's statistical department:

Gross sales	$135,000
Alteration and workroom costs	$1,000
Opening inventory at cost	$49,500
Closing inventory at cost	$61,000
New purchases at cost	$77,500
Inward freight	$1,500
Cash discounts	4%
General overhead	$11,000
Advertising	$9,000
Salaries	$20,000
Rent	$8,600
Customer returns and allowances	$15,000

Ms. Kane obtained, from outside research, profit and loss data on her competitor, China Seas, which had the following results for the same year:

Profit	6% or $7,350
Operating expenses	40%

Ms. Kane then prepared a skeletal profit and loss statement for her department and for that of her competitor China Seas. Upon completion of this task, she compared the two statements. Based on this study, where and how did Ms. Kane determine that she could take action that would give immediate results and have an impact on the department's profitability? Support the suggested action mathematically.

CASE STUDY 4
MERCHANDISING FOR A PROFIT

For the past two years, Ms. Rose has been the owner of My Secret Love, a trendy boutique specializing in moderate-priced handbags. Her previous training and experience as an assistant buyer in a major department store were instrumental in the development of a successful and profitable business. Lately, however, she has realized that current economic conditions are less favorable for her. Sales have been sluggish, and she could see that maintaining the current level of her expenses was becoming increasingly difficult. As a result, she decided to target another customer group for the next season by adding a high-priced designer line to her assortment. To properly merchandise this new classification, she wants to hire another part-time salesperson skilled in selling this type of goods and to use additional sales promotion techniques to launch the new line. Most important, however, she wants to maintain her current profit percentage, even though sales are soft and her expenses will increase.

In the first year, My Secret Love's net sales were $450,000, expenses were at 40.5%, and the profit margin was 4.5%. Ms. Rose was pleased with her venture. The second year, sales grew to $481,500 and her profit increased to 5.0%, with expenses totaling $192,600. She felt she was moving in the right direction. Now, her goal is to increase sales by 7%, with expenses estimated to reach 41%.

a. How, if at all, will her change in sales and expenses affect her profit?

b. As you review Ms. Rose's performance and future goals, what suggestions can you offer to help her meet them?

c. The opening of a new mini-mall near Ms. Rose's trading area is predicted. Therefore, as she does her projections for the next two years, she recognizes that the increased competition could decrease the rate of sales growth for her fourth year from 7% to 6%, yet she wishes to maintain a 5% net profit and offsetting expenses at 41%. Prepare a spreadsheet from the following data, using the above facts and figures.

	Year 1		Year 2		Year 3		Year 4	
	$	%	$	%	$	%	$	%
Growth rate				7%		7%		6%
Net sales	$450,000.00	100%	$481,500.00	100%	$515,205.00	100%	$546,117.30	100%
Cost of goods	247,500.00							
Gross margin	202,500.00							
Operating expenses	182,250.00							
Net profit	20,250.00							5%

Using Year 1 as a base, complete the chart for the subsequent years by calculating the following in dollars and as percentages:

a. Cost of goods sold.

b. Gross margin.

c. Operating expenses.

d. Net profit.

What can Ms. Rose do to retain the gross margin percentage that provides the net profit percentage? Compare the yearly results. What, if any, adjustments in the third and fourth years should be made to reach the 5% net profit goal?

QUICK TIPS FOR SETTING UP YOUR COMPUTER SPREADSHEET

Columns and rows: When using Excel or similar programs, it is important for you to begin to "think in a spreadsheet format"—e.g., setting up your data so that you can easily perform mathematical calculations across the columns or rows. Start by asking yourself, "How shall I label or name my data?" "In what order should my data be organized?"

Begin setting up your spreadsheet by properly labeling columns across the top and rows along the side. Labeling is important so that you understand and remember where and how to enter different pieces of data. Words cannot be used in the cells for which you later want to do any mathematical calculation, only numbers.

If a word or even a letter is entered in a cell where you want a formula performed, the term "#VALUE!" will appear, indicating that the machine cannot perform the function requested because it does not know how to read that cell.

A word about percentages: Percentage calculations are frequently required when doing retailing math, and it is important that you understand how to calculate and enter percentage figures on your spreadsheets.

When doing percentage calculations, a percent needs to be expressed as a decimal (e.g., 4% is expressed as 0.04) in order to do the math. Similarly, when calculating a percentage, we are solving for a fraction or a decimal figure, which must then be converted to a percentage. In this text, formulas are given to solve for a decimal, and these decimals must be multiplied by 100 in order to convert the figure to a percentage (e.g., 0.04 is multiplied by 100 in order to move the decimal point and convert the figure to 4%).

When entering percentages into an unformatted spreadsheet, numbers must also be expressed as decimals. If, however, a cell has been previously formatted as a percentage, enter a value as a whole number and the machine will know how to handle it as a percent. For example, if previously formatted, the machine will automatically convert 4 to 4%. If the cell was not formatted and you enter 4, and you later format it as a percentage, the machine will convert it to 400%.

Shortcuts: On the toolbar you will see some symbols that act as shortcuts to format cell(s) (such as "$" and "%"), as well as shortcuts to increase or decrease the number of decimal points shown (e.g., .←.0 .00; →.00 .0).

Rounding: You may choose a certain rounding format, limiting the number of decimal points or cents shown for a number. Even if the number shown in the cell is rounded off, however, the computer still knows that unrounded number. When a calculation is performed, the unrounded number will be used, and the final answer may be slightly different than you would have expected based on your (or your textbook) doing the arithmetic with a fully rounded number. Remember, the computer's arithmetic is never wrong.

Formula writing: There is some formula shorthand that you need to become familiar with:

Operation	Symbol
To add	+
To subtract	−
To multiply	*

Note: Any time you asterisk a number, your computer will think that you want it to multiply. If you want to make a note of a particular number, try a color, make it bold (B), or italicize (I).

Traditionally, we are accustomed to using "×" to denote multiplication. However, on the computer spreadsheet, "×" is a letter and has no mathematical meaning. If you enter "×," the computer will tell you that it is reading this as a word and you will see "#NAME?"

To divide	/

Note: Any time you use this slash with numbers, your computer will think that you want it to divide. That is why entering a date as "3/21" may not be accepted, and dates need to be specifically formatted.

All equations must begin with: =

Parentheses ( ) are used to accurately describe the order in which you want the computer to do a calculation: Numbers inside the ( ) are calculated first. In order to avoid confusion, get into the habit of always using parentheses when writing complicated formulas. For example:

$= a + b + c/100 - X$ should be written as $= (a + b + c)/(100 - X)$.

Otherwise, the computer will assume that you want a + b to be added to c/100 and then X subtracted from the total. Using actual numbers clearly illustrates this:

$$= (40 + 50 + 35)/(1.00 - 0.3)$$

$$= 178.57$$

Without the ( ), the computer will calculate this to be:

$$= 40 + 50 + 35/1 - 0.3$$

$$= 124.7, \text{ a very different answer!}$$

Entering formulas: Once your data is entered into your spreadsheet, you can easily direct the computer to perform whatever calculations you desire by entering the appropriate formula.

- Click the cell in which you want the solution to be entered, and a dark outline of that cell will appear.

- Begin your formula with = .

- Decide what mathematical calculation you want to make. Prepare the formula. Remember, each cell is described by column letter and row number.

   - Assuming you want to add a column of figures in Column B, the formula might be = B2 + B3 + B4.

- Click on the first cell conforming to your formula: B2.

- In the formula bar, directly above the spreadsheet columns, you will see a description of that cell, expressed as a letter/number combination that clearly describes the cell you have clicked—e.g., B2 (Column B, Row 2).

- Enter the mathematical command that you want (+, – , *, /) and the next cell in the operation. Complete your formula.

- The formula line will show each cell highlighted in a different color to assist you in following along.

- Don't forget to add parentheses where appropriate.

- Changes can easily be made to the formula by placing your cursor on the spot to be corrected and pressing Backspace (or Delete).

- When you have finished the formula and reviewed it for accuracy, press Enter. The formula on the spreadsheet will be replaced with the solution.

- You can still see the formula that you have entered, however, at the top of the page on the formula function line.

Autosum Σ: There are Excel commands to automatically do many complex mathematical operations. For our purposes, however, the operation that we will most frequently use is simple addition. When you have a column of numbers to add, you can enter the formula as, for example:

$$= B2 + B3 + B4 + B5 + B6 + B7 + B8 + B9$$

A shortcut to this notation is to use Autosum by clicking the symbol Σ, located on the formatting bar on the top of the sheet.

- As before, click the cell where you want the solution to be entered, and a dark outline of that cell will appear.

- Then click Σ. There is no need to type an = sign first.

- Σ assumes that it knows what numbers you want added.

  - It reads "= SUM(B2:B9)" which means that it will take a sum of cells B2 through B9.

  - It circles that set of cells to be added with a flashing box.

  - Σ makes its assumption based on cells that are "closest to it." You may want different cells (more or less) included in this calculation, and you can adjust the operation by either typing in the cell number/letter you want on the formula, or by dragging your mouse along the cells that you want.

  - Once you are sure that the formula is correct and includes all, or only, the cells that you want to be summed, press Enter.

Copying formulas: The Copy and Paste features can be very handy. You can literally copy a formula in one section of your spreadsheet and transfer (or Paste) it somewhere else on the sheet.

- Click on the formula you want to copy. A black box will appear. Click Copy.

- Go to the cell where you want to paste the formula. Click Paste.

- Remember that when using the Copy/Paste features, all formulas become relative to the column in which they have been placed. For example:

  Original formula, assuming solution cell is B4
  And the formula = B2 * B3
  When the same formula is copied and pasted into F4
  The formula will become = F2 * F3 and still works!

When you want to repeat a formula across columns or rows, use the Fill feature.

- Click on the formula you want to copy. A black box will appear.

- Drag your mouse right (or down), indicating how many columns (or rows) you want the formula to copy, or how far you want the "Fill" to go.

- Remember that when using Fill features, all formulas once again become relative to the column in which they have been placed. For example:

  Original formula, assuming solution cell is B4
  And the formula = B2 * B3
  When the formula is filled right the formulas will become:
  = C2 * C3
  = D2 * D3
  = E2 * E3

Saving your work: It is always important to remember to save your work. You should save frequently during your work session to be sure that you don't lose anything.

Your Mathematics for Retail Buying CD-ROM is protected; therefore, if you are working with the CD-ROM in your external drive, you will need to save your work to your hard drive.

- Go to File—Save As. . . . Select a name and designate a location from which you will be able to easily retrieve this file in the future.

If you are working with a blank CD-ROM and prefer to save your work directly there:

- Go to File—Save As—My Computer—Removable Disk X.

Quick tips summary: Mathematical concepts are consistent. When using Excel, however, its symbols and structures may differ from what you are most accustomed to using. Remember the following:

- The basic symbols are:

Operation	Symbol
To add	+
To subtract	–
To multiply	*
To divide	/

- Never use letters or words in a cell in which you want to do a calculation.

- Start all formulas with = .

- Use ( ) in complex formulas to ensure accuracy.

- There are many helpful shortcuts and many ways to perform calculations in Excel.

Once you understand the basic retailing math concepts, you will be able to easily enter them into spreadsheet format.

GLOSSARY OF CONCEPT FORMULAS

Billed cost = List price − Trade discount(s)

Book inventory

$$\begin{array}{c}\text{Book} \\ \text{inventory} \\ \text{at retail}\end{array} = \begin{array}{c}\text{Physical} \\ \text{inventory}\end{array} + \begin{array}{c}\text{Net retail} \\ \text{purchases} \\ \text{\small(Total merchandise} \\ \text{\small handled)}\end{array} + \begin{array}{c}\text{Other} \\ \text{stock} \\ \text{additions}\end{array} - \begin{array}{c}\text{Net} \\ \text{sales}\end{array} - \begin{array}{c}\text{Markdown} \\ \text{differences}\end{array} - \begin{array}{c}\text{Other} \\ \text{deductions} \\ \text{from stock}\end{array}$$

$$\begin{array}{c}\text{Book} \\ \text{inventory} \\ \text{at cost}\end{array} = \begin{array}{c}\text{Opening} \\ \text{retail book} \\ \text{inventory}\end{array} \times \left(100\% - \begin{array}{c}\text{Cumulative} \\ \text{markup \%} \\ \text{achieved on} \\ \text{stock}\end{array} + \text{Purchases} \right)$$

Cost of goods sold

$$\begin{array}{c}\text{Total cost of} \\ \text{goods sold}\end{array} = \begin{array}{c}\text{Billed} \\ \text{cost}\end{array} + \begin{array}{c}\text{Inward} \\ \text{transportation} \\ \text{charges}\end{array} + \begin{array}{c}\text{Workroom} \\ \text{costs}\end{array} - \begin{array}{c}\text{Cash} \\ \text{discount}\end{array}$$

Cost = Retail − \$ Markup

Cost = Retail × (100% − Markup %)

$$\text{Cost \%} = \frac{\text{\$ Cost}}{\text{\$ Retail}} \times 100$$

\$ Cost of goods sold = Cost of goods sold % × Net sales

$$\text{Cost of goods sold \%} = \frac{\text{\$ Cost of goods sold}}{\text{Net sales}} \times 100$$

$$\textbf{Cumulative markup \%} = \frac{\text{\$ Cumulative markup}}{\text{\$ Cumulative retail}} \times 100$$

Customer returns and allowances

$$\text{Customer returns and allowances \$} = \text{Total of all refunds or credits to the customer on individual items of merchandise} \times \text{Number of units actually returned}$$

$$\text{Customer returns and allowances \%} = \frac{\text{\$ Customer returns and allowances}}{\text{Gross sales}} \times 100$$

$$\text{\$ Customer returns and allowances} = \text{Gross sales} \times \text{Customer returns and allowances \%}$$

$$\textbf{Department's net sales \% of total store sales} = \frac{\text{Department's net dollar sales}}{\text{Store's total net dollar sales}} \times 100$$

Gross margin

$$\text{Gross margin} = \text{Net sales} - \text{Total cost of goods sold}$$

$$\text{\$ Gross margin} = \text{Gross margin \%} \times \text{Net sales}$$

$$\text{Gross margin \%} = \frac{\text{\$ Gross margin}}{\text{Net sales}} \times 100$$

$$\textbf{GMROI} = \frac{\text{Gross margin \%} \times \text{Turnover}}{100\% - \text{Markup \%}}$$

$$\text{Gross margin \%} = \frac{\text{Net sales} - \text{Total cost of goods sold}}{\text{Net sales}} \times 100$$

$$\text{Gross margin \%} = \frac{\text{Maintained markup} + \text{Cash discounts} - \text{Alteration costs}}{\text{Net sales}} \times 100$$

Gross sales

$$\text{Gross sales} = \text{Total of all the prices charged to consumers on individual items} \times \text{Number of units actually sold}$$

$$\text{Gross sales} = \frac{\text{Net sales}}{(100\% - \text{Customer returns and allowance \%})}$$

Markdown

$$\text{\$ Markdown} = \text{Original or present retail} - \text{New retail}$$

$$\text{\$ Markdown} = \text{Percentage off} \times \text{Present retail price}$$

$$\text{Total \$ markdown} = \text{First total \$ markdown} + \text{Second total \$ markdown}$$

$$\text{Planned \$ markdowns} = \text{Net sales} \times \text{Markdown \%}$$

$$\text{Markdown \%} = \frac{\text{\$ Markdown}}{\text{Net sales}} \times 100$$

$$\text{Markdown \%} = \frac{\text{\$ Markdown}}{\text{Total dollar sales of group's final selling prices}} \times 100$$

Markdown cancellation $=$ Higher retail $-$ Markdown price

Net markdown $=$ Gross markdown $-$ Markdown cancellation

$$\text{Planned total seasonal dollar markdowns} = \text{Planned total seasonal sales} \times \text{Total seasonal markdown \%}$$

$$\text{Total seasonal markdown \%} = \frac{\text{Last year (LY) total dollar markdowns}}{\text{LY total sales}} \times 100$$

Markup

$$\text{Averaging or balancing markup} = \text{Total planned (pieces, retail, cost, or markup \%)} - \text{Purchases to date}$$

$\$ \text{ Markup} = \text{Retail} - \text{Cost}$

$$\text{Initial markup \%} = \frac{\text{Gross margin \% + Retail reductions \%}}{100\% + \text{Retail reductions \%}}$$

$$\text{Initial markup \%} = \frac{\$ \text{ Gross margin} + \$ \text{ Retail reductions}}{\$ \text{ Sales} + \$ \text{ Retail reductions}} \times 100$$

$$\text{Initial markup \%} = \frac{\text{Gross margin} + \text{Alteration costs} - \text{Cash discount earned} + \text{Retail reduction}}{\text{Sales (100\%)} + \text{Retail reductions \%}}$$

$$\text{Markup \% on retail} = \frac{\$ \text{ Markup}}{\$ \text{ Retail}} \times 100$$

$$\text{Markup \% on cost} = \frac{\$ \text{ Markup}}{\text{Cost}} \times 100$$

$$\text{Maintained markup \%} = \frac{\text{Net sales} - \text{Gross cost of goods sold}}{\text{Net sales}} \times 100$$

$$\text{Maintained markup \%} = \frac{\text{Gross margin} - \text{Cash discounts} + \text{Alteration costs}}{\text{Net sales}} \times 100$$

$$\text{Maintained markup \%} = \text{Initial MU \%} - \text{Retail reduction \%} \times (100\% - \text{Initial MU \%})$$

$$\text{Retail markup \% on entire purchase} = \frac{\text{Total \$ markup}}{\text{Total retail}} \times 100$$

Net cost

Net cost $=$ Billed cost $-$ Cash discount

Net cost $=$ List price $-$ Trade discount(s) $-$ Cash discount

Net profit

Net profit $=$ Net sales $-$ Cost of goods sold $-$ Operating expenses

Net operating profit or net profit $=$ Gross margin $-$ All operating expenses

$$\text{Net profit \%} = \frac{\text{Net profit in dollars}}{\text{Net sales}} \times 100$$

Net Sales

Net sales $=$ Gross sales $-$ Customer returns and allowances

$$\textbf{Number of weeks supply} = \frac{\text{Weeks}}{\text{Desired turnover}}$$

Open-to-buy (OTB)

OTB $=$ Planned purchases for the month $-$ Outstanding orders to be delivered that month

$$\text{OTB for balance of month} = \text{Planned purchases for month} - \text{Merchandise received to date} - \text{Merchandise on order}$$

$$\text{OTB for balance of month} = \text{Planned EOM stock} + \text{Planned sales for balance of month} + \text{Planned markdowns for balance of month} - \text{Actual stock-on-hand} - \text{On order}$$

Operating expenses

Operating expenses $=$ Direct expenses $+$ Indirect expenses

$ Operating expenses $=$ Operating expenses % $\times$ Net sales

$$\text{Operating expenses \%} = \frac{\text{Direct and indirect expenses in dollars}}{\text{Net sales}} \times 100$$

Planned purchases

$$\text{Planned monthly purchases at retail} = \text{Planned EOM stock} + \text{Planned sales for month} + \text{Planned markdowns for month} - \text{Planned BOM stock}$$

$$\text{Planned monthly purchase at cost} = \text{Planned retail purchases} \times (100\% - \text{Planned markup \%})$$

$$\text{Purchase balance} = \text{Total planned (pieces, retail, cost, or markup \%)} - \text{Purchases to date}$$

Retail

Retail $=$ Cost $+$ $ Markup

$$\text{Retail} = \frac{\text{Cost}}{(100\% - \text{Markup \%})}$$

Average retail stock $= \dfrac{\text{Planned sales for period}}{\text{Turnover rate}}$

Average retail stock $= \dfrac{\left(\begin{array}{c}\text{Sum of beginning} \\ \text{inventories}\end{array} + \begin{array}{c}\text{Ending inventory} \\ \text{for given period}\end{array}\right)}{\text{Number of inventories}}$

Retail reduction % $= \dfrac{\text{Initial markup \% } - \text{ Maintained markup \%}}{\text{Sales (100\%) } - \text{ Initial markup \%}}$

Sales increase % $= \dfrac{\text{This year (TY) planned sales } - \text{ LY actual sales}}{\text{LY actual sales}} \times 100$

Seasonal planned sales $=$ LY sales $+$ Dollar increase

Dollar increase $=$ LY sales $\times$ Planned increase %

Shortage or overage

Shortage $=$ Closing book inventory at retail $-$ Physical inventory count

Shortage % $= \dfrac{\text{\$ Shortage}}{\text{\$ Net sales}} \times 100$

Estimated dollar shortage $= \begin{array}{c}\text{Estimated shortage} \\ \text{percentage}\end{array} \times$ Planned net sales

Stock ratios

Stock-sales ratio $= \dfrac{\text{Retail stock at given time in the period}}{\text{Sales for the period}}$

Planned stock $=$ Average weekly sales $\times$ Number of weeks supply

BOM stock $=$ Planned monthly sales $\times$ Stock-sales ratio

BOM stock $=$ Basic stock $+$ Planned sales for the month

Turnover $= \dfrac{\text{Net sales for period}}{\text{Average retail stock for the same period}}$

GLOSSARY OF TERMS

Additional markup Adjustment that raises the price on merchandise already in stock.

Advanced dating (seasonal discount) In which the invoice date is advanced so that additional time is allowed for payment and the deduction of the cash discount.

Allowance to customer A partial refund or credit compensating for a merchandising deficiency, such as missing buttons, dry cleaning, and so on.

Alteration and workroom costs A charge to a selling department when it is necessary to put merchandise in condition for sale (e.g., assembling, polishing, making cuffs).

Anticipation A discount earned by retailers, under certain conditions, for the payment of invoices prior to expiration of cash discount period.

Average cost The proportioning of different cost amounts that can carry retail prices that achieve the desired markup percentage.

Average retail Price that will achieve desired markup percentage.

Average retail stock Sum of retail inventories at the beginning of each year, season, month, or week.

Average stock The total of BOM dollar inventory figures divided by the number of stocks considered.

Averaging or balancing markups The adjustment of the proportions of goods purchased at different markups. A composite of the relationship between all cost and retail for a department or grouping of goods during a specified time.

Averaging retails The proportioning of different retail prices on purchases that may have two or more costs to achieve a desired markup percentage.

Basic stock method Stock size using a constant basic stock figure with a turnover rate.

Billed cost The manufacturer's price for goods offered to a retailer.

BOM stock The beginning of the month stock figure in dollars.

Book inventory (perpetual or running book inventory) Statistical records that show the value at retail of goods on hand at a given time.

Cash discount A percentage deducted from the cost of goods for conformance to prearranged terms of payment of an invoice between the vendor and retailer.

Charge-back Form on which the amounts of merchandise returned to resources by retailer for credit or refund is recorded.

Closing book inventory The value of merchandise in stock at the end of an accounting period. It can be expressed in cost or retail.

Closing physical stock The retail value of aggregate retail prices of a stock determined by a physical count at the end of a designated time period.

COD dating A form of dating in which payment must be made "on the spot" as delivery occurs.

Complement The difference between 100 and any number less than 100; e.g., the complement of 60 is 40.

Contribution or controllable margin The technique that evaluates the buyer's performance based on those expenses that are direct, controllable, or a combination of direct and controllable expenses. It is the amount a department contributes to indirect expenses and profit.

Controllable expenses Many, but not all, direct expenses are controllable. See *Direct expenses.*

Cost The amount a retailer pays a resource for purchases.

Cost complement The amount paid for a purchase, which can be calculated when dollar markup is subtracted from retail.

Cost of goods sold The cost of merchandise that has been sold during a given period.

Cumulative markup The markup percentage achieved on all goods available for sale from the beginning of a given period. It is the markup in dollars or percentages obtained on the accumulated inventory at the beginning of the given period, plus the markup of all the new purchases received season-to-date.

Customer allowances The amount of reduction in price the customer has been given after a sale has been made.

Customer returns Dollar amount value returned to retailer by customer for credit or refund.

Dating An agreement specifying time period for payment of an invoice.

Debit memo form A record of an accounting debt.

Department A grouping of related merchandise for which common records are kept.

Direct expenses Expenses that exist only within a given department and cease if that department is discontinued (e.g., department advertising).

Discount date The date by which an invoice must be paid to take advantage of the discount granted.

Dollar merchandise plan A "roadmap" indicating projected sales, stocks, markdowns, and purchases, as well as the desired markups, usually prepared biannually in advance of the selling season.

Employee discounts A percentage deducted from a regular retail price as a courtesy to employees of a retail organization. It ranges from 10% to 30% and is a "retail reduction."

EDP (electronic data processing) The planned conversion of factors (as by the computer) into storable form to achieve a desired result.

EOM End of month. Usually designates dollar value of stock at the end of a month.

EOM dating Computation of the cash discount period from the end of the month in which the invoice is dated rather than from the date of the invoice itself.

EOM stock End of month stock. Usually designates dollar value of stock at the end of a month.

Expenses The overhead of doing business, e.g., salaries, rent, advertising, delivery, utilities.

Extra dating A specific number of days granted during which a discount may be taken.

Final profit and loss statement The basic profit factors (i.e., sales, cost of goods, and expenses) are developed in detail so that every transaction is clearly seen.

Final selling price Price received when an item is sold.

Flash report Daily report indicating sales amount.

FOB (Free-on-board) A way of expressing who is responsible for payment of transportation and the point at which title is transferred.

FOB city or port of destination In which the vendor pays transportation charges to a specific city or destination.

FOB factory In which the retailer pays transportation.

FOB retailer In which the resource pays transportation.

GMROI (gross margin return on investment) The relationship between the average inventory at cost and gross margin. Gross margin divided by average inventory at cost.

Gross margin The remainder after subtracting total cost of goods sold from the total retail amount of sales. Also called gross profit. The difference between net sales and the cost of goods sold.

Gross markdown Original price reduction.

Gross sales Retail value of total initial sales prior to deduction of dollar amount returned by customers.

Indirect expenses Expenses that consist of some store expenses, which are pro-rated to all selling departments on the basis of sales volume.

Initial or original markup The difference between the cost of goods and the original retail price. The first price placed on merchandise for resale. Planned markups specified on orders for merchandise; a projected markup goal.

Initial or original retail The first price placed on merchandise for sale.

Inventory (n.) Synonymous with the term "stock."

Inventory (v.) To actively count and record quantities of merchandise.

Invoice A bill presented by a vendor to a retailer for goods purchased.

Inward freight The amount charged for transporting merchandise to designated premises, e.g., trucking, freight, postage, and so on. Charges are paid by either vendor or retailer according to an agreement between them at the time of purchase.

Journal or purchase record Consolidated listing of purchases by invoice amounts, transportation charges, discounts, vendors, and so on.

List price A theoretical retail price set by manufacturers.

Loading Intentionally increasing the amount of the invoice to a price that would allow a theoretically greater cash discount, but which results in paying the net amount that the vendor quotes.

LY Last year.

Maintained markup The difference between the cost of goods and the actual selling price of the merchandise sold.

Markdown A reduction in retail price. The lowering or reducing of the original or previous retail price on one item or group of items. The difference between the original or present retail price and the new retail price. Taken in dollars and can be expressed as a percentage.

Markdown cancellation The restoration of a markdown price to the former retail.

Markdown percentage Markdown expressed as a percentage of net sales.

Markup The difference between cost and retail price, expressed either in dollars or as a percentage.

Markup percentage Markup expressed as a percentage of net sales.

Markup cancellation A downward price adjustment that offsets an original inflated markup.

Merchandise loans Goods given temporarily to another department or division for purposes other than resale, such as display.

Merchandise plan A combination of a dollar merchandise plan and an assortment plan.

Merchandise transfers Goods "bought or sold" internally, from one department to another, for purposes of resale to the ultimate consumer.

Net What remains when nothing more is to be taken away.

Net cost When no additional discounts are earned on merchandise purchased.

Net loss When the operating expenses are greater than the gross margin.

Net markdown Difference between gross markdown and markdown cancellation.

Net payment date The date by which an invoice must be paid to acquire a favorable credit rating and avoid late penalties.

Net period Span of time between expiration of eligibility for cash discount and start of the penalty period.

Net profit The difference between gross margin and operating expenses.

Net sales The sales total after customer returns and allowances have been deducted from gross sales.

Net terms A condition of sale in which a cash discount is neither offered nor permitted.

On order Unfilled orders, also known as open orders.

Opening book inventory The value of merchandise in stock at the beginning of an accounting period. It can be expressed at retail or at cost.

Opening inventory The retail value of merchandise in stock.

Open-to-buy (OTB) The amount of unspent money available for purchasing merchandise.

Operating expenses Disbursals incurred in running an organization. There are two types, direct and indirect.

Operating income In retailing, this is the net sales.

Ordinary dating See *Regular dating*.

Overage Dollar difference between book stock figure and physical count when the latter is the larger of the two.

Perpetual inventory See *Book inventory.*

Physical inventory The retail dollar value of all goods physically present in a periodic stock count.

Planned purchases Also known as planned receipts, the dollar amount of merchandise that can be brought into a stock during a given period.

Planned receipts See *Planned purchases.*

Point-of-sale markdown Recording of the markdown as the reduced offering when an item is being sold.

POS Point-of-sale.

Prepaid Payment of transportation charges by vendor when merchandise is shipped.

Prestige price zone Refers to the high price lines in a stock assortment.

Price change form Form on which markdowns, markdown cancellation, additional markups, and markup cancellation, or any price change made, is recorded.

Price line A predetermined retail figure or a specific price point that is aimed at a specific customer market segment.

Price lining The predetermination of retail prices at which an assortment of merchandise will be carried.

Price range The spread from highest to lowest price lines.

Price zone Series of price lines likely to appeal to one group of a store's customers. These can be referred to as volume, promotional, or prestige price zones.

Profit The dollar amount remaining after costs and expenses are paid.

Profit and loss statement Statement prepared periodically by either department, store, or organization that summarizes the basic merchandising factors which affect profit results.

Promotional price zone Refers to the lower price lines in a stock assortment.

Purchase record A form used to preserve information about merchandise bought.

Quantity discount A percentage deduction from billed cost allowable when the dollar or unit amount on an order for goods (or a cumulative figure for a period of time) falls within certain predesignated limits.

Regular dating Discount date calculated from date of invoice. Also called *ordinary dating.*

Remit or remittance Payment.

Retail Price at which stores offer merchandise for sale.

Retail merchandising The science of offering goods to the ultimate consumer at the right price, in the right form, at the right location, and at an appropriate time.

Retail method of inventory An accounting system used in retail stores that values merchandising at current retail prices which can then be converted to cost value by markup formula.

Retail price The price at which goods are ultimately sold to the consumer.

Retail reductions Markdown plus stock shortages and employee discounts.

Return to vendor See *Charge-back*.

ROG dating Receipt of goods used in dating terms to denote the beginning of a discount period.

Running book inventory See *Book inventory*.

Sales volume Indicates in dollars how much merchandise has been sold.

Season letter A code letter indicating date of item's entry into stock.

Shortage Dollar difference between book stock figure and physical count figures, when the former is the larger of the two.

Shrinkage Lessening of retail value of stock-on-hand, generally due to theft or breakage. See *Shortage*.

Six-month seasonal dollar merchandise plan A budget scheduling the planned month by month sales, the amount of stock planned for each of these months and the projected reductions.

Skeletal profit and loss statement A quick method to determine profit or loss at any given time.

Stock Goods on hand at a given time, expressed as a dollar amount.

Stock-sales ratio The proportion between the BOM stock figure and the dollar amount of sales for the same month.

Terms of sale Arrangement between merchandise source or vendor and retailer relative to time period of invoice, cost of merchandise, shipping charges, and transportation arrangements.

Total cost of goods purchased Combined cost of merchandise purchased and inward transportation charges.

Total cost of goods sold Results from subtracting cash discounts and adding alteration and workroom costs to the gross cost of merchandise sold (total merchandise handled less the cost of the closing inventory).

Total merchandise handled Opening inventory at cost plus new purchases at cost plus inward freight, or the sum of the opening inventory plus the total cost of the purchases that is all merchandise available for sale.

Trade discount A percentage or series of percentages deducted from a list price, thereby determining cost price.

Transfers Change of ownership of merchandise between departments or stores.

Turnover The number of times at which the average retail stock has been sold and replaced.

Vendor A merchandise resource such as a manufacturer, importer, jobber, distributor, etc.

Vendor analysis An investigation of the profitability of each vendor's products sold by a retailer.

Volume The retail value of sales for a given period, usually expressed annually. See *Sales volume.*

Volume price zone A series of price lines, generally in the middle price lines where the largest percentage of sales occur.

Week's supply method A method of planning stock size on a weekly basis.

Workroom charges A charge to a selling department when it is necessary to put merchandise in condition for sale, e.g., assembling, polishing, putting on cuffs, etc. See *Alteration and workroom costs.*

SELECTED ANSWERS

UNIT I: ANALYSIS OF BASIC SALES ELEMENTS

Operating Income

1. 5.0%
3. $49,122.00
5. $40,000.00
7. 1.5% (juniors' department); 4.5% (misses' department)

Cost of Merchandise Sold

11. (a) $93.06; (b) $1,644.06
13. $59,045.00
15. (a) $1,374.00; (b) $1,420.26

Discounts

17. $122.50
19. Competitor B; $36.50 less
21. $972.00
23. $488.88
25. $4,419.80
27. $4,159.67
29. (b)

Dating

31. (a) $522.00; (b) $1,503.36
33. $624.00
35. May 12 discount expiration date; 70 days for discount
36. $5,320.00

Anticipation, Loading, and Shipping Terms

40. (a) $1,944.00; (b)$1,778.76
43. $4,443.75
49. $2,437.50

Practice Problems for Review

50. $6,446.86
51. December 5
53. (a) March 10; (b) March 30; (c) $5,674.39
55. $2,928.00
60. $1,404.00

UNIT II: RETAIL PRICING AND REPRICING OF MERCHANDISE

Retail Pricing

2. $29.95
4. $93.00
6. 45.0%

Markup

8. (a) $88.54; (b) $90.00; (c) 46.5%
12. $75.43; 50.0%
16. $44.00
18. 48.7%
20. $41.67
22. $23.07
24. (a) $25.00; (b) $10.83

Repricing of Merchandise

31. $1,225.00
37. $669.75
39. (a) $1,330.00; (b) 15.34%

Practice Problems for Review

45. $20.57
47. $8.57
49. 47.95% or 48%
51. (a) 47.0%; (b) 2.98% or 3.0%
52. 54.4%
54. $4,240.00
56. $67.90
58. (a) $117,000.00; (b) 0.5% more

UNIT III: BASIC MARKUP EQUATIONS USED IN MERCHANDISING DECISIONS

Initial Markup Concepts

1. 51.4%
3. 49.15% or 49.2%
5. 53.0%
7. 53.8%
9. 48.3%

Cumulative Markup

11. 53.7%
13. (a) 55.3%; (b) 54.9%
15. 50.1%

Maintained Markup

17. 37.3%
21. 13.4%

Average Costs

23. (a) $8,704.00; (b) $108.80 per dozen
25. $1,774.50
27. $27.41

Average Retail

28. $25.51
29. $26.00

Average Markup Percentage

31. 53.7%
33. 49.6%

Practice Problems for Review

35. 47.2%
37. 47.6%
38. 13.0%
40. (a) 41.6%; (b) 47.6%
42. 53.6%
45. $21.68
46. $800.00; 61.5%
47. $5.83
48. $47.14
50. $60.41
53. 49.5%
55. 49.6%
58. (a) $130,000.00; (b) $139,200.00

Unit IV: The Retail Method of Inventory

Maintaining a Perpetual Book Inventory Figure

1. $62,875.00
3. $95,000.00
5. (a) $23,000.00; (b) $11,730.00
7. (a) $1,311,000.00; (b) $672,543.00
9. $162,046.50
10. (a) $937,000.00; (b) $475,996.00

Shortages and Overages

13. 0.41%
15. 1.5%
17. 2.07% or 2.1%

Practice Problems for Review

19. $70,000.00
21. (a) 0.1% higher; (b) $2,000.00 more
25. (a) $284,100.00; (b) $282,550.80

Unit V: Dollar Planning and Control

Planning Sales

1. 10.0%
3. August: $900,000.00
    September: $840,000.00
    October: $960,000.00
    November: $1,080,000.00
    December: $1,500,000.00
    January: $720,000.00
5. 20.0%

Calculating Average Retail Stock Turnover and GMROI

8. $80,000.00
10. $300,000.00
12. 3.88 or 3.9
15. 2.5
16. (a) $40,000.00; (b) 4.95 or 5.0
18. 3.2
20. 1.10
22. 3.0

Calculating Stock-Sales Ratios

24. $312,000.00
26. 4.25 or 4.3

Finding Weekly Rate of Sales

28. $117,000.00
30. $126,150.00

Using Basic Stock Method

31. $275,000.00
33. $60,000.00

Planned Purchases

36. $80,000.00
38. (a) $20,000.00; (b) $9,700.00; (c) 0.36 or 0.4
40. (a) $28,000.00; (b) $33,000.00
42. $61,800.00

Calculating Retail Open-to-Buy

44. None
46. None
48. None

Practice Problems for Review

50. 10.4
52. $780,000.00
54. 10.2%
56. (a) $3,000.00; (b) $1,320.00
58. $37,000.00
60. 1.5
62. (a) 4.5; (b) 2.1
64. (a) $83,428.57; (b) 6.0; (c) 4.0
65. August: $217,250.00 BOM
    September: $230,050.00 BOM
    October: $266,550.00 BOM
    November: $233,450.00 BOM
    December: $234,750.00 BOM
    January: $216,550.00 BOM
67. $88,000.00

UNIT VI: MERCHANDISING FOR A PROFIT

Operating Expenses

3. 0 (zero)
5. $2,500.00

Skeletal Profit and Loss

7. (a) $9,000.00; (b) 41.25% or 41.3%
9. $38,800.00; 48.5%

Final Profit and Loss Statements

16. $3,000 profit; 1.62%

Practice Problems for Review

20. $200,000.00
21. $5,620.00
22. $7,000.00; 1.75%
25. $110,000.00
28. $50,000.00
35. 3.37%

INDEX

markdowns (*continued*)

    second markdown, calculating, 88–89

    timing of, 86

    typical, by category, *227*

markup dollar calculations

    cost calculations, 74

    vs. percentage calculations, 147–148

    retail price calculations, 73–74

markup percentage equations, 63, 67–73

    on cost, 67–68

    cumulative markups, 120

    vs. dollar calculations, 147–148

    formulas, 114

    on a group of items with varying prices
        or costs, 70–73

    with individual cost and individual
        retail, 68–69

    initial markups, 117–119

    maintained markup, 122–123, 124

    on retail using retail method of
        inventory, 67

markups

    additional, 95

    averaging or balancing, 134–141

    cancellations, 95

    case studies, 156–160

    cumulative markup, 114, 119–121

    defined, 67

    effects of, 114

    formulas, 56, 62–63

    initial markup, 115–119

    maintained markup, 121–124

    managing, 115

    percentage vs. dollar calculations,
        147–148

    planning, 228–230

mathematical symbols in software, 335

merchandise plan worksheet, annual,
    233

merchandise statistics reports, 237–240,
    238

merchandising, profitable pricing in, 60

merchandising for profit case study,
    329–330

monthly sales distribution, department
    store, *213*

N

net cost, 20–24

    all formulas, 2

    billed cost and cash discount formula, 20

    list price and cash discount formula, 21

    list price and quality discount formula,
        23

    quality and cash discount formula, 22

net loss. *See* Net operating profit

net operating profit

    defined, 3, 295

    formulas, 295

    inventory valuation and, 199

    results, buyer, 47

net payment dates, 30–31

net profit. *See* Net operating profit

net sales, 7–9

    defined, 4, 7, 292

    formulas, 7–8, 290

    shortages and overages as percentage
        of, 191

    volume, comparing percentages of, 301

net terms, 25

number of weeks supply, 208

O

on order, 257

opening book inventory, 166

Open-to-buy (OTB)

    case study, 284

    defined, 209, 257

    formulas, 208, 266, 267

    reports, *258, 260*

    reports, explanation of, 257, 259, 260–264

    retail calculating, beginning of
        month, 265

    retail calculating, during month,
        266–267

operating expenses

    defined, 3, 292

    direct expenses, 292

    formulas, 290

    indirect expenses, 293

operating income. *See* Net sales

operating profit, net. *See* Net operating
    profit

ordinary dating, 28
original markup. *See* Initial markup
OTB. *See* Open-to-buy (OTB)
Outstanding Transfer List Form, *172*
overage, 165. *See also* Shortages and
    overages

P

payment dates, net, 31
percentages in spreadsheet software,
    331
performance, sales, 9
perpetual book inventory, 166–167
physical inventory, 164–165
    in calculating shortages or overages, 190
    company averages, 165
    count sheet, 165
plan, annual merchandise worksheet,
    233
plan, seasonal budget, 209
plan sales comparison, 9
planned gross profit percentage,
    228–230
planned purchases, 232–240
    adjusting, 237
    case study, 285–287
    at cost, calculating, 232
    formulas, 208, 231, 232
    monthly purchases at retail, 231
    purpose of, 209
    six-month seasonal dollar merchandise
        plans, 232–237
planned receipts. *See* planned purchases
planning sales, 210–213
planning stocks, 214
point of sale (POS) markdown, 91–92
POS credit slip, *92*
POS markdown receipt, *92*
postdating, 30–31
prestige price zone, 57–58
price, retail, 56, 60, 62, 137–139
price change entry, *175*
price change forms, 174–176
price change printout, *96*
price change procedures, 96
price change worksheet, buyer's, *174*

price lining, 57–58
    price line reports, 60, 61
    report by classification, *61*
    strategy advantages, 59
    structure chart, *58*
price range, 57–58
price zone, 57–58
pricing, 56–57
    case studies, 109–112
    factors influencing, 59
    factors relationship, 60
    formulas, 56
    price line structuring, 57–58
    profit and, 75
profit, net. *See* net profit
profit and loss statements, 300–306, *305*
    analysis case study, 328
    basic formula of, 300
    components of, 292–295
    final, 303–306
    skeletal, 301–303
profits, 56
    approaches to increasing, 313–316
    calculations, use and importance of, 291
    margins, by percentage of companies,
        313
    merchandising for, case study, 329–330
    performance analysis case study, 324
    pricing factors and, 75
    repricing and, 97
promotional price zone, 57–58
purchase order, *44*
purchase planning. *See* planned pur-
    chases
purchase records, 170, *171*

R

receipt of goods (ROG) dating, 30
receipts, planned. *See* planned purchases
records, purchase, 170, *171*
reductions, price. *See* Markdowns
regular dating, 28
reports, merchandise statistics, 237–240,
    238
reports, price line, 60, 61
repricing, 84, 96, 97